Architecture and Energy

Bauen in Zeiten des Klimawandels

Building in the age of climate change

Architecture and Energy

Bauen in Zeiten des Klimawandels

Building in the age of climate change

Herausgegeben von
Edited by
Werner Sobek
Annette Becker
Peter Cachola Schmal

Redaktion
Editor
Kjell Reiter

Mit Beiträgen von
With contributions by
Heinrich Bökamp
Brian Cody
Gustav Düsing
Maxim von Gagern
Andrea Gebhard
Oliver Geden
Andres Herzog
Claudia Kemfert
Regine Leibinger
Werner Sobek
Cord Soehlke
Angèle Tersluisen
Katharina Volgger

HIRMER

Inhalt

Table of contents

Vorwort

Foreword

Eine Frage des Klimas

Die vielfältigen Konflikte und Krisen unserer Welt drängen das Bewusstsein und das Nachdenken über die Folgen der Erderwärmung immer wieder in den Hintergrund. Doch schreitet die globale Erwärmung unvermindert voran. Ihre ersten Auswirkungen sind deutlich zu erkennen, die Folgen insgesamt unübersehbar.[1] Dass es immer wieder Stimmen gibt, die die naturwissenschaftlichen Fakten und die gesellschaftlichen wie wirtschaftlichen Auswirkungen des Klimawandels zu relativieren versuchen, mag menschlich sein. Es nützt jedoch nichts, die Aufmerksamkeit der Menschen abzulenken und die Situation schönzureden. Stattdessen gilt es den vom Menschen selbst verursachten Klimawandel als Fakt anzuerkennen. Wir müssen versuchen, diesen Klimawandel zu verlangsamen und Wege finden, wie wir in Zukunft in einer anderen

1 Wie der im April 2025 veröffentlichte Bericht des EU-Erdbeobachtungsprogramms Copernicus zeigte, haben Extremwetterlagen und die Erwärmung in Europa im Jahr 2024 einen neuen Höchststand erreicht. Siehe Copernicus Climate Change Service (C3S) and World Meteorological Organization (WMO), 2025: European State of the Climate 2024; https://climate.copernicus.eu/esotc/2024 [Abruf: 23.4.2025].

A climate question

The wide range of conflicts and crises in the world today have repeatedly forced awareness and consideration of global warming to take a back seat. Yet the warming of our planet continues relentlessly all the same. While its effects can already be seen clearly, the full consequences still exceed our comprehension.[1] Perhaps it is only human that certain voices continue to relativise the scientific facts and the social and economic impacts of climate change. However, there is no point in distracting people's attention and trying to talk the situation up. Instead, the focus must be on recognising that anthropogenic climate change is a fact. We must try to slow climate change down and find ways to live in what will be a different world. Finding those ways is one of the central questions relating to the future of humankind. It calls for a great effort by society as a whole. That said, it could also lead to a completely new form of peaceful coexistence worldwide.

Since at least the seventh century BCE, humans have mined coal, albeit initially only in small volumes. The coal mining that started at the end of the thirteenth century in the Ruhr region in northeast Germany was likewise on a minor scale. Not until the beginning of the Industrial Revolution in the eighteenth century did coal mining and burning coal assume proportions that had a noteworthy impact on the environment. The "fossil age" that started then not only brought affluence, prosperity, and population growth, but also set anthropogenic

1 As is shown in the April 2025 report by the EU's climate monitoring and data collection service Copernicus, extreme weather events and global temperatures reached record highs in Europe in 2024. See Copernicus Climate Change Service (C3S) and World Meteorological Organisation (WMO), 2025: *European State of the Climate 2024*; https://climate.copernicus.eu/esotc/2024 (accessed 23 April 2025).

Welt leben können. Dies ist eine der zentralen Zukunftsfragen der Menschheit. Es wird unseren Gesellschaften größte Anstrengungen abverlangen, kann aber weltweit auch zu einer neuen Art des friedfertigen Miteinanders führen.

Schon vor 2.500 Jahren förderten die Menschen Kohle. Doch erst mit Beginn der Industriellen Revolution im 17. Jahrhundert nahmen Kohleabbau und -verbrennung umweltrelevante Ausmaße an. Das damals einsetzende „fossile Zeitalter" hat nicht nur für Wohlstand, Prosperität und Bevölkerungswachstum gesorgt, sondern mit den großen Mengen an Treibhausgasen, die dabei freigesetzt wurden, den menschengemachten Klimawandel in Gang gesetzt. Um den immer größer werdenden „Energiehunger" unserer Industriegesellschaften zu befriedigen, wurde der Energieträger Kohle alsbald mit Erdöl und Erdgas ergänzt. Alle drei Energieträger werden verbrannt, um Wärme zu erzeugen. Bei der Verbrennung von Kohle, Erdöl und Erdgas entsteht, neben anderen Emissionen, das klimaschädliche Gas Kohlendioxid. Einmal in die Atmosphäre entlassen, ist es ein wesentlicher Faktor für die Erderwärmung. Diese wird also nicht durch den Energieverbrauch als solchen, sondern durch die Emission klimaschädlicher Gase bewirkt.[2] Es ist wichtig, dies zu verstehen, da es bedeutet, dass Energie, die nicht emissionsbehaftet ist, klimatologisch nicht von Bedeutung ist.

Um den Klimawandel bewältigen zu können, sind Energien zu nutzen, die nicht über Verbrennung erzeugt werden: die *erneuerbaren Energien*, die auf der Nutzung von Windkraft, Solareinstrahlung und anderen Quellen beruhen. Bei Beibehaltung der verbrennungsbasierten Energie gilt es, die entstehenden Gase „einzufangen". Gelingt dies nicht, muss auf deren Nutzung verzichtet werden.

2 Vgl. IPCC: Sections, in: Climate Change 2023: Synthesis Report. Contribution of Working Groups I, II and III to the Sixth Assessment Report of the Intergovernmental Panel on Climate Change, Genf 2023, S. 35–115.

Die Treppe „Luikerweg" von Rademacher de Vries Architects (Amsterdam) ist Teil der Rekultivierung eines Zementsteinbruchs in den Niederlanden. | The "Luikerweg" staircase by Rademacher de Vries Architecten (Amsterdam) is part of the renaturalisation of a limestone quarry in the Netherlands.

Da das Auffangen – auch *carbon capture* – noch in den technischen Anfängen steckt und zudem bei einigen der angewandten Technologien mit hohem Energieverbrauch behaftet ist, erscheinen die Verringerung der Nutzung verbrennungsbasierter Energie und die Steigerung des Anteils erneuerbarer Energien derzeit als einziger Ausweg.[3]

Wie gehen wir mit Energie um?

Dass die Menschheit auch in Zukunft nicht auf Energie verzichten kann, erzwingt die zunehmende Verwendung erneuerbarer Energie. Vor allem Strom wird hier eine zentrale Rolle spielen.[4] Um unsere bisherigen Verhaltensweisen beibehalten zu können, müssen die bisher genutzten Energiemengen durch erneuerbare Energie ersetzt werden, und zwar so, dass die Energie dann in hinreichender Menge abgerufen werden kann, wenn sie benötigt wird. Der notwendige Ausbau der Systeme für die Erzeugung, Speicherung und Verteilung von Energie wurde in den vergangenen Jahrzehnten versäumt.[5] Der Ausstieg aus der verbrennungsbasierten Bereitstellung von Raumwärme und Warmwasser führt zu einem Einstieg in strombasierte Systeme wie Wärmepumpen. Da momentan noch Strom gespart werden muss, fordert der Gesetzgeber, Gebäude so auszustatten, dass der Energieverbrauch für Raumwärme reduziert wird.[6] Der Hintergrund hierfür ist, dass deren

3 Z. B. im Maßnahmen- und Gesetzespaket Green Deal der letzten Legislaturperiode der EU-Kommission, das u. a. für eine drastische Reduzierung der Treibhausgasemissionen sorgen soll und neue Ausbauziele für erneuerbare Energien enthält; https://commission.europa.eu/strategy-and-policy/priorities-2019-2024/european-green-deal_de [Abruf: 23.4.2025].

4 Die Fraunhofer-Gesellschaft geht davon aus, dass sich der Strombedarf in den Industrieländern durch Elektrifizierung und Digitalisierung bis 2050 verdreifachen wird; https://www.fraunhofer.de/de/forschung/artikel-2025/energie-fuer-unsere-zukunft.html [Abruf: 23.4.2025]

5 Auch der Baukulturbericht 2024/25 hat gezeigt, dass große Teile der Infrastruktur in Deutschland in unzureichendem Zustand sind; Bundesstiftung Baukultur (Hg.): Baukulturbericht 2024/25. Infrastrukturen, Potsdam 2024, S. 7f.; https://www.bundesstiftung-baukultur.de/fileadmin/files/BKB-24/Baukulturbericht_202425_Infrastrukturen_Auflage_3.pdf [Abruf: 23.4.2025].

6 Vgl. Gesetz zur Einsparung von Energie und zur Nutzung erneuerbarer Energien zur Wärme- und Kälteerzeugung in Gebäuden (Gebäudeenergiegesetz, GEG).

climate change in motion by releasing large volumes of greenhouse gases into the atmosphere.

In order to quench the ever-greater "thirst for energy" in our industrial societies, coal as an energy source was soon supplemented by natural gas and then oil. In the course of time, all three of these energy sources were burned to generate heat. In part, this heat was used to drive piston engines and turbines that in turn served as a source of mechanical power and/or electricity.

The combustion of coal, oil, and natural gas releases, among other emissions, carbon dioxide into the atmosphere. This climate-damaging gas is a substantial factor driving global warming.

In other words, global warming does not result from energy consumption per se but is caused by the emission of climate-damaging gases.[2] It is important to understand this, as it means that energy which does not entail emissions is irrelevant in climatological terms.

In order to manage climate change, we need to use those energies that are not caused by combustion: These so-called *renewable energies* rely on wind power, solar irradiation, and other sources. If we continue to utilise combustion-based energy sources, then we need to "capture" the gases that are released. If we do not succeed in that, then we must stop using combustion-based fuels. Since *carbon capture* is still in its technological infancy and because it also requires, in the case of some of the technologies involved, high energy inputs, at present the only way forward would seem to be to reduce the use of combustion-based energy and increase the share of renewable energies in our overall energy mix.[3]

2 Cf. IPCC: Sections, in *Climate Change 2023: Synthesis Report. Contribution of Working Groups I, II and III to the Sixth Assessment Report of the Intergovernmental Panel on Climate Change* (Geneva, 2023), pp. 35–115.

3 For example, in the package of measures and laws covered by the Green Deal in the last EU Commission legislative period, which among other things is set to achieve a drastic reduction in greenhouse gas emissions and states new targets for expanding renewable energy generating capacity; https://commission.europa.eu/strategy-and-policy/priorities-2019-2024/european-green-deal_de (accessed 23 April 2025).

Das Collegium Academicum in Heidelberg, ein selbstverwaltetes Studentenwohnheim in Holzbauweise, wurde 2023 von DGJ Architektur (Frankfurt am Main) fertiggestellt. | In 2023, Heidelberg's Collegium Academicum, a self-managed student residence hall constructed from wood, was completed by DGJ Architektur (Frankfurt am Main).

In Nordhausen wird das Plattenbauquartier Ossietzky-Wohnhof zu einem klimagerechten Quartier weiterentwickelt. | In Nordhausen, the Ossietzky-Wohnhof housing estate is being transformed into a climate-friendly neighbourhood.

Bereitstellung in Deutschland einen Anteil von ca. 25 Prozent am gesamten Endenergieverbrauch hat, die Reduktion des Wärmeverbrauchs also eine große Hebelwirkung besitzt.[7] Der Gesetzgeber schreibt dafür detaillierte, in ihrer Umsetzung teils sehr kostenintensive Maßgaben vor, die natürlich auch architektonische Auswirkungen haben.

Und wie reduzieren wir die Emissionen?

Mit der Reduktion des Verbrauchs von verbrennungsbasierter Energie geht eine Verringerung von Treibhausgasen einher. Es ist wichtig zu vermerken, dass mit dem Ausstieg also nicht das Ende der Emission von Treibhausgasen verbunden ist. Aufgrund chemischer Reaktionen, etwa bei der Herstellung von Zement, entstehen durch menschliches Handeln auch weiterhin viele klimaschädliche Gase.

Unser Blick muss sich deshalb auf die Reduktion der Treibhausgasemissionen *insgesamt* richten. Die Verminderung muss auf internationaler Ebene angegangen werden. Der wohl bekannteste in diesem Zusammenhang abgeschlossene Vertrag ist das Klimaschutzabkommen von Paris 2015. Hier wurde ein Emissionsreduktionspfad, also eine jährliche Minderung der Emissionen vereinbart. Werden diese Vorgaben tatsächlich umgesetzt, kann die Erwärmung des Erdklimas voraussichtlich auf 1,5 Grad Celsius begrenzt werden.[8]

Zur einfacheren Erfassung der Treibhausgasemissionen werden diese einzelnen Sektoren wie Verkehr, Industrie, Energiewirtschaft und Gebäuden zugewiesen. In Deutschland verfehlen die Sektoren Verkehr und Gebäude seit Jahren die vorgegebenen Grenzwerte.[9]

7 Vgl. Deutsche Energie-Agentur (Hg.): Dena-Gebäudereport 2025. Zahlen, Daten, Fakten zum Klimaschutz im Gebäudebestand, 2024, S. 57ff.; https://www.dena.de/infocenter/gebaeudereport-2025/ [Abruf: 23.4.2025].

8 Vgl. Übereinkommen von Paris vom 12. Dezember 2015, Artikel 2; https://unfccc.int/sites/default/files/resource/parisagreement_publication.pdf [Abruf: 23.4.2025].

9 Vgl. Dena 2024 (wie Anm. 7), S. 52.

How do we use energy?

Given that humanity will not be able to avoid using energy, exiting the current reliance on fossil fuels means we must instead firmly enter the renewable age. Above all, electricity will play a key role in this context.[4] In order to retain our behavioural patterns to date, the volume of energy used hitherto must be covered henceforth from renewable sources, and the latter must be available in the requisite volumes as and when it is needed. In past decades, the opportunity to expand energy generation, storage, and distribution systems was missed.[5]

If we exit the combustion-based provision of heating for rooms and warm water, we need to enter into wide-scale use of electricity-based systems such as heat pumps. Since at present we still need to reduce electricity consumption levels, lawmakers are demanding that buildings be fitted out such as to reduce the energy consumption levels required for room heating.[6] The background to this: In Germany, providing heating accounts for about 25% of total final energy consumption, thus reducing the heating requirement has great leverage.[7] The legislature has issued detailed specifications for reducing heating requirements for buildings. Putting these measures into practice will, in part, be highly cost-intensive, and they will of course influence architecture going forwards.

4 Fraunhofer-Gesellschaft assumes that the electricity requirement in the industrialized nations will triple by 2050 owing to electrification and digitisation; https://www.fraunhofer.de/de/forschung/artikel-2025/energie-fuer-unsere-zukunft.html (accessed 23 April 2025).

5 The *Baukulturbericht* 2024/25 has also shown that large parts of German infrastructure are not in an adequate shape; Bundesstiftung Baukultur, ed., *Baukulturbericht 2024/25. Infrastrukturen* (Potsdam, 2024), pp. 7–8; https://www.bundesstiftung-baukultur.de/fileadmin/files/BKB-24/Baukulturbericht_202425_Infrastrukturen_Auflage_3.pdf (accessed 23 April 2025).

6 See the German Act on Saving Energy and Using Renewable Energy to Heat and Cool Buildings (Building Energy Act, GEG).

7 Cf. Deutsche Energie-Agentur, ed., *Dena-Gebäudereport 2025. Zahlen, Daten, Fakten zum Klimaschutz im Gebäudebestand*, 2024, pp. 57ff.; https://www.dena.de/infocenter/gebaeudereport-2025/ (accessed 23 April 2025).

Welche Auswirkungen hat das Bauen?

Werden die Emissionen, die bei der Errichtung und Nutzung von Bauwerken entstehen, über die genannten Sektoren hinaus betrachtet, so zeigt sich, dass ein Großteil der Emissionen dort anfällt.[10] Das Bauen spielt folglich bei der Reduzierung der Emissionen eine zentrale Rolle und ist wesentlicher Schauplatz der Energie- und Emissionswende. Im Hinblick auf die von Gebäuden verursachten Emissionen sind drei Handlungsfelder von zentraler Bedeutung:

1. Errichtung: Für den Bau von Gebäuden werden große Mengen an Ressourcen und Energie benötigt. Auch der Transport trägt zu den Emissionen bei, die in der Wertschöpfungskette der Baustoffe entstehen. Lange Transportwege und steigender Energieaufwand bei der Herstellung von Baustoffen haben dazu geführt, dass der Anteil dieser „grauen" Energie an den gesamten Emissionen eines Gebäudes in den letzten Jahren immer größer geworden ist.

2. Nutzung: Wenn wir über den Energieverbrauch von Gebäuden sprechen, meinen wir in den meisten Fällen die Energie, die für deren Betrieb aufzuwenden ist. Dieser Bedarf setzt sich aus der Bereitstellung von Strom und Wärme zusammen. Die Wärmeversorgung stellt eine der größten Herausforderungen dar, da ein Großteil der Wärmeenergie in Deutschland nach wie vor über fossile Energieträger bereitgestellt wird.

10 Der Anteil der Gebäude an der Gesamtemissionsbilanz in Deutschland einschließlich Bau, Nutzung und Abriss/Demontage wird von den Institutionen unterschiedlich eingeschätzt, liegt aber im Konsens bei mindestens 40 Prozent.

And how can we reduce emissions?

Reducing our dependence on combustion-based energy sources will lead to a lowering of greenhouse gas emissions. It is important to note here that exiting fossil-fuel combustion does not spell the end of greenhouse gas emissions per se. Given the chemical reactions innate in the production of cement or steel, in agriculture, animal husbandry, and many other areas, many climate-damaging gases will, through human agency, continue to be released into the atmosphere.

We must therefore focus on reducing greenhouse gas emissions as a whole. Achieving such a decrease must occur at the global level. Probably the best-known climate protection treaty in this context is the 2015 Paris Agreement, which included agreement on an emission reduction path, meaning an annual decrease in emissions. If these stipulations are in fact met, global climate warming should be limited to 1.5°C compared to the level before the Industrial Revolution.[8]

In order to simplify the calculation of greenhouse gas emissions, these are assigned to individual fields, such as transportation, industry, the energy sector, and buildings. In Germany, the transportation and buildings sectors continue to overshoot the threshold values set for them.[9] So much remains to be done in this regard.

What impact does construction have?

If we look beyond the aforementioned sectors and consider emissions generated during the construction and use of buildings, it becomes clear that they are

8 Cf. the Paris Agreement of 12 December 2015, Article 2; https://unfccc.int/files/meetings/paris_nov_2015/application/pdf/paris_agreement_english_.pdf (accessed 23 April 2025).

9 See Dena 2024 (see note 7), p. 52.

Für einen Kindergarten von Lendager Arkitekter (Kopenhagen, vgl. S. 44ff.) wurden Materialien einer abgerissenen Schule wiederverwendet. | This kindergarten, designed by Lendager Arkitekter (Copenhagen, see pp. 44ff.), was built using materials recycled from a demolished school.

Ein ehemaliger Supermarkt in Karwe wurde von Studio Other Spaces (Berlin) unter Beibehaltung und Sanierung der vorhandenen Bausubstanz mit einer neuen Hülle versehen. | Studio Other Spaces (Berlin) gave a former supermarket in Karwe a new façade while retaining and modernising the existing substance of the building.

Die Fassade des Pariser Pavillon Jardins des Atelier du Pont (Paris) besteht aus Holzrahmen, die das begrünte Flachdach tragen. | The façade of the Jardins des Atelier du Pont (Paris) pavilion in Paris boasts a wooden frame with a greened flat roof.

3. Rückbau: Beim Abbruch von Gebäuden müssen nicht nur Baustoffe entsorgt werden. Es entstehen auch Emissionen, sei es durch Abbrucharbeiten, den Abtransport des Materials oder andere Prozesse. Hinzu kommt, dass ein Neubau, der häufig mit dem Rückbau einhergeht, durch den intensiven Einsatz von Ressourcen zu neuen Emissionen beiträgt.

Diese Emissionen müssen dringend reduziert werden. Das gilt für Bauwerke über ihren gesamten Lebenszyklus hinweg. Die Grenzen dieser Betrachtung haben über das einzelne Gebäude hinauszugehen, da der Einsatz von Ressourcen, die Energieerzeugung und -versorgung oder die Einbeziehung regionaler Faktoren auch Fragen der Stadt-, Quartiers- und Landschaftsplanung betreffen. Letztlich stellen diese Herausforderungen im Hinblick auf die notwendige Energie- und Emissionswende eine Frage in den Mittelpunkt: Wie wollen und müssen wir in Zeiten des Klimawandels bauen?

Architektur! Und warum dieses Buch?

Mit unserem Projekt wollten wir Folgendes erfahren und vermitteln: Wenn der Architektur und dem Bauen insgesamt eine Schlüsselrolle bei der Reduktion von Emissionen zukommt, was können und müssen Planende dann tun und wie sehen mögliche Maßnahmen konkret aus? Wie gehen Architektinnen und Architekten mit den Herausforderungen des Klimawandels um? Wie können Gebäude ressourcenschonend geplant werden? Lässt sich der Energieverbrauch an die Architektur eines Gebäudes koppeln? Wie sieht eine Null-

responsible for a large proportion of emissions.[10] Construction therefore plays a key role in reducing emissions and is a critical area for the energy and emissions transition. As regards the emissions caused by buildings, three fields of action are of central importance:

1. Construction: Large volumes of resources and energy are required to construct buildings. Transportation of the materials also contributes to the emissions that arise in the construction materials value-added chain. Long transport routes and the growing energy inputs needed to produce construction materials have led in recent years to a continual increase in the proportion of emissions generated by this *grey energy* in the total emissions balance of buildings.

2. Use: When we talk about buildings' energy consumption, in most cases we are referring to the energy required to operate them. This energy is required to generate two things: electricity and heat. In this context, providing heat is one of the greatest challenges because, in Germany, a large proportion of the energy required to provide heating continues to be from fossil fuels.

3. Demolition: Tearing down buildings involves two things. First, we need to dispose of building materials and, second, we create emissions, be it through the demolition work itself, when transporting the materials away from site, or by other processes. Furthermore, the very act of

10 Estimates of the share that buildings account for in Germany's total emissions balance including construction, use, and demolition/disassembly differ from one institution to the next, but the consensus is that it is at least 40%.

Emissions-Architektur aus? Den unmittelbar am Bauen Beteiligten kommt bei der Beantwortung dieser Fragen eine Schlüsselrolle zu. Aber wir alle müssen die Zusammenhänge zwischen Energieverbrauch, klimaschädlichen Emissionen, Bauen und Architektur verstehen.

Dazu dient das vorliegende Buch ebenso wie das begleitende Ausstellungsprojekt. Beides soll zu einem Mehr an Wissen, zu einem Umdenken und zum Perspektivwechsel beitragen. Entwürfe – wie die hier gezeigten –, die über das Notwendige der Energiewende hinausgehen und das baukulturell Wünschenswerte betonen, spielen eine wichtige Rolle für die Akzeptanz einer neuen, emissionsgerechten Architektur. Deshalb zeigen wir anhand innovativer und wegweisender Architekturprojekte praktische Umsetzungsmöglichkeiten. Ziel ist es, attraktives Bauen und Klimaneutralität in Einklang zu bringen. Die vorgestellten beispielhaften Lösungen sollen dazu beitragen, dieses Ziel in der Breite voranzutreiben und das allgemeine Bewusstsein für die Möglichkeiten klimagerechten Bauens zu schärfen.

Das Buch stellt Bauten vor, die sich durch ihre zukunftsweisende Gestaltung auszeichnen. Die inhaltlichen Zusammenhänge „Energie – Emissionen – Gebäude – Architektur" werden erklärt und vermittelt. Es werden Lösungsansätze zur Reduktion von Emissionen und Energiebedarf sichtbar, die beispielsweise in Energieträgern, Materialqualitäten oder einem effizienten Betrieb liegen.

Bei der Auswahl der Projekte haben wir uns auf bereits realisierte Projekte im europäischen Raum beschränkt. Sie befinden sich in städtischen und

demolition often leads to a subsequent new build, which, as outlined above, itself contributes to releasing new emissions given the intensive use of resources required.

We must urgently reduce these emissions. In this context, we must consider buildings across their entire life cycle. This focus must go beyond the individual building itself, as the utilisation of resources, energy generation, and energy supplies or the inclusion of regional factors also affect issues relating to urban, neighbourhood, and landscape planning. In the final instance, with a view to the energy and emissions transformation that is necessary, these challenges place one question at the absolute centre of things: How do we want to build—or rather, how must we build in the age of climate change?

Architecture! And why this book?

This book and exhibition project arose in response to those challenges outlined above. Our goal was to address the following questions and communicate our findings more widely: If architecture and construction as a whole play a key part in reducing emissions, then what can and must planners do, and what shape will the actual measures take? How do architects tackle the challenges of climate change? How can buildings be planned in such a way as to reduce resource consumption? Can energy utilisation be linked to the architecture of a building? What does zero-emissions architecture look like?

Those directly involved in construction have a key role to play in answering these questions. However, we must all seek to understand the inter-

ländlichen Gebieten und variieren in Größe, Finanzierung und Bauaufgabe. Es sind Wohnungsbauten darunter, Kindergärten und Schulen. Es werden Lebensmittelmärkte, Bürogebäude, Rathäuser, öffentliche Plätze oder ganze Quartiere gezeigt. Und wir gehen der Frage nach, welche Auswirkungen dies alles auf die Landschaftsgestaltung hat. Dabei war es uns wichtig, überwiegend serienmäßig hergestellte Baumaterialien zu zeigen und keine Sonderanfertigungen. Auch der soziale Anspruch der Bauprojekte spielte eine große Rolle.

Acht Piktogramme (Legende siehe Umschlaginnenseite) verweisen auf die verschiedenen Ansätze der Projekte zur Umsetzung einer emissionsarmen und energiebewussten Architektur. Jeder Ansatz stellt einen Lösungsweg dar, unterscheidet sich in der Umsetzung und markiert eine wichtige Perspektive auf die Herausforderungen, die der Klimawandel an das Bauen und die Architektur stellt.

Es war uns ein besonderes Anliegen, vielfältige Wege aufzuzeigen: von der einfachen Bauweise über den Einsatz von Technik bis hin zur Umnutzung des Bestandes oder der aktiven Einbeziehung der Natur. Ein „Wettbewerb" unterschiedlicher Ansätze kann den Weg zur Emissionsminderung nur beflügeln.

Wir sind bei unserer Arbeit auf viele spannende Ansätze gestoßen, auch und insbesondere in der Forschung, und bedauern, dass wir sie aus Platzgründen nicht umfassender darstellen können. Unser Anspruch bestand ganz dezidiert darin, das jetzt Machbare und sofort Umsetzbares zu präsentieren. Ein zweiter Punkt kam hinzu: Diskussionen über die Energieversorgung gestalten sich rasch kompliziert, teilweise auch polemisch. Andres Herzog (S. 146ff.) beschreibt eben diese Schwierigkeit in der Kommunikation und

connection of energy consumption, climate-damaging emissions, construction, and architecture.

That is the purpose of the present book and the exhibition project, both of which are intended to help us increase our knowledge, prompt us to think in new ways, and change our perspective.

Proposals such as those described in the present publication—which go beyond the energy transformation we so desperately need, emphasising also what is desirable in our built culture—most certainly help foster acceptance of a new architecture that does justice to reducing emissions. This is why we are using innovative and trailblazing architectural projects to present how progress can be achieved in practical terms. The objective: to strike a balance between attractive buildings and climate neutrality. The exemplary solutions illustrated here are intended to help ensure that a wider audience becomes familiar with this objective and to heighten general awareness of the opportunities that exist for climate-friendly construction.

The book presents buildings that stand out for their pioneering design for tomorrow. The interrelationships of "Energy—Emissions—Buildings—Architecture" are carefully explained. Moreover, it highlights possible solutions to reducing emissions and energy requirements, for example, that derive from the energy sources, types of materials, and operational efficiency.

Selecting the projects

In the selection process, we limited ourselves to projects that have already been completed in Europe. They are located in both urban and rural areas, and

wie man sie überwinden kann. Aus einer anderen Perspektive, aber mit den gleichen Problemen konfrontiert, beschreibt Regine Leibinger (S. 64ff.) das Verhältnis eines Architekturbüros zu seinen Auftraggebern.

Wir bedanken uns bei den beteiligten Architekturbüros für die anregende Zusammenarbeit und die Bereitstellung von Plänen, Fotografien und energietechnischen Informationen zu den einzelnen Projekten. Unserem wissenschaftlichen Beirat danken wir für die engagierten Diskussionen. Ohne sie alle wäre dieses Projekt nicht möglich gewesen. Wir wünschen der Publikation eine ebenso interessierte Leserschaft.

Die Herausgeber

differ in terms of size, financing, and construction task. They include housing, kindergartens, and schools—not to mention food markets, office buildings, city halls, public squares, entire neighbourhoods, and much more besides. And we explore the question of what impact all of this has on landscape architecture. We felt it important, first and foremost, to present construction materials that are mass-produced and not customised variants for a one-off purpose. The social intentions behind the construction projects were also important to us.

The different approaches the projects take in implementing low-emission and energy-aware architecture can be seen at a glance in eight pictograms (see key on back flap). Each approach constitutes a path to a solution; they differ in terms of method, and offer a significant perspective on the challenge that climate change poses for construction and architecture.

It was of special importance to us to highlight a diversity of approaches: from simple constructions to those requiring a lot of technology, through to converting existing structures or actively incorporating nature. A degree of "competition" between different methods can help move us further along the path to reducing emissions.

In our preparatory work we came across many exciting approaches, particularly in research, and we regret that for reasons of space we cannot present them more extensively. We consciously set out to showcase what is feasible today and could immediately be realised. There was a second point, too: Discussions about energy provisioning can swiftly get complicated, if not polemical. Andres Herzog (pp. 146–53) describes precisely this difficulty in communications and how we can overcome it. From a different perspective,

but confronting the same problems, Regine Leibinger (pp. 64–68) describes the relationship between an architecture practice and its clients.

We would like to thank the participating architecture practices for their stimulating ideas and for providing plans, photographs, and technical energy specifications on the individual projects. We are also most grateful to our scientific advisory council for the in-depth discussions. Without them, this project would simply not have been possible. We hope this publication reaches very many interested readers.

The editors

Werner Sobek

Bauen im Spannungsfeld von Energieeffizienz und Emissionsreduktion

Construction at the intersection of energy efficiency and emissions reduction

Das Bauschaffen ist seit mehreren Jahrzehnten von einer zunehmend weiter ausgreifenden Forderung nach *Energieeffizienz* geprägt. Warum Wohngebäude energieeffizient sein sollen, wird bei Nachfrage aber häufig nicht deutlich. Das Spektrum der Antworten spannt sich von „Umweltschutz“ und „weniger Emissionen“ bis hin zu „bezahlbaren Heizkosten“. Angesichts einer derart diffusen Ausgangslage erscheint es sinnvoll, sich zunächst näher mit den Ursachen und der Begründung der Forderung nach Energieeffizienz zu beschäftigen. Dies umso mehr angesichts der Tatsache, dass die Menschheit eigentlich kein Energieproblem hat ...

Energie

Der dem Laien eher abstrakt vorkommende Begriff *Energie* bezeichnet die Fähigkeit von etwas, Arbeit zu verrichten oder Strahlung (zumeist Wärmestrahlung) freizusetzen. Energie kann nicht erzeugt und nicht vernichtet werden. Energie kann nur von einer Form in eine andere Form, also zum Beispiel von Wärme in Kraft umgewandelt werden.[1] Die an diesen Vorgängen beteiligte Energiemenge wird dabei niemals kleiner oder größer. Dieses Prinzip wird auch *Energieerhaltungssatz* genannt.

Die Sonne strahlt ungefähr 10.000-mal mehr Energie auf die Erde ein als die Menschen für alle ihre Bedürfnisse benötigen. Windenergie, Wasserkraft, Wellenenergie, Geothermie und andere kommen hinzu. Damit ist klar, dass die Menschheit kein Energieproblem als solches hat. Sie hat allerdings ein *Energieträgerproblem*. Dies aber ist etwas Anderes.

1 Der Begriff „erneuerbare Energie“ ist also, von seiner inhaltlichen Aussage her betrachtet, Unfug.

For several decades now, construction activities have been characterised by increasing calls for greater energy efficiency. However, if asked, advocates of energy-efficient housing often cannot say why this need be the case. The range of answers extends from “environmental protection” and “fewer emissions” to “affordable heating costs”. Given such diffuse statements, it seems sensible to focus more closely on the causes and justifications for these calls for *energy efficiency*, especially if one bears in mind that humanity does not have an energy problem in the first place.

Energy

Energy, which the layperson may feel is an abstract concept, describes the ability of something to perform a task or release radiation (mostly heat radiation). Energy cannot be created and it cannot be destroyed.[1] Physics tell us that energy can only be converted from one form into another, e.g., from heat into power. The volume of energy involved in these processes never becomes smaller or larger. This principle is also referred to as the *law of conservation of energy*.

The sun radiates about 10,000 times more energy onto Earth than humans need to cover all their needs. Add wind energy, hydropower, wave energy, geothermal energy, and other sources to the equation, and it is clear that humanity does not have an energy problem per se. What it does have is an *energy source problem*. But that is something different.

1 In other words, the term “renewable energy” is essentially nonsense.

Energieträger

Ein Energieträger ist ein Stoff oder eine Substanz, die in sich Energie speichert, welche man an einem anderen Ort und zu einem anderen Zeitpunkt mit geeigneten Mitteln freisetzen kann. Der über lange Zeit wichtigste in Deutschland genutzte „technische“ Energieträger war Kohle. Diese wurde nach dem Zweiten Weltkrieg zunächst durch Erdöl, dann in kleineren Mengen durch Kernkraft, später zunehmend durch Erdgas und schließlich durch die sogenannten *erneuerbaren Energien* abgelöst. Die Reihenfolge, in der die einzelnen Energieträger dominierten bzw. ihre Dominanz verloren, hat nur bedingt etwas mit ihrer Verfügbarkeit am Markt zu tun. Weitaus stärker war diese Entwicklung von wirtschaftsstrategischen Interessen und Einflüssen geprägt.

Energie als wirtschaftsstrategischer Gegenstand

Bereits der Übergang (zumindest in Westdeutschland) von Steinkohle zu Erdöl war Teil eines Gesamtkonzepts der USA, das auch den Marshallplan (1948–1952) beinhaltete. Durch den mit Druck herbeigeführten Wechsel des Hauptenergieträgers erhielten diese einerseits die Möglichkeit, die Bundesrepublik erforderlichenfalls durch Androhung von Lieferbeschränkungen unter Druck zu setzen, andererseits vergrößerte dies natürlich auch den Markt für ihre Erdölexporte. Entsprechend hart reagierten die USA, als die Sowjetunion der Bundesrepublik nach großen Erdgasfunden in der Zeit um 1960 die Lieferung von billigem Erdgas in großen Mengen anbot. Durch massive Sanktionsdrohungen, die auf zwei eigens dafür verabschiedeten Gesetzen, dem *Foreign Assistance Act* (1961) und dem *Trade Expansion*

Energy sources

An *energy source* is a material or substance that stores energy which, given suitable means, can then be released at another place and at another time. For many years, Germany's most important "technical" energy source was coal. After World War II, coal was replaced initially by oil, then in smaller volumes by nuclear power, later increasingly by natural gas, and finally by so-called *renewable energy sources*. The sequence in which the individual energy sources were dominant, and/or forfeited their dominance, is only partially the result of their availability in the market. It was far more strongly driven by strategic economic interests and influences.

Energy as an object of economic strategy

Germany's transition from hard coal to oil was itself part of an overall US strategy that included the Marshall Plan. At the time, the United States had a monopoly on petroleum. The switch from hard coal to oil as the main energy source gave the United States, on the one hand, the option of "keeping a handle" on (West) Germany by threatening to throttle supply and, on the other, the opportunity to expand their selling market. The US response was therefore severe when the Soviet Union, after discovering major gas fields in the period around 1960, offered to supply West Germany with greater volumes of cheap natural gas. The massive threat of sanctions based on two specially enacted laws, the Foreign Assistance Act (1961) and the Trade Expansion Act (1962), "persuaded" West Germany under Konrad Adenauer to turn down the Russian offer in 1962. As for exiting hard coal, all that remained for West Germany was to switch to

Act (1962) basierten, brachten die USA die Bundesregierung unter Konrad Adenauer 1962 zum Verzicht auf die russische Offerte. Zur Erzeugung von Raumwärme und Warmwasser im Gebäudebereich verblieb mit dem Ausstieg aus der Steinkohle also nur noch der Energieträger Erdöl. Die folgenden Jahre waren entsprechend gekennzeichnet durch den massenhaften Einbau von Erdöltanks in die Vorgärten und Keller deutscher Wohn- und Nichtwohngebäude.

Im weiteren Verlauf der 1960er-Jahre wurden in der Sowjetunion weitere große Erdgasvorkommen entdeckt. Da das Land nicht über eine geeignete Röhrenfabrikation verfügte, wurde der Bundesrepublik Deutschland die langfristige Lieferung von billigem Erdgas im Austausch gegen die Lieferung geeigneter Rohre angeboten. Unter der Regierung von Willy Brandt unterzeichnete man im Jahr 1970 als „Röhren-Erdgas-Geschäft" den ersten Vertrag. Die USA hatten die zugehörigen Verhandlungen sehr kritisch begleitet. Das dank der erfolgreichen Öffnung nach Osten unter der Regierung Brandt erstarkte politische Selbstwertgefühl auf der deutschen Seite führte jedoch dazu, dass die USA schließlich nichts unternahmen, um den Vertrag zu behindern, was beispielsweise durch Anwendung der beiden noch immer bestehenden oben genannten Gesetze möglich gewesen wäre.

Infolge der Verstaatlichung der bis dato im Besitz von vier US-Firmen befindlichen ARAMCO (Arabian American Oil Company) durch König Faisal ibn Abd al-Aziz ging das Erdölmonopol 1970 auf Saudi-Arabien über. Um einen militärischen Konflikt mit den USA zu vermeiden, hatte König Faisal sich bereit erklärt, den Gegenwert von ARAMCO in mehreren Jahresraten

oil as an energy source for warming rooms and heating water in buildings. The years that followed were thus characterised by the widespread installation of oil tanks in the front gardens and cellars of German residential and non-residential buildings.

As the 1960s continued, additional large gas fields were found in the Soviet Union. Since they did not have suitable pipeline production facilities, the Soviet Union offered long-term supplies of cheap natural gas to West Germany in return for deliveries of pipes. In 1970, under the Willy Brandt–led government, the first contract was signed for such a "pipes for natural gas" deal. The United States followed these negotiations very "critically". However, because of the stronger political self-confidence in Germany after Brandt's successful opening eastwards, the United States eventually did not prevent the deal, something it could have done by applying the terms of the still-valid Foreign Assistance Act and Trade Expansion Act.

In 1970, King Faisal of Saudi Arabia nationalised ARAMCO (Arabian American Oil Company), which had until then been owned by four US corporations, and the oil monopoly thus passed into Saudi hands. To avoid military conflict with the United States, King Faisal declared his willingness to pay the previous owners the value of ARAMCO in several annual instalments. While the former owners thus emerged from the takeover without incurring a loss, the United Stated had lost its oil monopoly, and it only accepted the deal because King Faisal also promised to sell oil exclusively in US dollars. This marked the birth of the petrodollar. The petrodollar had a seigniorage function, meaning it functioned like the right to mint. Every rise in demand for oil thus

an die vormaligen Anteilseigner zu bezahlen. Während also die ehemaligen Besitzer verlustfrei aus der Übernahme herausgingen, hatten die USA ihre Dominanz im Ölmarkt verloren. Sie akzeptierten dies nur deshalb, weil König Faisal zusagte, fortan alles Erdöl ausschließlich in US-Dollar zu handeln. Das war die Geburt des *Petrodollar*. Dieser hat eine Seigniorage-Funktion, funktioniert also wie das Münzrecht. Jede Steigerung der Nachfrage nach Erdöl führt zu leistungsfreien Einnahmen in den USA in derselben Höhe. Bei einer Produktionssteigerung von 1 Prozent entspricht das derzeit etwa 30 bis 40 Milliarden US-Dollar jährlich. Seit 1970 (die Produktionssteigerung betrug seither durchschnittlich 2 Prozent) summierten sich die leistungsfreien Deviseneinnahmen durch die Petrodollar-Seigniorage auf ca. 1.500 bis 2.000 Milliarden US-Dollar.

Ebenfalls im Jahr 1970 wurde in Bagdad die *OPEC* (Organisation der erdölexportierenden Länder) gegründet. Bereits im Herbst 1973 nutzten die Länder der OPEC ihre neu erlangte Macht: Sie drosselten ihre Lieferungen an die Länder, die Israel im „Jom-Kippur-Krieg" unterstützten. Die dadurch bewirkte erste Erdölpreiskrise war mit Preissteigerungen und einer breiten Verunsicherung der Bevölkerung in Bezug auf die Stetigkeit künftiger Öl-lieferungen verbunden. Zusammen mit den zu dieser Zeit anlaufenden umfangreichen Gaslieferungen aus Russland führte dies dazu, dass die Erzeugung von Raumwärme und Warmwasser in vielen deutschen Gebäuden auf das preiswerte Erdgas umgestellt wurde. Die Konsequenz war jetzt der massenhafte Ausbau von Erdöltanks aus den Vorgärten und Kellern deutscher Wohn- und Nichtwohngebäude.

led to the United States booking income for no effort on the same scale. Assuming an annual increase in production of 1%, that would amount to some $30–40 billion annually. Since 1970 (production has on average climbed by 2%) these no-effort revenues from petrodollar seigniorage have totalled about $1.5–2 trillion.

And it was in 1970 that OPEC (Organization of the Petroleum-Exporting Countries) was founded in Baghdad. By the fall of 1973, the OPEC member states used their new-found power: They cut back oil deliveries to countries that supported Israel in the Yom Kippur War. The resulting oil crisis brought price hikes as well as widespread uncertainty about the reliability of future oil supplies. Together with the extensive gas supplies from the Soviet Union that began at this point, this caused many German buildings to switch over to the more inexpensive fuel of natural gas for heating rooms and water. This in turn resulted in the mass removal of oil tanks from the front gardens and cellars of German buildings.

The shock caused by this first oil crisis prompted the West German government to pass its Law on Energy Saving (EnEG)[2] in 1976. The EnEG applied only to new housing construction and the energy inputs they required to heat rooms and water.

The West German government decided to support the EnEG by diversifying the countries it obtained energy from and diversifying the energy sources. The latter related mainly to ending its reliance on oil and furthering its use of gas. When the Soviet Union offered to significantly boost supply volumes as part of an additional "pipes for natural gas" deal, the United States used a new package

2 Cf. *Gesetz zur Einsparung von Energie in Gebäuden* (Gebäudeenergiegesetz EnEG) of 22 July 1976, came into force on 1 November of the same year. The EnEG laid the foundations for energy standards to be set for buildings in Germany. It created the legal framework on the basis of which other statutory regulations such as the Regulation on Heat Protection (WSchVO) of 1995–2001 and the Regulation on Energy Saving (EnEV) of 2002–20 could then be issued.

Der durch die erste Erdölkrise bewirkte Schock veranlasste die Bundesregierung, 1976 ein *Energieeinspargesetz* (EnEG)[2] zu verabschieden. Das EnEG umfasste nur Wohnungsneubauten und dort den zur Erzeugung von Raumwärme und Warmwasser erforderlichen Energiebedarf. Es diente, ganz offiziell, der Stabilisierung des Bundeshaushalts und der Lockerung der Abhängigkeit Deutschlands von den Erdöllieferstaaten. Es hatte nichts mit irgendwelchen ökologischen Überlegungen zu tun.

Als begleitende Maßnahme zum Energieeinspargesetz beschloss die Bundesregierung unter Helmut Schmidt eine Diversifizierung der Lieferstaaten und der von diesen bezogenen Energieträger. Letzteres betraf hauptsächlich die Reduzierung der Erdölnutzung und die Zunahme der Erdgasnutzung. Als die Sowjetunion anbot, ihre Liefermengen im Rahmen eines weiteren „Röhren-Erdgas-Geschäfts" durch den Bau zusätzlicher Pipelines deutlich zu erhöhen, versuchten die USA unter Ronald Reagan, dies durch ein neues Sanktionspaket, den eigens dafür beschlossenen *Siberian Gas Pipeline Sanctions Act* (1982), zu unterbinden. Nur aufgrund des heftigen und massiven Widerstands in Europa, insbesondere vonseiten Deutschlands und Frankreichs, wurden diese Sanktionsdrohungen nicht umgesetzt, sodass die Pipelines wie geplant gebaut und zusätzliches Gas geliefert werden konnte.

Durch die umfangreichen und kontinuierlichen Lieferungen von Erdgas zu sehr günstigen Preisen entstand in Deutschland eine hohe Versorgungssicherheit, und der deutschen Industrie erwuchs durch niedrige Energiekosten ein bemerkenswerter Marktvorteil. Das führte zu erneuten Sanktionsandrohungen seitens der USA, beispielsweise dem *Countering America's*

2 Vgl. Gesetz zur Einsparung von Energie in Gebäuden (Gebäudeenergiegesetz EnEG) vom 22.7.1976, in Kraft getreten am 1.11.1976. Das EnEG bildete die Grundlage für die energetischen Anforderungen an Gebäude in Deutschland. Mit ihm wurde der rechtliche Rahmen geschaffen, auf dessen Basis andere Gesetze wie die Wärmeschutzverordnung (WSchVO) von 1995 bis 2001 und die Energieeinsparverordnung (EnEV) von 2002 bis 2020 erlassen werden konnten.

of sanctions to try to prevent this with the Siberian Gas Pipeline Sanctions Act (1982). Only as a result of fierce and massive opposition from Europe, specifically Germany and France, were these threatened sanctions not put in place, and the pipelines were built as scheduled and supplied the additional gas.

The extensive and continuous supplies of natural gas at very favourable prices led to great supply security in Germany, lowering energy costs and giving its industrial sector an appreciable market edge. This led to renewed US threats of sanctions, such as the Countering America's Adversaries Through Sanctions Act (2017), the Protecting Europe's Energy Security Act (2019), and the Protecting Europe's Energy Security Clarification Act (2021). One focus of the latter two laws was to prevent the Nord Stream 2 pipeline, which would have further shored up German industry's energy cost advantages and further strengthened Germany's supply security.

Directly following Russia's invasion of Ukraine in 2022, the German federal government announced it was going to swiftly reduce imports of Russian gas to zero. The Russian gas suppliers responded by cutting back deliveries, quickly stopping the supply. The reduction in procured volumes and deliveries led to a drastic decrease in stored gas volumes and simultaneously, at short notice, to the gas volumes required from other suppliers. This phase of gas shortages and the switch away from gas is sometimes termed the "gas crisis". In terms of its impact, but not of its causes, the gas crisis is comparable with the first (1973) and second (1979) oil price shocks.

Today, Germany procures its natural gas from many different countries. Significant amounts of gas obtained by fracking are imported from the

Adversaries Through Sanctions Act (2017), dem *Protecting Europe's Energy Security Act* (PEESA, 2019) sowie dem *Protecting Europe's Energy Security Clarification Act* (PEESCA, 2021). Ein Schwerpunkt der beiden letztgenannten Gesetze war die Verhinderung der Pipeline Nord Stream 2, durch welche die Energiekostenvorteile der deutschen Industrie weiterbestanden hätten sowie die Versorgungssicherheit Deutschlands noch gestiegen wäre.

Unmittelbar nach dem Beginn des Krieges in der Ukraine im Jahr 2022 kündigte die Bundesregierung an, die Abnahmemengen von russischem Erdgas zügig bis auf null zu drosseln. Die russischen Gaslieferanten antworteten ihrerseits mit einer Reduzierung der Lieferungen, sodass es alsbald zu einem Lieferstopp kam. Die Reduktion der Abnahmemengen bzw. Lieferungen führte zu einer drastischen Verringerung der Gasvorräte bei gleichzeitig kurzfristiger Beschaffung der benötigten Gasmengen von anderen Lieferanten. Diese Phase der Verknappung und des Umstiegs wird auch als *Gaskrise* bezeichnet. Diese ist in ihren Auswirkungen, aber nicht ihren Ursachen mit dem ersten (1973) und dem zweiten (1979) Ölpreisschock vergleichbar.

Heute bezieht Deutschland Erdgas aus vielen verschiedenen Ländern. Wesentliche Mengen werden in Form von Fracking-Gas aus den USA bezogen. Die USA haben hierdurch zwar nicht das Monopol auf die deutschen Erdgasimporte erhalten, besitzen jetzt aber einen entscheidenden Hebel zur Beeinflussung der deutschen Politik. Der durch die Sanktionen gegen Russland erzwungene Bezug von Fracking-Gas hat zu einer Wiederbelebung der bis dato am Weltmarkt chancenlosen amerikanischen Fracking-Industrie geführt. Die in Deutschland aufgerufenen Preise für Fracking-Gas liegen deutlich

United States. The United States has not cornered a monopoly on German natural gas imports, but it has gained a decisive lever with which to influence German policymaking.

The imports of gas obtained by fracking, which became necessary as a result of the sanctions against Russia, have led to a revival in the US fracking industry, which until then had no hopes on the world market. The price Germany is paying for such gas is appreciably higher than the prices paid beforehand for Russian pipeline gas. The strongly fluctuating prices for gas obtained by fracking have at times been more than triple what was paid for Russian natural gas. So, while the US fracking industry is delighted by this thriving revenue stream, German industry and households are suffering from significantly higher energy costs.

Since a flip backwards in favour of hard coal and oil on a large scale hardly seems political possible, and would be ecological madness anyway, there have been increasing calls in Germany since 2023 for the reactivation of decommissioned nuclear power stations. The electricity this would provide, its proponents claim, could reduce the country's reliance on gas obtained by fracking. This is only partially correct, as the electricity volumes required go far beyond those that the reactivated nuclear power stations, in combination with the currently available renewable-energy sources, could provide. Moreover, decommissioned nuclear power stations cannot simply be "switched back on".

For almost two decades now, an increasing number of plants for generating renewable energy have been installed. These are mainly offshore wind

höher als die vormals für russisches Erdgas zu leistenden Entgelte. Die stark fluktuierenden Preise für Fracking-Gas betrugen teils mehr als das Dreifache dessen, was für Erdgas aus Russland zu bezahlen gewesen war. Während sich also heute die Fracking-Industrie in den USA über sprudelnde Einnahmen freut, leiden die deutsche Industrie ebenso wie die Haushalte unter deutlich gestiegenen Energiekosten.

Da eine Rückorientierung auf die Verbrennung von Steinkohle und Erdöl im großen Stil politisch kaum durchsetzbar erscheint und zudem ökologischer Irrsinn wäre, tauchen in Deutschland seit 2023 vermehrt Forderungen nach einer Reaktivierung stillgelegter Kernkraftwerke auf. Mit dem von ihnen gelieferten Strom, so die Behauptung, könne die Abhängigkeit von Fracking-Gas-Importen reduziert werden. Dies ist nur teilweise richtig, denn die heute benötigten Strommengen gehen weit über das hinaus, was von den Kernkraftwerken in Kombination mit derzeit bereitstellbaren Mengen an erneuerbarer Energie erzeugt werden könnte. Zudem kann man die stillgelegten Kernkraftwerke nicht einfach wieder „einschalten".

Seit knapp zwei Jahrzehnten werden in Deutschland vermehrt Anlagen zur Gewinnung erneuerbarer Energie installiert. Dabei handelt es sich im Wesentlichen um Windkraftwerke auf See oder auf dem Land sowie um Photovoltaikanlagen. Alle drei Anlagentypen „produzieren" Strom. Der politische Hintergrund für die umfassende Installation von Wind- und Solarkraftwerken bestand einerseits in der Schaffung einer alternativen Energieversorgung, die eine Abkopplung von den Abhängigkeiten, die durch den notwendigen Import von Erdöl und Erdgas bestanden, bewirken sollte. Ein zweiter Grund bestand

parks, on-land wind farms, and photovoltaic plants. All three plant types "produce" electricity. The political background for the extensive installation of wind-power and solar-power plants have entailed, on the one hand, the creation of alternative power supplies that were destined to cut dependencies deriving from the necessary import of oil and natural gas. On the other hand, the intention was to reduce climate-damaging emissions as agreed to in the 1997 Kyoto Protocol.

Energy and climate protection

Already in 1976, the Law on Energy Saving (EnEG) essentially hinged on the demand for energy efficiency. Energy efficiency means the best possible exploitation of an energy source. Boosting efficiency thus means improving the exploited yield.

Initially, the EnEG served exclusively to steady the government budget and ease Germany's dependence on supplies from oil-exporting countries, and it was not until many years later that the law was expanded to include national *climate protection goals.*

Climate protection goals are stipulations for reducing the emission of gases that are damaging to the climate. They have nothing whatsoever to do with energy efficiency. Energy efficiency is therefore also not to be confused with climate protection, although it is repeatedly described in this way, in particular by German lawmakers.

From the point of view of climate protection, an effort to achieve energy efficiency is specifically undertaken if the emphasis is on reducing energy consumption attributable to the use of *combustion-based energy*. The use of

in der im Kyoto-Protokoll von 1997 vereinbarten Reduktion der Emission klimaschädlicher Gase.

Energie und Klimaschutz

Bereits das Energieeinspargesetz EnEG von 1976 hatte als inhaltlichen Kern die Forderung nach Energieeffizienz, also die in einem Energieträger enthaltene Energie möglichst gut auszunutzen. Effizienzsteigerung bedeutet die Verbesserung der Ausbeutung.

Das EnEG, das zunächst ausschließlich der Stabilisierung des Bundeshaushalts und der Lockerung der Abhängigkeit Deutschlands von den Erdöllieferstaaten diente, wurde erst viele Jahre später um den Aspekt des Erreichens nationaler *Klimaschutzziele* erweitert.

Klimaschutzziele sind Vorgaben für die Reduktion der Emission klimaschädlicher Gase. Mit Energieeffizienz haben sie nichts zu tun. Energieeffizienz ist deshalb auch nicht gleichbedeutend mit Klimaschutz, obwohl dies immer wieder, insbesondere auch vom deutschen Gesetzgeber, so dargestellt wird.

Unter Klimaschutzgesichtspunkten ist das Bemühen um Energieeffizienz genau dann und nur dann richtig, wenn es um die Reduktion jenes Verbrauchs geht, der aus der Nutzung von *verbrennungsbasierter Energie* stammt. Die Nutzung *nicht-verbrennungsbasierter Energie* ist klimatologisch irrelevant. Sie bedarf deshalb auch keiner Unterwerfung unter ein Effizienzprinzip. Jedwedes Gesetz zur Einsparung von Energie sollte diese Dinge präzise auseinanderhalten – was leider nicht geschieht, weshalb die Zusammenhänge

non-combustion-based energy is not of relevance in climatological terms and therefore does not need to be subjected to an efficiency principle. Any legislation on saving energy should distinguish carefully between these things. Not that this has happened, which is why the terms are continuously being confused in everyday parlance.[3]

Regrettably, communications from both politicians and the media fail to make clear why legislators today regard energy-efficiency policies as necessary. The three reasons are easy to name, however. The goals are

1. to reduce procurement of oil and natural gas in order to avoid supply and sanctions issues;
2. to continuously reduce the use of combustion-based energy and thus the climate-damaging gases that arise through the combustion process; and
3. to limit not only the use of oil and natural gas by the generalised call for energy efficiency, but also the use of renewable energy, essentially electricity, that is not available in the requisite quantity.

The two latter points bear addressing in detail.

3 The argumentation is confusing as early as section 1, titled "Object and Objective", of the German Building Energy Law GEG. If one were to exclude the word "efficiency boosting", which I have underscored in the sentence below, then the thrust of the second sentence would be unambiguous. In its present form it is anything but, as no one knows what "efficiency-boosting measures to reduce greenhouse gas emissions" are meant to be. Section 1 (1) of the law states: "The objective of this law is to make a significant contribution to achieving national climate protection goals. The intention is to achieve this through economic, socially compatible, and efficiency-boosting measures to reduce greenhouse gas emissions as well as the increasing use of renewable energies or unavoidable waste heat to supply energy to buildings."

in der täglichen Kommunikation permanent durcheinandergebracht werden.[3]

Bedauerlicherweise wird politisch wie medial nicht klar kommuniziert, warum Energieeffizienzpolitik heute seitens des Gesetzgebers als erforderlich angesehen wird. Die drei Gründe dafür sind jedoch einfach zu benennen. Man will

1. den Bezug von Erdöl und Erdgas reduzieren, um die Liefer- und Sanktionsproblematik zu umgehen,
2. durch die kontinuierliche Reduktion der Nutzung verbrennungsbasierter Energie die bei der Verbrennung entstehenden klimaschädlichen Gase reduzieren und
3. durch die generalisierte Forderung nach Energieeffizienz nicht nur die Nutzung von Erdöl und Erdgas, sondern auch die Nutzung der nicht in hinreichendem Umfang lieferbaren erneuerbaren Energie, im Wesentlichen Strom, beschränken.

Auf die beiden letztgenannten Punkte wird nachfolgend näher eingegangen.

3 Bereits in § 1 „Zweck und Ziel" des Gebäudeenergiegesetzes (GEG) wird verwirrend argumentiert. § 1 (1) lautet: „Ziel dieses Gesetzes ist es, einen wesentlichen Beitrag zur Erreichung der nationalen Klimaschutzziele zu leisten. Dies soll durch wirtschaftliche, sozialverträgliche und effizienzsteigernde Maßnahmen zur Einsparung von Treibhausgasemissionen sowie der zunehmenden Nutzung von erneuerbaren Energien oder unvermeidbarer Abwärme für die Energieversorgung von Gebäuden erreicht werden." Würde man das von mir unterstrichene Wort „effizienzsteigernde" weglassen, dann wäre der zweite Satz in seiner Aussage eindeutig. In der vorliegenden Form ist er es nicht, da niemand weiß, was „effizienzsteigernde Maßnahmen zur Einsparung von Treibhausgasemissionen" sein sollen.

Das Emissionsproblem

Mit dem 2005 in Kraft getretenen Protokoll von Kyoto,[4] das als internationales Abkommen im Jahr 1997 im Rahmen der

4 Auf der Klimaschutzkonferenz von Kyoto 1997 wurde das Kyoto-Protokoll verabschiedet, mit dem erstmals verbindliche Ziele für die Reduzierung von Treibhausgasemissionen in den Industrieländern festgelegt wurden.

The emissions problem

The Kyoto Protocol[4] enacted in 2005, which was passed as an international agreement in 1997 in the framework of the United Nations Framework Convention on Climate Change, was the first multinational acknowledgement of the fact that humanity has a massive emissions problem. Emissions of carbon dioxide, nitrous oxides, and fluorinated hydrocarbons have contributed to the earth's warming climate, which entails many serious consequences, such as periods of drought, torrential rainfall, melting glaciers, etc. The consequences of these consequences are collapses in grain, fruit, and vegetable production as a result of heat and drought periods, severe damage to buildings and infrastructure facilities as a result of torrential rainfall, and much more besides.(fig. 1)

In 2009, relatively soon after the passing of the Kyoto Protocol, the European Union resolved a comprehensive climate package to implement the agreed-upon changes. One section of the climate package included the demand that member states enact emission-reduction laws. It then took the German federal government ten years before it issued the (first) Federal Climate Protection Act (2019). For the first time, this law set binding targets for reducing greenhouse gas emissions, albeit targets that fell short of those enshrined in the Kyoto Protocol. The Federal Constitutional Court ruled that the threshold values set were too low, eventually rejecting the law as being "in violation of the Constitution". With the revised, and thus second, Federal Climate Protection Act (2021), the corresponding threshold values were tightened and adjusted to align with the 2016 Paris Agreement on climate change. However, in the aftermath of its being enacted, the law was not heeded

4 The Kyoto climate protection conference took place in 1997. It resolved the Kyoto Protocol, in which for the first time binding targets were set for the reduction of greenhouse gas emissions in the industrialised nations.

Klimarahmenkonvention der Vereinten Nationen UNFCCC verabschiedet worden ist, wurde erstmals auf multinationaler Ebene die Tatsache anerkannt, dass die Menschheit ein massives Emissionsproblem hat. Emissionen von Kohlendioxid, Methan und Distickstoffoxid (Lachgas) und Fluorkohlenwasserstoffen führen zu einer Erwärmung des Erdklimas, die wiederum eine ganze Reihe weiterer Folgen, unter anderem Dürreperioden, Starkregenfälle, Gletscherschmelzen usw. nach sich zieht. Die Folgen dieser Entwicklungen sind Einbrüche in der Getreide-, Obst- und Gemüseproduktion infolge von Hitze- und Dürreperioden, schwere Schäden an Gebäuden und Infrastruktureinrichtungen durch Unwetter und vieles mehr.(Abb. 1)

Die Europäische Union hat zur Umsetzung des Kyoto-Protokolls bereits 2009 – und damit vergleichsweise zügig – ein umfassendes *Klimapaket* verabschiedet. Ein Teil dieses Klimapakets bestand in der Aufforderung an die Mitgliedsstaaten, Emissionsreduktionsgesetze zu erlassen. Die Bundesregierung benötigte daraufhin zehn Jahre bis zum Erlass des (ersten) *Bundes-Klimaschutzgesetzes* (2019). Damit wurden in Deutschland erstmals verbindliche, allerdings deutlich unter den Vorgaben des Kyoto-Protokolls liegende Ziele zur Reduzierung des Treibhausgasausstoßes festgelegt. Das Bundesverfassungsgericht stufte die festgelegten Grenzwerte als viel zu niedrig ein und verwarf das Gesetz schließlich als „verfassungswidrig". Mit dem überarbeiteten, nun zweiten *Bundes-Klimaschutzgesetz* (2021) wurden die entsprechenden Grenzwerte verschärft und an die Forderungen des Pariser Abkommens angeglichen. Dessen Festlegungen wurden in der Folge allerdings weder vom Gesetzgeber selbst noch von sonst jemandem beachtet oder

or adhered to, neither by the legislature itself nor by anyone else. In 2023, the law was again changed in the context of political horse-trading[5] within the ruling coalition, details of which were not revealed to the public. The resulting changes rendered one of the most important laws of recent decades almost completely ineffective, an incomprehensible and, given the world's climate situation, essentially irresponsible outcome.

The switch to electricity

To reduce emissions of climate-damaging gases means exiting from combustion-based processes as a way of supplying energy. That in turn means an almost complete switchover to energy provisioning largely based on electricity. This is a trend that should be unequivocally welcomed, and we have known for a long time that it is necessary. Regrettably, lawmakers have failed to swiftly advance the expansion of renewable-energy sources, and, at the same time, build or expand the grids necessary to transport and distribute the electricity. For that reason, we now face a situation in which we cannot transition away from combustion-based energy as swiftly as we should. Hence, the legislature has chosen a bail-out route: Electricity consumption to generate heat for rooms shall be limited by construction measures, essentially by thermal insulation. This means continuing the energy-efficiency policy in the field of construction, albeit for different reasons: The focus is on preventing the collapse of the electricity supply system.

In the pending phase of accelerated grid expansion and faster supply of electricity, it will be imperative to accept at least temporary supply-volume

5 On 31 August 2023, over sixty German professors of constitutional and international law published an open letter to the German federal government. They drew attention to its duty to fulfil its international and constitutional obligations and demanded "as scholars of constitutional and international law that the federal legislative organs not dilute the Climate Protection Act", https://jurios.de/2023/09/04/juraprofessorinnen-setzen-sich-fuer-klimaschutz-ein.

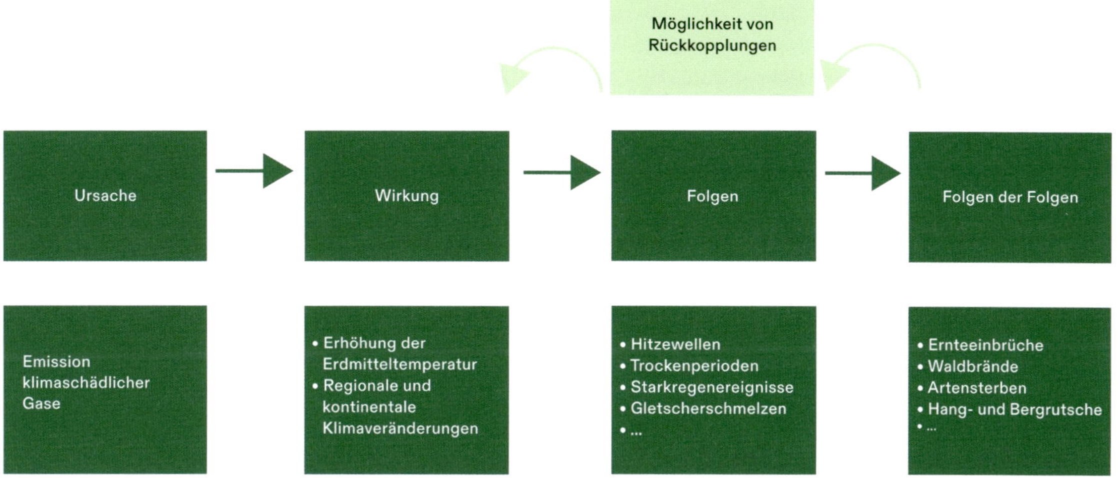

Abb. 1 Die Ursache-Wirkung-Folgenbeziehung am Beispiel der Emission klimaschädlicher Gase in die Atmosphäre. Die Darstellung weist auch auf mögliche Rückkopplungseffekte hin. So können etwa durch Waldbrände wie 2023/24 in Kanada große Mengen an CO_2 freigesetzt werden, die einer weiteren Erhöhung der Erdmitteltemperatur Vorschub leisten. |
Fig. 1 The cause-and-effect relationship, taking as example the emission of climate-damaging gases in the Earth's atmosphere. The representation also points to possible feedback loops. For example, forest fires, such as occurred in Canada in 2023 and 2024, release large volumes of CO_2, which in turn triggers a further increase in the Earth's mean temperature.

restrictions. A conscious budgeting of electricity, characterised by low-energy appliances, the provision of warm water and room heat whenever electricity is available, automatic room-temperature regulation, and much more besides will be needed until such a time as the electricity required for the switchover to electromobility and electrically powered buildings can be sourced from renewable energy.

Needless to say, electricity supplies can be supplemented by procuring electricity from outside the country, which, with the exception of electricity from French nuclear power stations, comes with a high CO_2 encumbrance. A sufficient provision of electricity could thus be ensured, even if the idea should be rejected for ecological reasons. This would not alter the dilemma of insufficient transport and distribution grid capacities.

With the transition to electromobility and electrically powered buildings, the price of electricity would invariably have to change, too. Energy from electricity at present costs the end consumer about seven to ten times as much as does energy from oil or natural gas. The price of electricity includes a series of duties ranging from network fees to offshore liability charges. If at least part of these levies were to be reduced or applied equally to other energy sources, then operating buildings with electricity could become an economically attractive proposition.

Saving electricity—but only in buildings?

A fact that is hardly the subject of public discussion to date is that lawmakers have not restricted the consumption of energy in the field of electromobility.

eingehalten. Im Jahr 2023 wurde das Gesetz im Rahmen eines der Öffentlichkeit nicht vermittelten politischen Geschachers[5] innerhalb der Regierungskoalition erneut geändert. Die vorgenommenen Änderungen führen im Grunde zur Wirkungslosigkeit eines der wichtigsten Gesetze der vergangenen Jahrzehnte, was angesichts der Klimasituation in der Welt völlig unverständlich und letztlich unverantwortlich ist.

Der Umstieg auf Elektrizität

Die Reduktion der Emission klimaschädlicher Gase bedeutet den Ausstieg aus den verbrennungsbasierten Prozessen zur Bereitstellung von Energie. Das wiederum bedeutet einen nahezu vollständigen Umstieg auf eine weitestgehend auf Elektrizität basierende Energieversorgung. Dies ist eine uneingeschränkt zu begrüßende Entwicklung, deren Notwendigkeit seit Langem bekannt ist. Bedauerlicherweise hat es der Gesetzgeber jedoch versäumt, den Ausbau der erneuerbaren Energien schnell voranzubringen und gleichzeitig die für den Transport der Elektrizität erforderlichen Trassen und Verteilernetze zu bauen bzw. auszubauen. Deshalb stehen wir heute vor dem Resultat, dass wir aus der Nutzung verbrennungsbasierter Energie nicht so schnell aussteigen können, wie wir wollen bzw. sollten. In dieser Situation wählt der Gesetzgeber einen Ausweg: Der Stromverbrauch zur Erzeugung von Raumwärme soll durch bauliche Maßnahmen, im Wesentlichen durch Wärmedämmung, beschränkt werden. Das bedeutet die Fortsetzung der Energieeffizienzpolitik im Bauwesen, jetzt aber aus anderen Gründen: Es geht darum, den Zusammenbruch der Elektrizitätsversorgung zu verhindern.

5 Am 31. August 2023 veröffentlichten mehr als 60 deutsche Professorinnen und Professoren einen offenen Brief an die Bundesregierung. Sie wiesen diese auf die Pflicht zur Erfüllung ihrer völker- und verfassungsrechtlichen Verpflichtungen hin und forderten „als Wissenschaftlerinnen und Wissenschaftler des Verfassungs- und Völkerrechts die gesetzgebenden Organe des Bundes auf, das Klimaschutzgesetz nicht abzuschwächen"; https://jurios.de/2023/09/04/juraprofessorinnen-setzen-sich-fuer-klimaschutz-ein/ [Abruf: 6.2.2025].

If, and this is the case at present, there is a shortfall in electricity supplies that requires efficiency measures in the construction sector, then the high electricity consumption of electric vehicles, which are becoming ever larger and heavier, cannot be neglected. Social tension is inevitable if one person with a very large electric vehicle uses an excessive amount of electricity[6] and another person has to spend a great deal to ensure their home is energy efficient, all in order to save electricity that the first person simply wastes.

Energy-efficiency policymaking

From the outset, energy policies in Germany have been geared to energy efficiency. They set out to achieve energy efficiency in buildings through a plethora of individual and highly detailed measures and threshold values. The Building Energy Act GEG 2024[7] itself currently consists of 115 articles (seventeen of them have since been deleted) including a list of fines and eleven appendices. The wording of the law is so complicated that even in the case of simple questions it requires guidance from third parties.(fig. 2) It is hardly surprising that the legislation, whose stipulations far exceed the bounds of comprehensibility,[8] has not been welcomed either by the experts or the general public. Not even the objectives stated in article 1 meet the modest linguistic standards one might expect.[9]

6 The German population's fear of having a limited range with their cars has led to electric vehicles now being offered with a range of 1,000 km. If one assumes that a range of 100 km requires about 120 kg of battery then it becomes clear how much battery weight is uselessly moved back and forth in Germany each day, with a corresponding increase in electricity consumption.

7 The full name reads: Act on Saving Energy and the Use of Renewable Energies to Generate Heat and Cooling in Buildings (Building Energy Act GEG). Issued on 8 August 2020. Last amended on 16 October 2023.

8 One of the almost innumerable impossible formulations in the GEG is that which governs overall energy requirements. Article 15 actually states: "(2) The highest value for the annual primary energy requirement of a residential building to be erected shall be calculated as per para. 1 in line with articles 20, 22–24, article 25 paras. 1–3 and 10, articles 26–29, articles 31 and 33."

9 On this, see note 3.

In der vor uns stehenden Phase eines beschleunigten Netzausbaus und beschleunigter Bereitstellung von Elektrizität ist es unumgänglich, Liefermengenbeschränkungen zumindest zeitweise zu akzeptieren. Ein bewussteres Haushalten mit Strom, gekennzeichnet durch sparsame Geräte, eine Warmwasser- und Raumwärmeaufbereitung dann, wenn Strom verfügbar ist, automatische Raumtemperaturregelungen und vieles mehr, ist so lange erforderlich, bis der durch den Umstieg auf Elektromobilität und elektrisch betriebene Gebäude bedingte Strombedarf über erneuerbare Energien gedeckt werden kann.

Natürlich kann man die Stromversorgung durch Bezug aus dem Ausland, der, mit Ausnahme französischen Atomstroms, in hohem Maße CO_2-behaftet ist, ergänzen. Die hinreichende Bereitstellung von Strom könnte damit abgesichert werden, auch wenn dies ökologisch abzulehnen ist. Das Dilemma besteht dann aber immer noch in der nicht ausreichenden Kapazität der Transport- und Verteilernetze.

Mit dem Übergang zur Elektromobilität und zu elektrisch betriebenen Gebäuden wird eine Neugestaltung der Zusammensetzung des Strompreises unumgänglich. Energie aus Strom kostet für den Endverbraucher derzeit das etwa Sieben- bis Zehnfache der Energie aus Heizöl oder Erdgas. Der Strompreis beinhaltet eine Reihe von Abgaben wie Netzentgelte bis hin zu einer Offshore-Haftungsumlage. Würde man zumindest einen Teil dieser Abgaben reduzieren oder die anderen Energieträger entsprechend belasten, dann würde der Betrieb von Gebäuden mit Strom auch ökonomisch attraktiv werden.

It is hard to understand why the legislature restricted the scope of the act only to operating buildings, meaning the phase in which the buildings are used. It omits consideration of the fact that a considerable amount of energy (the common term here is *grey energy*) is required to construct the buildings. The proportion of grey energy in new builds that adhere to the Energy Savings Ordnance EnEV amount to a multiple of about twenty, and for new builds that adhere to the improved building energy standards, a multiple of about thirty of the annual energy consumption required to provide heat, warm water, and light in the interior.[10]

The effort to achieve energy efficiency during a building's use phase refers mainly to the energy consumption required to provide heating, which accounts for the lion's share, or approximately 70%, of domestic energy consumption.(fig. 3)

Thanks to its energy efficiency policies, Germany succeeded in the two decades from 2002 to 2022[11] in reducing heat consumption per person in housing by about 24%.[12] (fig. 4) This translates into an annual reduction in consumption of approximately 1.2%. During that same period, the mean winter temperature rose by about 2.4°C, which enabled a "natural" lower energy consumption for generating heating of around 14% over the same period.[13] We can deduce that efficiency improvements and financially incentivised savings measures

10 Source: https://www.bbsr.bund.de/BBSR/DE/forschung/programme/zb/Auftragsforschung/5EnergieKlimaBauen/2017/graue-energie/01_start.html?pos=2.

11 No figures are yet available for the years 2023 and 2024.

12 Fig. 4 indicates that: 2002: 8,500 kWh and 2022: 6,300 kWh. The reduction over this twenty-year period thus runs at about 26% compared to the initial value.

13 Rule of thumb: Savings in energy to provide heating: 6% per 1°C increase in mean winter temperature.

Stromsparen nur im Bauwesen?

Ein gesellschaftlich kaum diskutierter Aspekt ist die Tatsache, dass der Gesetzgeber den Energieverbrauch im Bereich der Elektromobilität nicht beschränkt. Wenn es wie aktuell einen zumindest temporären Engpass im Bereich der Stromversorgung gibt, der Effizienzmaßnahmen im Gebäudebereich erzwingt, dann kann der hohe Stromverbrauch der immer größer und schwerer werdenden Elektrofahrzeuge nicht unbeachtet bleiben. Soziale Spannungen sind vorhersehbar, wenn der eine mit seinem großen Elektrofahrzeug übermäßig viel Energie verbraucht[6] und der andere sein Habitat mit großem finanziellen Aufwand auf energetische Effizienz trimmen soll, um den Strom zu sparen, den der andere vergeudet.

Energieeffizienzpolitik

Die Gebäudeenergiepolitik in Deutschland ist seit Anbeginn auf Energieeffizienz ausgerichtet. Energieeffizienz im Bauwesen soll dabei durch eine Vielzahl einzelner, detailliert beschriebener Maßnahmen und Grenzwerte erreicht werden. Allein das Gebäudeenergiegesetz (GEG)[7] von 2024 besteht derzeit aus 115 Paragrafen (17 davon wurden gestrichen) einschließlich Bußgeldverordnung und weiteren elf Anhängen. Das Gesetz ist derart kompliziert formuliert, dass es selbst für einfache Fragestellungen von Dritten bereitgestellter Wegweisungen bedarf. (Abb. 2) Dass eine Gesetzgebung, deren Regelungen das Niveau von Verständlichkeit bei Weitem

6 Die Besorgnis der deutschen Bevölkerung führte dazu, dass mittlerweile Elektrofahrzeuge mit einer Reichweite von 1000 km angeboten werden. Geht man davon aus, dass 100 km Reichweite ungefähr 120 kg Batteriegewicht erfordern, dann wird offensichtlich, wieviel in Deutschland täglich – mit entsprechendem Stromverbrauch – nutzlos hin- und hertransportiert wird.

7 Die vollständige Bezeichnung lautet: Gesetz zur Einsparung von Energie und zur Nutzung erneuerbarer Energien zur Wärme- und Kälteerzeugung in Gebäuden (Gebäudeenergiegesetz, GEG), ausgefertigt am 8.8.2020, zuletzt geändert am 16.10.2023.

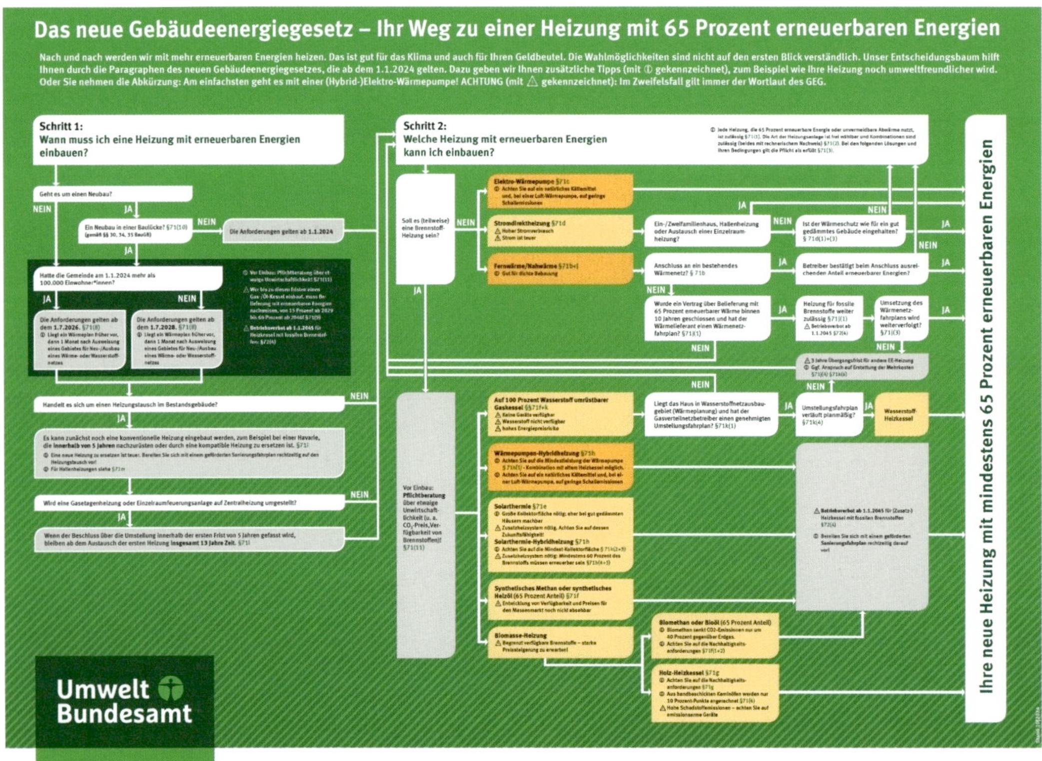

Abb. 2 | Fig. 2 Diese vom Umweltbundesamt (UBA) bereitgestellte Grafik soll den Bürgern dazu verhelfen, das neue Gebäudeenergiegesetz besser zu verstehen. | This diagram compiled by the German Federal Environmental Agency is supposed to help citizens understand at least parts of the new Building Energy Act.

überschritten haben,[8] weder von den Fachleuten, die es umzusetzen haben, noch von der Bevölkerung selbst gutgeheißen wird, liegt auf der Hand. Nicht einmal die in § 1 des Gesetzes gegebene Zielformulierung erfüllt die sprachlichen Anforderungen, die man bei bereits bescheidener Erwartungshaltung erhoffen kann.[9]

Nicht nachvollziehbar ist, dass sich der Gesetzgeber bei seinen Regelungen nur auf den Betrieb der Gebäude beschränkt, also auf deren Nutzungsphase. Er lässt außen vor, dass erhebliche Mengen an Energie (man spricht von *grauer Energie*) für die Herstellung der Bauwerke erforderlich sind. Der Anteil der grauen Energie beträgt bei Neubauten, die die Energieeinsparverordnung (EnEV) einhalten, etwa das Zwanzigfache, und bei Neubauten, die verbesserte Gebäudeenergiestandards einhalten, das ca. Dreißigfache des jährlichen Energieverbrauchs für Raumwärme und -kälte, Warmwasser sowie Beleuchtung.[10]

Das Streben nach Energieeffizienz in der Nutzungsphase von Gebäuden bezieht sich hauptsächlich auf den Energieverbrauch bei der Bereitstellung von Raumwärme. Diese hat mit ca. 70 Prozent den größten Anteil am häuslichen Energieverbrauch.[(Abb. 3)]

Mit der Energieeffizienzpolitik ist es in Deutschland in den Jahren 2002 bis 2022[11] gelungen, den Wärmeverbrauch für Wohnen pro Person um ca. 24 Prozent zu reduzieren.[12 (Abb. 4)] Das entspricht einem Verbrauchsrückgang von jährlich etwa 1,2 Prozent. Im selben Zeitraum ist die Wintermitteltemperatur um ca. 2,4 Grad angestiegen,

8 Eine der beinahe unzähligen unzumutbaren Formulierungen des GEG ist die Regelung des Gesamtenergiebedarfs. Im betreffenden § 15 heißt es tatsächlich: „(2) Der Höchstwert des Jahres-Primärenergiebedarfs eines zu errichtenden Wohngebäudes nach Absatz 1 ist nach Maßgabe des § 20, der §§ 22 bis 24, des § 25 Absatz 1 bis 3 und 10, der §§ 26 bis 29, des § 31 und des § 33 zu berechnen."

9 Siehe Anm. 3.

10 Quelle: https://www.bbsr.bund.de/BBSR/DE/forschung/programme/zb/Auftragsforschung/5EnergieKlimaBauen/2017/graue-energie/01_start.html?pos=2 [Abruf: 6.2.2025].

11 Für 2023 und 2024 liegen noch keine Zahlen vor.

12 Aus Abbildung 4 lässt sich ablesen: 2002 = 8500 kWh und 2022 = 6300 kWh. Die Minderung beträgt im Zeitraum von zwanzig Jahren also, bezogen auf den Ausgangswert, ca. 26 %.

led to a reduction in consumption of roughly 10% over twenty years and thus an average annual decrease of a mere 0.5%.[14]

Energy requirement and energy consumption

The energy savings laws for the construction industry limit, as do the state subsidy systems, the energy *requirement* and not the energy *consumption*. The energy requirement comprises that volume of energy that is necessary to heat an apartment to a specific temperature for the inhabitants' comfort, assuming they behave "correctly". Since inhabitants typically do not behave "correctly" in terms of what the legislature envisaged, the actual energy consumption can be up to 30% higher than the requirement. The difference between requirement and consumption, meaning between "could" and "is", is termed the *energy requirement gap*.[15]

The legislature limits the energy *requirement* per square metre of living space and not per person. This approach is antisocial in the sense that it gives preferential treatment to those who can afford a large apartment and the attendant heating costs. It is, moreover, inacceptable at the macro level of society, as the "permissible" level of emissions of climate-damaging gases must not be pegged to the individual citizen's financial resources.[16] These problems would be solved by restricting energy *consumption* per person.

14 Given that the sums deployed to this end are far in excess of €400 billion, it bears asking whether this approach is the right one.

15 The term *energy requirement gap* is more confusing than it is self-explanatory. It is remarkable how, in discussions around these matters, new terms are repeatedly introduced that actually do not express what they are supposed to mean.

16 The emission of climate-damaging gases can be considered a crime against the atmosphere and therefore as an action against the basis of everyone's lives. It is therefore inacceptable that one person emits more than is permissible under the emission reduction path agreed for society as a whole. In particular, emission rights trading at the private level is inacceptable, as it would lead to emission behaviour that depended on that person's disposable income.

was einen „natürlichen“ Minderverbrauch an Energie zu Erzeugung von Raumwärme von ca. 14 Prozent in der besagten Zeitspanne ermöglicht.[13] Man kann hieraus grob abschätzen, dass Effizienzsteigerungen und finanziell getriebene Einsparmaßnahmen zu einer Verbrauchsreduzierung von ca. 10 Prozent in zwanzig Jahren bzw. durchschnittlich gerade einmal 0,5 Prozent pro Jahr geführt haben.[14]

Energiebedarf und Energieverbrauch

Die Energieeinspargesetze für das Bauwesen begrenzen, analog zu den staatlichen Fördermaßnahmen, den *Bedarf* und nicht den *Verbrauch* von Energie. Der Energiebedarf stellt jene Energiemenge dar, die zum Beheizen einer Wohnung mit einer bestimmten Komforttemperatur bei „korrektem“ Verhalten der Bewohner erforderlich ist. Da diese sich aber typischerweise nicht korrekt im Sinne des Gesetzgebers verhalten, liegt der tatsächliche Energieverbrauch um bis zu 30 Prozent höher. Die Differenz zwischen Bedarf und Verbrauch, also zwischen „könnte“ und „ist“, wird *Energiebedarfslücke* genannt.[15]

Der Gesetzgeber beschränkt den Energiebedarf pro Quadratmeter Wohnraum und nicht pro Person. Dieser Ansatz ist insofern unsozial, als er diejenigen bevorzugt, die sich eine große Wohnung sowie die zugehörigen Heizkosten leisten können. Er ist zudem gesamtgesellschaftlich inakzeptabel, da die „zulässige“ Höhe der Emission klimaschädlicher Gase nicht an die finanziellen Möglichkeiten der

13 Faustformel: Einsparung an Energie zur Aufbereitung von Raumwärme = 6 Prozent pro Grad Celsius Erhöhung der Wintermitteltemperatur.

14 Angesichts der hierfür eingesetzten Mittel in Höhe von weit mehr als 400 Mrd. Euro muss die Frage gestellt werden, ob der eingeschlagene Weg der richtige ist.

15 Der Ausdruck „Energiebedarfslücke“ ist weniger selbsterklärend als verwirrend. Es ist bemerkenswert, warum immer wieder neue Begriffe in die Debatte eingeführt werden, die etwas anderes ausdrücken als eigentlich gemeint ist.

Reducing the energy requirement in the use phase—by thermal insulation

The preferred measures in past decades to lower ambient heating *requirements* relied on construction measures such as good thermal insulation and measures relating to the facilities technology such as an efficient heating system and automatic ambient temperature regulation. Thermal insulation was achieved by utilising materials that possess a low heat transition and thus “thermal insulating properties”. The thermal insulation of building components that come into contact with the outside air or the soil is typically made up of multi-layer elements that involve a load-bearing part, such as a masonry wall; elements with low heat-transition properties, such as a layer of insulation; and components that seal the building against wind and moisture. Frequently the individual components are bonded by adhesives and are then referred to as composite elements, outfitted with multi-layer coating systems, making them hard to recycle later.

Lowering the energy requirement in the use phase as a result of rising mean winter temperatures

At present, the annual mean temperature in Germany is about 10°C. The mean summer temperature runs at 19°C and the mean winter temperature at approximately 2°C. We can assume that the mean winter temperature in Germany will rise by around 1.3–2.4°C by the year 2045.[17] This will translate into a lower heating energy requirement by 2045 of about 10–14%.[18]

As indicated in and discernible from figure 4, heat consumption per person since 2012, and thus over the last ten-plus years, has not fallen, although

17 Werner Sobek, *non nobis – über das Bauen in der Zukunft*, vol. 2 (AV Edition: Stuttgart, 2023).

18 Rule of thumb: For every 1°C increase in mean winter temperature, there is an approximately 6% savings in heating energy.

Energieverbrauch für Wohnen nach Anwendungsbereichen 2020
in %
1
8
6
15
70
Raumwärme
Warmwasser
Sonst. Prozesswärme
Sonst. Betrieb von Elektrogeräten
Beleuchtung
Rundungsbedingte Abweichung möglich.
© Statistisches Bundesamt (Destatis), 2024

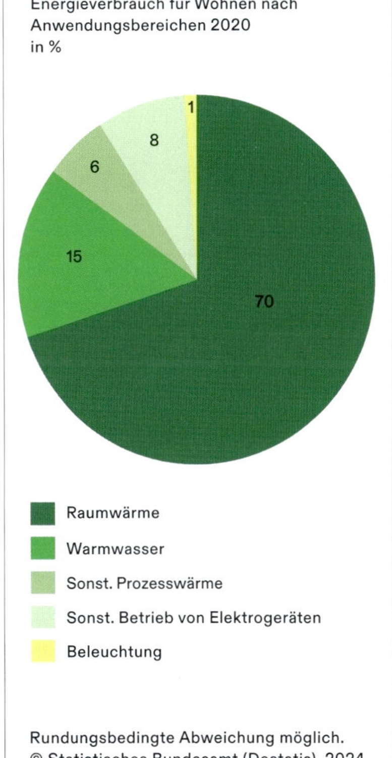

Abb. 3 Prozentuale Aufteilung des Energieverbrauchs in der Nutzungsphase von Wohngebäuden in Deutschland. Die Bereitstellung von Raumwärme hat gegenüber Warmwasser, Raumkühlung und Beleuchtung den größten Anteil. | Fig. 3 Distribution (in percent) of energy consumption in residential buildings in Germany during the use phase. The provision of ambient heating accounts for a far larger share than that of warm water, cooling, and lighting.

Abb. 4 Nach einem spürbaren Rückgang im Zeitraum 2002 bis 2013 ist der Wärmeverbrauch pro Person seit 2014 mehr oder weniger konstant geblieben. | Fig. 4 After an appreciable fall in the period of 2002 to 2013, heat consumption per person has more or less remained constant since 2014.

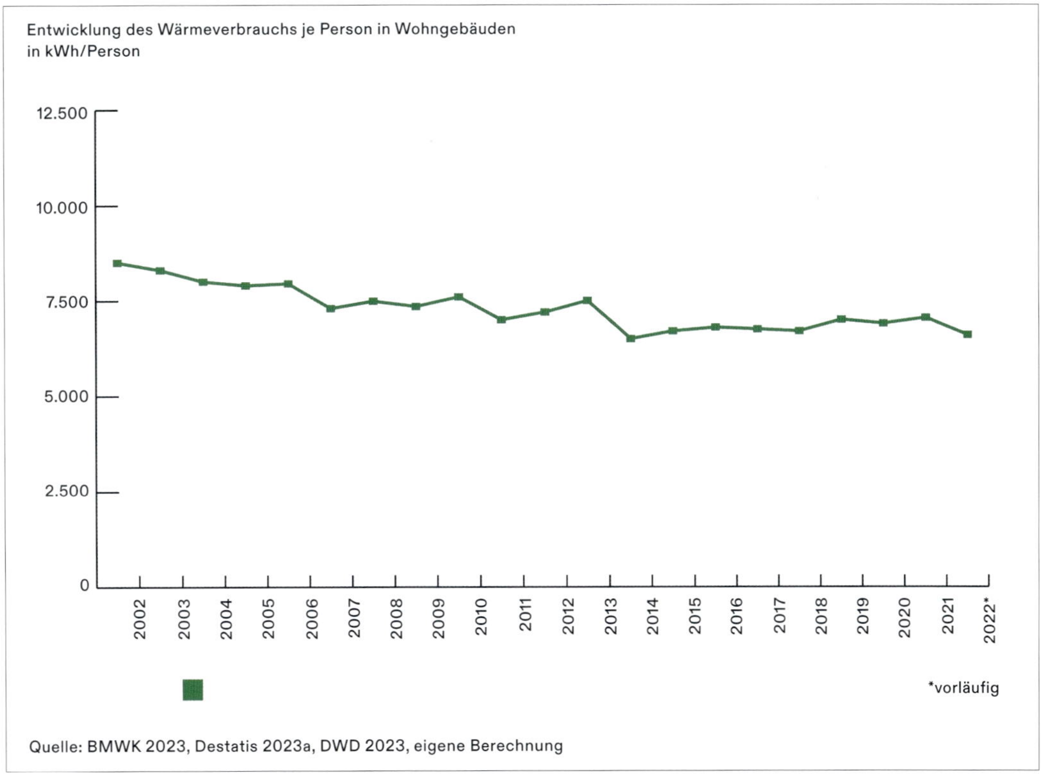

Entwicklung des Wärmeverbrauchs je Person in Wohngebäuden
in kWh/Person
12.500
10.000
7.500
5.000
2.500
0
2002
2003
2004
2005
2006
2007
2008
2009
2010
2011
2012
2013
2014
2015
2016
2017
2018
2019
2020
2021
2022*
*vorläufig
Quelle: BMWK 2023, Destatis 2023a, DWD 2023, eigene Berechnung

einzelnen Bürger gebunden werden darf.[16] Mit einer Beschränkung des Energieverbrauchs pro Person wären diese Probleme gelöst.

Senkung des Energiebedarfs in der Nutzungsphase durch Wärmedämmung

Die in den vergangenen Jahrzehnten bevorzugten Mittel zur Senkung des *Raumwärmebedarfs* beruhten auf baulichen Maßnahmen wie einer guten Wärmedämmung und anlagentechnischen Maßnahmen wie einer effizienten Heizungsanlage und der automatischen Regelung der Raumtemperaturen. Wärmedämmung wird dadurch erzielt, dass Materialien verwendet werden, die einen geringen Wärmedurchgang und damit eine „wärmeisolierende Eigenschaft" aufweisen. Die Dämmung von Gebäudeteilen, die mit der Außenluft oder dem Erdreich in Verbindung stehen, wird typischerweise durch mehrschichtige Bauteile gebildet, die sich aus tragenden Teilen wie einer Mauerwerkswand, Elementen mit geringem Wärmedurchgang wie einer Dämmschicht sowie Bauteilen, die gegen Wind und Feuchte abdichten, zusammensetzt. Die einzelnen Komponenten werden häufig miteinander verklebt, man spricht dann von Verbundbauteilen, sowie mit mehrschichtigen Anstrichsystemen versehen, wodurch ihr späteres Recycling erschwert wird.

16 Die Emission klimaschädlicher Gase kann als Verbrechen gegen die Atmosphäre und damit als Handlung gegen die Lebensgrundlage aller angesehen werden. Es ist deshalb nicht akzeptabel, dass einzelne mehr emittieren als dies der gesamtgesellschaftlich vereinbarte Emissionsreduktionspfad zulässt. Insbesondere ist ein Emissionsrechtehandel im privaten Bereich inakzeptabel, da er zu einem Emissionsverhalten führen würde, dessen Höhe vom verfügbaren Einkommen abhängt.

Senkung des Energiebedarfs in der Nutzungsphase infolge steigender Wintermitteltemperaturen

Die Jahresmitteltemperatur in Deutschland beträgt derzeit ca. 10 Grad. Die Sommermitteltemperatur liegt bei 19 Grad und die Wintermitteltemperatur bei ca. 2 Grad. Man kann heute davon ausgehen, dass die Wintermitteltemperatur

the mean winter temperature has risen over the same period. In other words, citizens are heating more despite all the demands for climate protection.

Lowering the energy requirement by using thermal inertia

It seems obvious to consider whether a building that has a high heat-storage capacity and absorbs heat during the day from the outside environment and solar radiation could release the heat again at night and thus, in the ideal case, dispense with any heating system at all. One could even transpose this idea onto an entire annual cycle. In Germany, this could work if, alongside the building's heat-storage capacity, external walls had adequate thermal insulation, and if one also factored in heat radiated by bodies and appliances inside the home.[19]

The installation of large storage masses in buildings requires a greater volume of materials, which in turn requires greater energy inputs for their production and transport, and thus higher emissions. It thus bears estimating in advance if, for each individual case, the additional inputs required for the construction would pay (non-monetary) dividends in the course of the building's use.

19 A milestone in realising this idea is Building 2226 by architecture firm Baumschlager Eberle in Lustenau, Austria (see pp. 142ff.). It requires no heating, and the ambient air is warmed by the people present inside, the lighting, and the office appliances.

Covering the energy requirement by solar gains and PV on the building

The first "solar houses" of the 1960s and 1970s already relied on front conservatories or comparable glazed structures to "capture" the energy radiated by the sun and store it in solid elements of the building. This technology can be used to heat buildings during cooler weather, too. In this way, the degree to which the interior cools at night can be reduced.

in Deutschland bis 2045 um ca. 1,3 bis 2,4 Grad ansteigen wird.[17] Das führt gleichzeitig zu einer Absenkung des Heizenergiebedarfs um ca. 10 bis 14 Prozent.[18]

Wie bereits angesprochen, ist der Wärmeverbrauch pro Person im Zeitraum von 2012 bis 2022 (bei Redaktionsschluss lagen die Daten für 2023 noch nicht vor) nicht gesunken, obwohl die Wintermitteltemperaturen gestiegen sind.(Abb. 4) Die Bürgerinnen und Bürger heizen derzeit also, entgegen allen Klimaschutzforderungen, mehr als früher.

Senkung des Energiebedarfs durch Nutzung der thermischen Trägheit

Es ist naheliegend zu überlegen, ob ein Gebäude durch eine hohe Wärmespeicherkapazität die tagsüber über die Außenlufttemperatur und die solare Einstrahlung aufgenommene Wärme nachts wieder abgeben könnte, somit im Extremfall sogar ohne eine Heizung auskommt. Man könnte diesen Gedanken sogar auf einen Jahreszyklus übertragen. In Deutschland kann dies dann funktionieren, wenn neben der Wärmespeicherkapazität von Gebäuden eine hinreichende Wärmedämmeigenschaft der Außenwände und die Heizung durch die im Gebäude befindlichen Menschen und Geräte hinzutritt.[19]

Die Installation großer Speichermassen in Gebäuden erfordert einen größeren Materialaufwand, was mit erhöhtem Energieaufwand für Herstellung und Transport sowie mit erhöhten Emissionen verbunden ist. Es ist deshalb in jedem Einzelfall vorher abzuschätzen, wie die beim Bau getätigten Mehraufwendungen sich im Lauf der Nutzung des Gebäudes (im nicht-monetären Sinn) amortisieren.

17 Werner Sobek, non nobis – über das Bauen in der Zukunft, Bd. 2, Stuttgart 2023.

18 Faustformel: Die Einsparung an Heizenergie beträgt pro Grad Celsius Erhöhung der Wintermitteltemperatur ca. 6 Prozent.

19 Einen Meilenstein bei der Umsetzung dieses Konzepts stellt das Gebäude 2226 der Architekten Baumschlager Eberle in Lustenau dar (vgl. S. 142ff.). Es benötigt keine Heizung; die Raumluft wird durch die anwesenden Menschen, die Beleuchtung und die Bürogeräte erwärmt.

Attaching PV (photovoltaic) elements to generate electricity is already mandatory for new builds in various German states. For existing buildings, this obligation applies whenever a roof is fundamentally renewed.

Generating electricity by on-building systems is probably the most ineffective PV method. This stems from the cost-intensive installation outlays, plus the PV cells have to be attached on and through the roof's and walls' thermal insulation, causing a myriad of penetration points that function as thermal bridges. Moreover, the alignment of the PV systems is determined by the line of the façades and/or roofs, which of course are determined more by urban planning considerations than optimising solar yields. Finally, most PV systems are not designed to integrate appealingly into the building's outer surfaces. It would be preferable to install the PV plant close to settlements and cities at the sides of link roads, railroad tracks, or, if designed as agrivoltaics, on fields. In all these cases, costs are lower and the design integration of such building measures appreciably easier. Moreover, the PV cells can be better aligned to the path of the sun leading to higher panel yields.

Impact of energy efficiency policies on building emissions

The heat consumption shown in figure 4 is made up of combustion-based heat and heat from renewable energy sources. The constant increase in the proportion of such renewable sources in residential buildings spells a decrease in ambient heat provided through combustion. One could therefore assume that the emission of climate-damaging gases has likewise fallen.

Deckung des Energiebedarfs durch solare Gewinne und Photovoltaik am Gebäude

Bereits die ersten „Solarhäuser" der 1960/70er-Jahre arbeiten mit vorgesetzten Wintergärten oder vergleichbaren verglasten Konstruktionen, um die durch die Sonne eingestrahlte Energie „einzufangen" und in massiven Bauteilen zu speichern. Mit dieser Technik lässt sich ein Gebäude auch bei kühler Witterung erwärmen. Gleichzeitig kann das nächtliche Abkühlen der Innenräume auf diese Weise reduziert werden.

Das Anbringen von PV-Elementen zur Erzeugung von Elektrizität ist mittlerweile in einer Reihe von Bundesländern bei Neubauten vorgeschrieben. Bei Bestandsbauten gilt die Verpflichtung dann, wenn die Dächer grundlegend saniert werden.

Die Erzeugung von Strom mittels Photovoltaik am Gebäude ist wahrscheinlich die ineffektivste Art ihrer Nutzung. Das betrifft einerseits den kostenintensiven Montageaufwand, andererseits müssen die PV-Zellen auf und durch die Wärmedämmung von Dach und Wand befestigt werden, was eine Vielzahl von Durchdringungspunkten, die auch Wärmebrücken sind, bewirkt. Des Weiteren ist die Ausrichtung der PV-Anlagen an die Lage der Fassaden bzw. der Dächer gebunden. Diese sind aber zumeist aufgrund städtebaulicher Überlegungen und weniger mit dem Gedanken der Optimierung solarer Gewinne festgelegt. Schließlich werden die PV-Anlagen in den meisten Fällen wenig geschickt gestalterisch in die Gebäudeoberflächen integriert. Sinnstiftender wäre es, die PV-Anlagen in der Nähe von Siedlungen und Städten entlang der Verbindungsstraßen, der Bahnlinien oder, in Form von Agri-PV, über Wiesen

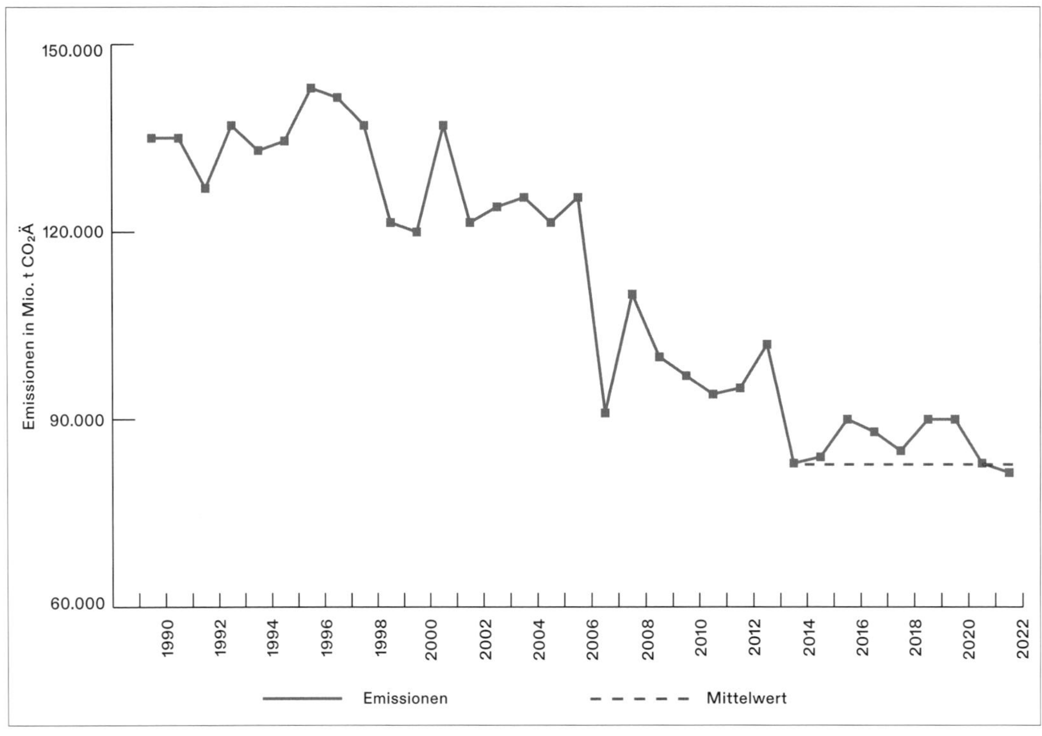

Abb. 5 | Fig. 5 Entwicklung der Treibhausgasemissionen der Haushalte in Deutschland seit 1990. Auffällig ist, dass die klimaschädlichen Emissionen seit 2014 so gut wie nicht zurückgegangen sind. | Trend for greenhouse gas emissions by German homes since 1990. It is striking that climate-damaging emissions have as good as flatlined since 2014.

und Weiden zu installieren. Die Kosten sind in allen diesen Fällen geringer und die gestalterische Integration der Baumaßnahmen ist bedeutend einfacher. Zudem können die PV-Zellen besser auf die optimale Himmelsrichtung eingestellt werden, wodurch man höhere Erträge erzielt.

Auswirkungen der Energieeffizienzpolitik auf die Emissionen von Gebäuden

Der in Abbildung 4 (S. 35) gezeigte Wärmeverbrauch setzt sich aus verbrennungsbasierter Wärme und aus Wärme, die auf Basis erneuerbarer Energien bereitgestellt wird, zusammen. Die stetige Zunahme des Anteils der erneuerbaren Energie in Wohngebäuden bedeutet einen Rückgang der mittels Verbrennung bereitgestellten Raumwärme. Man könnte also davon ausgehen, dass die Emission klimaschädlicher Gase ebenfalls rückläufig ist.

Betrachtet man die in Abbildung 5 dargestellte Entwicklung, so stellt man fest, dass die Emissionen in der Nutzungsphase von Wohngebäuden seit 2014 kaum geringer geworden sind. Die nach 1990 zunächst deutliche Reduktion des Emissionsvolumens ist seitdem quasi zum Stillstand gekommen. Die Energieeffizienzpolitik des letzten Jahrzehnts hat also nicht zu einer Emissionsreduktion geführt.

Neben den Maßnahmen zur Reduzierung klimaschädlicher Emissionen in der Nutzungsphase sind die „grauen" Emissionen,[20] also die Emissionen, die bereits durch die Herstellung der Gebäude entstehen, zu betrachten. Im Gebäudesektor machen sie ca. 8 bis 14 Prozent aller in Deutschland getätigten Emissionen aus und stellen somit eine signifikante Menge dar. Für ihre Reduktion gibt es bis heute allerdings keine gesetzlichen Vorgaben.

20 Sehr häufig werden irrtümlicherweise die *grauen Emissionen* mit denjenigen gleichgesetzt, die bei der Bereitstellung der *grauen Energie*, die zur Herstellung der Gebäude erforderlich ist, entstehen (hier spricht man auch von *energiebedingten Emissionen*). Das ist falsch, denn die *grauen Emissionen* umfassen auch die durch chemische Prozesse bei der Gewinnung und Herstellung von Baustoffen entstehenden *prozessbedingten Emissionen*. Sie setzen sich also aus *energiebedingten* und *prozessbedingten Emissionen* zusammen.

If one considers the trend shown in figure 5, then it becomes clear that emissions in the use phase of residential buildings have as good as flatlined since 2014. After 1990 there was initially a significant reduction in the volume of emissions, but this has essentially come to a standstill over the last decade, despite energy efficiency policies.

Alongside measures to reduce climate-damaging emissions in the use phase, grey emissions,[20] meaning those emissions that arise during the manufacture of the building, also need to be taken into account. Grey emissions in the buildings sector make up about 8–14% of all emissions in Germany and thus constitute a significant variable. To date, however, there are no statutory regulations on reducing grey emissions.

Outcomes of energy efficiency policymaking to date

The above remarks show that neither the reduction of imports of fossil-fuel-based energy sources called for in terms of economic strategy, nor the expansion and savings measures required to stabilise the power grid, nor the emission reductions called for in the construction sector have been achieved on the scale envisaged. The approaches taken to date have proved particularly unsuitable as regards key climate-damaging emissions that cause global warming, and the construction sector is responsible for almost 50% of them.

The historically driven focus on energy efficiency was a meaningful measure in terms of economic strategy, but, in light of climate change, proved to be insufficient when it comes to building activity. For this reason, climate-damaging emissions must immediately be given pride of place in deliberations

20 Frequently, but erroneously, *grey emissions* are confused with those emission that are released when providing the *grey energy* required to make the buildings (people also speak here of *energy-related emissions*). This is wrong, as the *grey emissions* also cover the *process-related emissions* that arise from the chemical processes involved in obtaining and manufacturing building materials. In other words, the *grey emission* are made up of the sum total of *energy-related* and *process-related emissions.*

Ergebnisse der bisherigen Energieeffizienzpolitik

Die vorstehend gemachten Ausführungen zeigen, dass weder die aus wirtschaftsstrategischen Gründen geforderte Reduktion des Imports fossiler Energieträger noch die zur Stromnetzstabilisierung erforderlichen Ausbau- und Einsparmaßnahmen oder die vom Bauwesen einzufordernde Emissionsreduktion im angestrebten Umfang erreicht wurden. Insbesondere hinsichtlich der für die Erderwärmung wesentlichen klimaschädlichen Emissionen, die zu knapp 50 Prozent durch das Bauwesen verursacht werden, erweisen sich die bisherigen Vorgehensweisen als untauglich.

Die historisch bedingte Fokussierung auf Energieeffizienz war eine wirtschaftsstrategisch sinnvolle Maßnahme, die sich jedoch als unzureichend herausgestellt hat, wenn es um klimagerechtes Bauen geht. Deshalb müssen ab sofort alle klimaschädlichen Emissionen ins Zentrum der Betrachtungen und der zugehörigen gesetzlichen Regelungen gerückt werden. Dabei gilt es nicht nur, die Emissionen in der Nutzungsphase der Gebäude bis 2045 auf Null bzw. Netto-Null zu reduzieren, sondern auch die Emissionen bei der Herstellung sowie dem Um- und Rückbau entsprechend zu behandeln.[21] Dies erfordert einen Paradigmenwechsel, weg von der Energieeffizienz hin zur Emissionsreduktion.

Von der Energieeffizienz zur Emissionsreduktion

Die Situation, in der sich unsere Gesellschaft heute befindet, erfordert es, die klimaschädlichen Emissionen so schnell wie möglich zu reduzieren, um so die Klimaerwärmung „einzubremsen“. Gleichzeitig muss der Stromverbrauch

21 Das GEG regelt nur die Heizungsart und den Energiebedarf in der Nutzungsphase.

and related statutory regulations. The emphasis must not only be on reducing emissions in the buildings' use phase to zero and/or net zero by the year 2045, but also on treating the emissions released for manufacture and/or demolition of the properties accordingly. This will require a paradigm shift away from energy efficiency in favour of reducing emissions.

From energy efficiency to emissions reduction

The situation in which society finds itself today makes it imperative that we reduce climate-damaging emissions as swiftly as possible in order to put a brake on "global warming". At the same time, electricity consumption must temporarily be reduced in order to avoid power-grid collapses. We can derive three simple rules from these insights:

- The emission of climate-damaging gases when constructing, operating, converting, or demolishing buildings should only be allowed if it obeys an emission-reduction path set by the legislature.
- The pace of expansion and provision of renewable energies must be increased sharply.
- During the transition period, citizens must accept that there will not always be enough electricity available.

In essence, lawmakers have understood the above rules. However, they have not gone through with the shift from calling for energy efficiency to calling for a reduction in emissions. This is the only possible explanation for the fact

vorübergehend reduziert werden, um Zusammenbrüche der Stromnetze zu vermeiden. Aus diesen einfachen Erkenntnissen kann man drei einfache Regeln ableiten:

- Die Emission klimaschädlicher Gase bei Errichtung, Betrieb, Um- und Rückbau von Gebäuden ist nur noch bei Einhaltung eines vom Gesetzgeber vorgegebenen Emissionsreduktionspfades erlaubt.
- Ausbau und Bereitstellung erneuerbarer Energien müssen massiv beschleunigt werden.
- Die Bürgerinnen und Bürger müssen für eine Übergangszeit akzeptieren, dass nicht immer genügend Elektrizität zur Verfügung steht.

Im Grunde genommen sind die vorstehenden Regeln auch vom Gesetzgeber verstanden worden. Er hat allerdings den Wechsel von der Forderung nach Energieeffizienz zu einer Forderung nach Reduzierung der Emissionen nicht vollzogen. Nur so ist zu erklären, dass es bis heute keine Regelungen zum Energieverbrauch bei Herstellung, Um- und Rückbau gibt und somit auch keinerlei (!) Regelungen zur Reduktion der Emissionen bei Herstellung, Betrieb, Um- und Rückbau. Die wesentlichen Themen werden also nicht erfasst, während es beim Unterthema *Energieverbrauch von Wohngebäuden in der Nutzungsphase* eine überbordende Komplexität an Regelungen gibt, die ausschließlich aus Maßnahmenkatalogen und nicht aus Zielformulierungen bestehen.

that there are still no regulations covering energy consumption for the production, conversion, and demolition of buildings, and that there are absolutely no regulations on reducing the emissions released in the production, operation, conversion, and demolition of buildings.[21] Put differently, the key issues are not subject to regulation, while the sub-topic of *energy consumption by residential buildings in the use phase* is subject to a veritable labyrinth of regulatory regimes that exclusively consist of lists of measures rather than defined targets.

What now or what next?

The paradigm shift we need is quite straightforward. An emissions reduction law for the construction sector could be captured in a single paragraph:

> *The emission of climate-damaging gases when erecting, operating, converting, and demolishing buildings is only permissible if it is in line with the emissions-reduction path set by the legislature. Any overshoots are subject to fines or must be offset by compensation measures.*

There would be no need for an energy-efficiency law for the construction sector as the supply of combustion-based energy is then regulated by the prospective Emissions Reduction Act and procurement of non-combustion-based energy would be regulated by the customary market mechanisms.

21 The GEG only regulates the type of heating and the energy requirement in the building's use phase.

Wie weiter?

Der notwendige Paradigmenwechsel ist einfach zu beschreiben. Ein Emissionsreduktionsgesetz für das Bauwesen könnte aus einem einzigen Paragrafen bestehen:

> *Die Emission klimaschädlicher Gase bei Errichtung, Betrieb, Um- und Rückbau von Gebäuden ist nur bei Einhaltung eines vom Gesetzgeber vorgegebenen Emissionsreduktionspfades erlaubt. Überschreitungen sind gebührenpflichtig oder müssen durch Kompensationsmaßnahmen ausgeglichen werden.*

Ein Energieeffizienzgesetz für das Bauwesen kann entfallen, weil die Bereitstellung verbrennungsbasierter Energie über das Emissionsreduktionsgesetz und der Bezug nicht-verbrennungsbasierter Energie durch die üblichen Marktmechanismen geregelt werden.

Die hier vorgestellten Beispiele

Architekten und Ingenieure, aber auch Behörden und Bauherren haben in den vergangenen Jahrzehnten immer wieder versucht, energieeffiziente Gebäude zu errichten oder Bestandsgebäude mittels einer energetischen Sanierung entsprechend umzuwandeln. Sie gingen dabei häufig über das hinaus, was gesetzlich vorgeschrieben war. In der Regel war dies anstrengend, erforderte Mut und Durchsetzungskraft.

The examples shown in the exhibition

In the preceding decades, architects and engineers, not to mention public authorities and developers, have repeatedly attempted to construct energy-efficient buildings or to convert existing buildings by modernising the relevant energy systems. In the process, they frequently went further than the statutory requirements. As a rule, this involved a lot of effort and required courage and tenacity.

The exhibition presents a selection of such projects. In our opinion, the buildings chosen demonstrate what can already be achieved. They are intended as inspiration and to give people the courage to do what is required. And they are intended to show that, when we are talking about the buildings of tomorrow, the focus must not be on efficient but rather effective energy management. At the technical level the emphasis is on strict emissions reductions, construction of recycling-ready buildings, and construction with recycled materials. At the non-technical level, it is all about creating a human habitat that is in harmony with nature.

Diese Publikation zeigt einen Teil solcher Bauprojekte. Die ausgewählten Gebäude sollen zeigen, was heute bereits möglich ist. Sie sollen Anregung sein und Mut machen, selbst mehr zu tun als das, was gefordert wird. Und sie sollen zeigen, dass es nicht um einen effizienten, sondern um den effektiven Umgang mit Energie geht, wenn wir vom Bauen in der Zukunft sprechen. Es geht, auf der technischen Ebene, um strikte Emissionsreduktion, um recyclinggerechtes Bauen und um Bauen mit Rezyklaten. Es geht, auf der nichttechnischen Ebene, um die Schaffung menschlicher Heimat, die im Einklang mit der Natur steht.

Kindergarten | Kindergarten

Søborg, Dänemark
Søborg, Denmark

Bauaufgabe | Task
Neubau eines Kindergartens mit recycelten Materialien | New construction of a kindergarten using recycled materials

Entwurf Hochbau | Architects
Lendager Arkitekter ApS, Kopenhagen | Copenhagen

Entwurf Energiekonzept | Energy design
NIRAS A/S, Allerød

Auftrag | Client
Gladsaxe Municipality, Søborg

Fertigstellung | Completion
2022

Finanzierung | Financing
Öffentliche Mittel | Public funding

Energie/Emissionen
Kreislaufwirtschaft; Nutzung vorhandener Ressourcen; Form-follows-availability-Architektur

Energy/Emissions
Circular economy; utilisation of existing resources; form-follows-availability architecture

Nach einer vorläufigen Machbarkeitsstudie zu den Möglichkeiten des Umbaus und der Umnutzung der bestehenden Schule in einen neuen Kindergarten wurde entschieden, dass die beste Option der Rückbau und die Umgestaltung in eine neue Gebäudestruktur sei. Dieser komplexe, prozessbasierte Ansatz in Verbindung mit einer projektspezifischen Risiko- und Potenzialbewertung wurde von Lendager geleitet und in enger Zusammenarbeit mit einer Reihe von Interessengruppen, darunter einer ambitionierten Bauherrenorganisation, umgesetzt. Das Ergebnis war eine Ausschreibung für einen nachhaltigen Abbruchprozess, der später vom Dänischen Verband der Bauherren (DACC) als vorbildlich für einen konkreten Weg zur Förderung der Kreislaufwirtschaft in der gebauten Umwelt gelobt wurde. Die Ergebnisse dieses spezialisierten

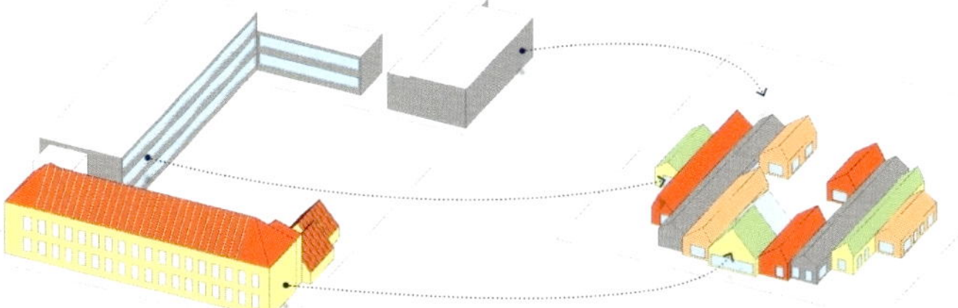

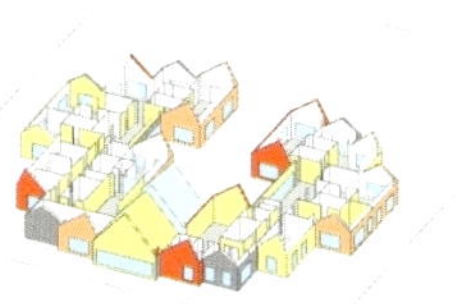

Bestandsbau der GL. Gladsaxe Schule *Materialien für Fassaden und Dächer* *Materialien Innenraum*

Material- und Recyclingkonzept | Materials and recycling concept

Beratungsprozesses flossen in die architektonische Entwicklung des neuen Gebäudes ein und ermöglichten eine Architektur nach den Prinzipien der „form-follows-availability" (Form folgt der Verfügbarkeit) zu erhalten und den inhärenten Wert dessen zu nutzen, was zuvor als Abfall galt. Das Ergebnis ist ein Gebäude, das sowohl architektonisch wertvoll ist als auch eine neue Ästhetik ausdrückt, die den inhärenten materiellen und kulturellen Wert bei der Neugestaltung unserer kollektiven baulichen Umgebung respektiert und anerkennt. Holzbalken der ehemaligen Sporthalle, Stahlfassadenelemente aus den 1960er-Jahren, Dachziegel, die alte Schuluhr und viele weitere Elemente wurden in das neue Design integriert. Dies ist nicht nur im Sinne der Nachhaltigkeit sinnvoll, sondern stellt zugleich eine respektvolle Geste gegenüber der Qualität der Gladsaxe Old School dar, die nun in einer Neuinterpretation ein zweites Leben erhält.

After a preliminary feasibility study regarding the potential for rebuilding and repurposing of the existing school into a new kindergarten, it was decided that the best option was to deconstruct and reconfigure into a new structure. This complex process-based approach coupled with a project-specific risk and potential assessment was led by Lendager and realised in close cooperation with a range of stakeholders, including an ambitious client organisation. The result of this was a tender for a sustainable demolition process, which later has been praised by the Danish Association of Construction Clients (DACC) for being a prime example of a pathway to promoting circularity in the built environment. The results of this specialised consulting process was coupled to the architectural development of the new building and enabled the architecture to adhere to principles of form-follows-availability, capitalising the inherent value in what otherwise was waste. This has resulted in a building that creates architectural value as well as a new aesthetic that respects and recognises the inherent material and cultural value in the reconfiguration of our collective built surroundings. Old wooden rafters from the sports hall, steel façade elements from the 1960s, tiles from the roofs as well as the old school clock—and several other elements have been reimplemented into the new design. This does not only make sense in terms of sustainability but also represents a respectful gesture to the quality of Gladsaxe Old School, which now gets an afterlife through reinterpretation.

Grundriss Erdgeschoss |
Floor plan—ground floor

DAM **Was finden Sie an Ihrem Projekt besonders bemerkenswert?**
Lendager Arkitekter Bemerkenswert ist die Tatsache, dass für das Projekt Materialien aus einer stillgelegten Schule genutzt werden konnten, um einen nachhaltigen und ästhetisch wertvollen Kindergarten zu errichten. Das Projekt ist ein Beispiel für zirkuläres Bauen und wird als Vorbild für die Förderung von Nachhaltigkeit gelobt.

DAM **Welche Aspekte waren Ihnen bei der Entwicklung des Projekts wichtig?**
Lendager Arkitekter Zu den wichtigsten Aspekten gehörten die Erfüllung von Nachhaltigkeitszertifizierungen, die Maximierung der Materialwiederverwendung und die Achtung des kulturellen Wertes des Ursprungsgebäudes. Die Zusammenarbeit mit den Interessengruppen und die Einhaltung des Prinzips „form-follows-availability" waren ebenfalls von entscheidender Bedeutung.

DAM **What do you find particularly remarkable about your project?**
Lendager Arkitekter The project's success in repurposing materials from a decommissioned school into a sustainable and aesthetically valuable kindergarten is remarkable. It exemplifies circularity in construction and has been praised as a model for promoting sustainability.

DAM **Which aspects were important to you when developing the project?**
Lendager Arkitekter Key aspects included meeting sustainability certifications, maximising material reuse, and respecting the cultural value of the original building. Collaboration with stakeholders and adherence to "form-follows-availability" principles were also crucial.

Bildungszentrum | Educational centre

Weil der Stadt, Deutschland
Weil der Stadt, Germany

Bauaufgabe | Task
Neubau eines Bildungszentrums mit Seminarraum, Landesbibliothek für Pomologie und Büroräume in Holzbauweise | New construction of an educational centre with seminar room, state library for pomology, and offices in timber construction

Entwurf Hochbau | Architects
lohrmannarchitekten, Stuttgart

Entwurf Energiekonzept | Energy design
Die Planschmiede, Vaihingen An Der Enz; Ingenieurbüro Bauphysik 5, Backnang

Auftrag | Client
Landesverband für Obstbau, Garten und Landschaft Baden-Württemberg e.V., Stuttgart

Fertigstellung | Completion
2023

Finanzierung | Financing
Öffentliche Fördermittel | Public funding

Energie / Emissionen
Nachwachsende, lokal erzeugte Materialien; regionale Wertschöpfungsketten; Heizungsbedarf durch Luft-Wasser-Wärmepumpe; Strombedarf über Photovoltaikanlage

Energy / Emissions
Renewable, locally produced materials, regional value chains, heating provided by air-to-water heat pump, electricity provided by photovoltaic system

Das vom Land Baden-Württemberg als Modellvorhaben geförderte Bauprojekt setzt einen klaren Akzent zum Thema Nachhaltigkeit und spiegelt in diesem Zusammenhang die Werte der Dauerhaftigkeit und des Bewährten wider. Diese Herangehensweise zielt darauf ab, robuste und ressourcenschonende Gebäude zu errichten, die nicht nur umweltfreundlich, sondern auch in ihrer Nutzung und ihrer technischen Ausstattung (Lowtech-Konzeption) zurückhaltend und

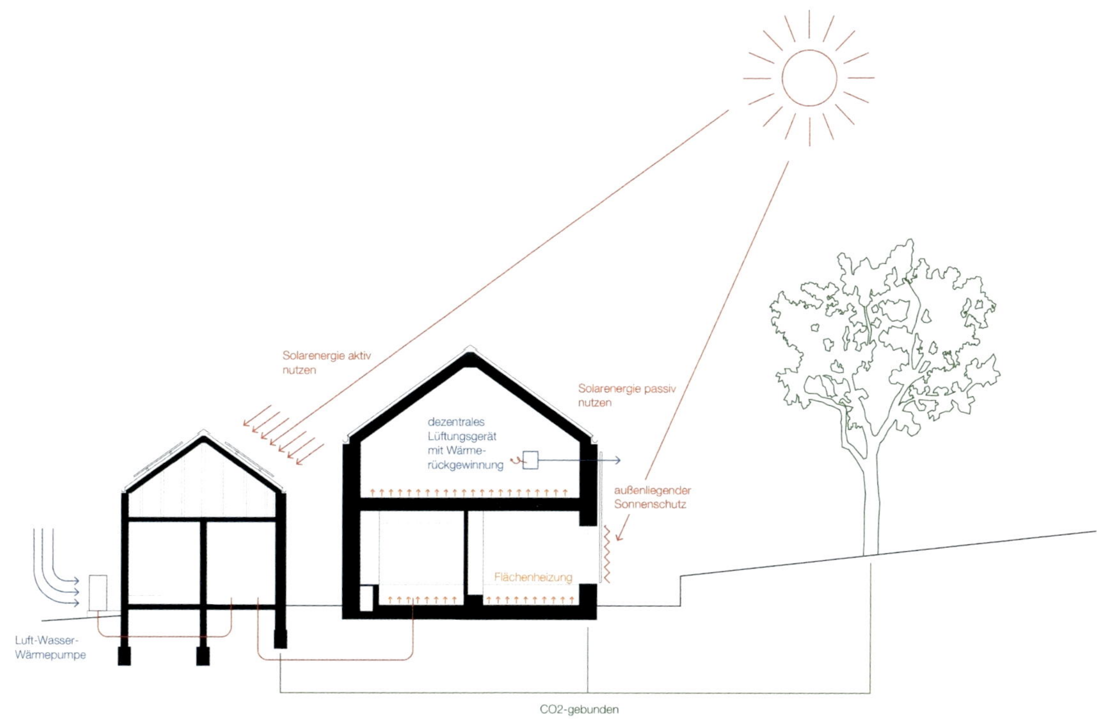

Energetisches Null-Emissionskonzept |
Energy consumption: the Zero-Emissions concept

anpassungsfähig sind. Das Gefüge aus verschiedenen nachwachsenden, lokal erzeugten Materialien nutzt das Potenzial regionaler Wertschöpfungsketten konsequent auch in Bezug auf die Nutzung der Produkte der heimischen Kulturlandschaft. Die sinnlich erfahrbare Materialvielfalt unterschiedlicher Holzarten generiert ein warmes und naturverbundenes Raumklima. Darüber hinaus zeichnet sich das Projekt durch ein energetisches Null-Emissionen-Konzept aus, das aus einer reversiblen Luft-Wasser-Wärmepumpe, einer PV-Anlage und einer minimierten, dezentralen Lüftung mit Wärmerückgewinnung besteht, sodass die benötigte Wärme und Energie selbst erzeugt werden kann, ohne weitere Emissionen auszustoßen.

Subsidised by the state of Baden-Württemberg as a model programme, this construction project emphasises sustainability and thus reflects the values of durability and tradition. Such an approach aims to create robust and resource-efficient buildings that are not only environmentally friendly but also restrained and adaptable in their use and technical requirements (low-tech concept). The diverse use of renewable, locally produced materials taps into the potential of regional value chains, including products from the local cultural community. The variety of materials, including a wide range of different wood types, creates a friendly, warm, and natural indoor experience. In addition, the project has a zero-energy emission concept consisting of a reversible air-to-water heat pump, a photovoltaic system, and a minimised, decentralised ventilation system with heat recovery, so that the required heat and energy can be generated on site without further emissions.

DAM **Was finden Sie an Ihrem Projekt besonders gelungen?**
lohrmannarchitekten Das Bildungszentrum ist ein gelungenes Beispiel für dauerhafte, zurückhaltende und nachhaltige Architektur, die sich respektvoll in die Landschaft sowie in den kultur- und baugeschichtlichen Kontext einfügt. Das Gebäude repräsentiert gleichermaßen das Gestrige, das Heute und das Morgen auf subtile Art und Weise.

DAM **Was war Ihnen bei der Erarbeitung des Projektes wichtig?**
lohrmannarchitekten Unser Anspruch war stets, einen Ort zu entwickeln, der die Werte der Arbeit des Vereins reflektiert, ein Gebäude, das poetisch in einen freundschaftlichen Dialog mit seinem natürlichen Umfeld tritt und eine vielfältige Nutzung ermöglicht, die über die reine Funktionalität hinausgeht.

DAM **What do you find particularly successful about your project?**
lohrmannarchitekten The education centre is a successful example of enduring, understated, and sustainable architecture that respectfully integrates with the landscape as well as the cultural and architectural context. The building subtly represents yesterday, today, and tomorrow all at once.

DAM **What was important to you when developing the project?**
lohrmannarchitekten Our aim was to develop a place that reflects the values of the association's work: a building that enters into a friendly, poetic dialogue with its natural environment and allows for a wide range of uses beyond pure functionality.

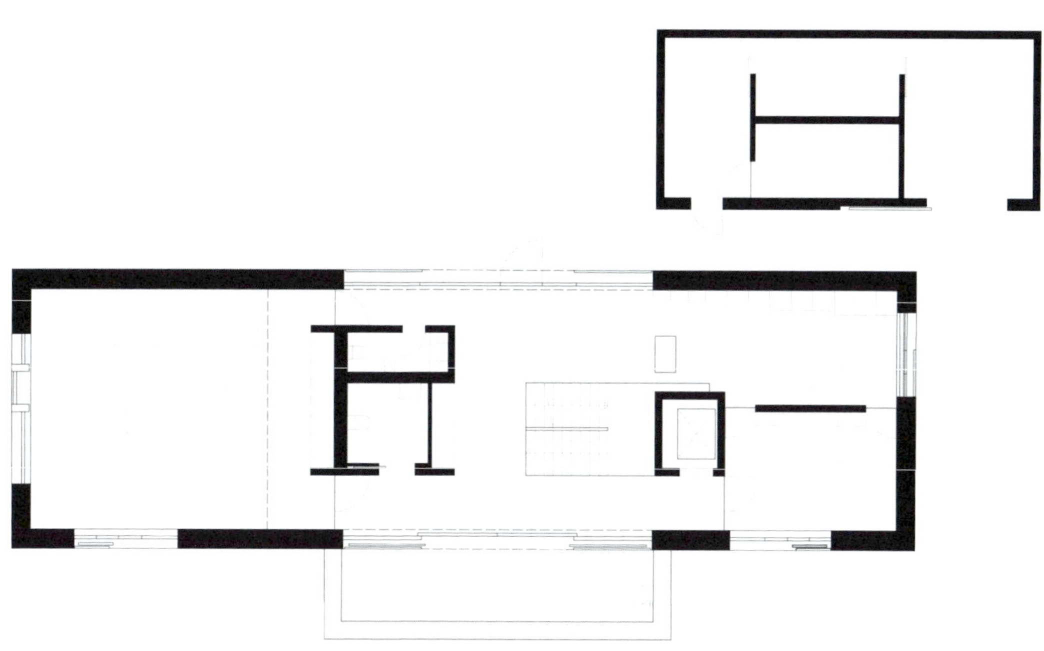

Grundriss Erdgeschoss |
Floor plan—ground floor

Pforzheimer
30

Wohnhochhaus
High-rise residential building

Pforzheim, Deutschland
Pforzheim, Germany

Bauaufgabe | Task
Aufstockung eines Wohnhochhauses aus den 1970er-Jahren und Generalsanierung zum Energieeffizienzhaus | General refurbishment and expansion of a 1970s high-rise residential building to create an energy-efficient house

Entwurf Hochbau | Architects
Freivogel Mayer Architekten, Ludwigsburg

Entwurf Energiekonzept | Energy design
Transsolar, Stuttgart

Auftrag | Client
Pforzheimer Bau und Grund, Pforzheim

Fertigstellung | Completion
2014

Finanzierung | Financing
Privat | Private

Energie / Emissionen
Heizwärme durch Fassadenabsorber; Eisspeicher als Energiespeicher; Deckung des Strombedarfs mittels Photovoltaikmodulen und Kleinwindkraftanlage; Verzicht auf Verbundkonstruktionen und Einsatz recyclingfähiger Baustoffe

Energy / Emission
Heating through façade absorbers, ice storage as energy storage, meeting electricity needs with photovoltaic modules and small wind turbines, no composite constructions, and use of recyclable building materials

Zu den Qualitäten dieses Wohnhochhauses aus den 1970er-Jahren zählen die zentrale Lage nahe dem Hauptbahnhof sowie die Aussicht über Stadt und Nordschwarzwald. Die Grundrissstruktur ist den heutigen Anforderungen gewachsen, die Bausubstanz solide; allerdings gab es Undichtigkeiten an Fassade/Fenstern und sanierungsbedürftige Bäder. Hinzu kamen hohe Energie-, Verbrauchs- und Betriebskosten. Zentraler Baustein des Entwurfskonzepts ist eine hoch gedämmte, hinterlüftete Gebäudehülle und die Schaffung großzügiger

überdachter privater Freiräume jeweils als Betonfertigteilkonstruktion. Die neue Gebäudehülle trägt zu einer deutlichen Steigerung des Wohnkomforts bei (Schall-, Sonnen- und Wärmeschutz), gleichzeitig wird das Stadtbild nachhaltig aufgewertet. Vorherige Elektronachtspeicherheizungen und Warmwasserboiler in den Wohnungen wurden komplett durch eine neue Haustechnikanlage ersetzt. Es erfolgte eine Umstellung auf Erzeugung der Heizwärme und der Brauchwassererhitzung über einen nicht sichtbaren, in die Betonfertigteilfassade integrierten Fassadenabsorber. Ein Eisspeicher unter den angrenzenden Parkplätzen dient als saisonaler Zwischenspeicher für die gewonnene Energie. Zur Deckung des Strombedarfs wurden Photovoltaikmodule und eine Kleinwindkraftanlage auf dem Dach eingesetzt. Durch Verzicht auf Verbundkonstruktionen und den Einsatz recyclingfähiger Baustoffe wird graue Energie reduziert.

Advantages of this 1970s residential tower block include its central location near the main railway station and its view over the city and the northern Black Forest. The floor plan meets today's requirements and the building fabric is solid, although there are leaks in the façade and windows and the bathrooms are in need of renovation. In addition, there are high energy consumption and operating costs. The central elements of the design concept are a highly insulated, rear-ventilated building shell and the creation of spacious, sheltered, private open spaces, each in the form of a prefabricated concrete structure. The new building envelope significantly improves the comfort of living (protection against noise, sun, and heat), while also enhancing the cityscape in the long term. Electronic storage heaters and hot-water boilers in the flats have been replaced by a completely new building services system. In future, heating and domestic hot water will be generated by an invisible façade absorber integrated into the prefabricated concrete façade. An ice store under the car park next door serves as seasonal buffer storage for energy produced. Photovoltaic modules and a small wind turbine on the roof cover the electricity needs. Grey energy is reduced by eliminating composite structures and using recyclable building materials.

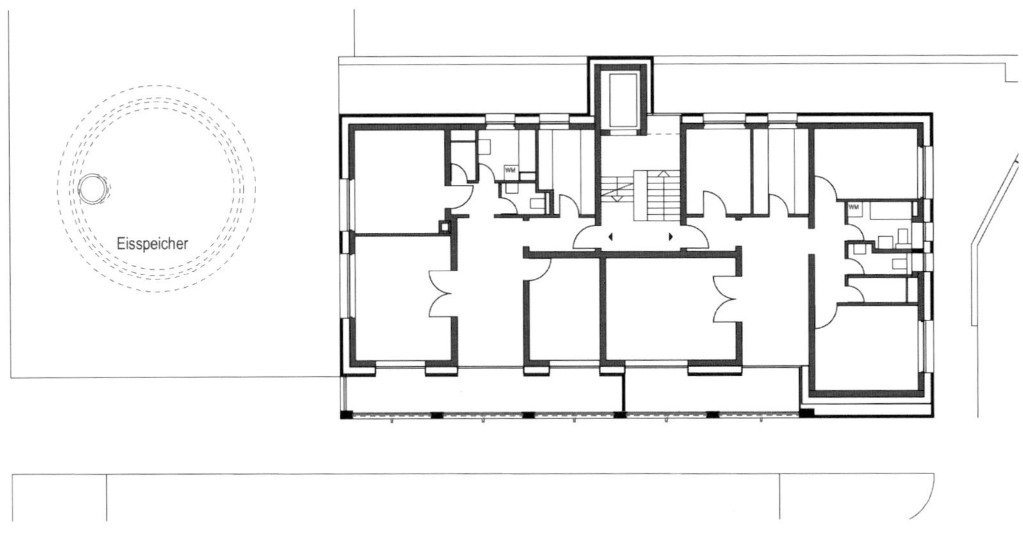

Grundriss Regelgeschoss | Floor plan—standard floor

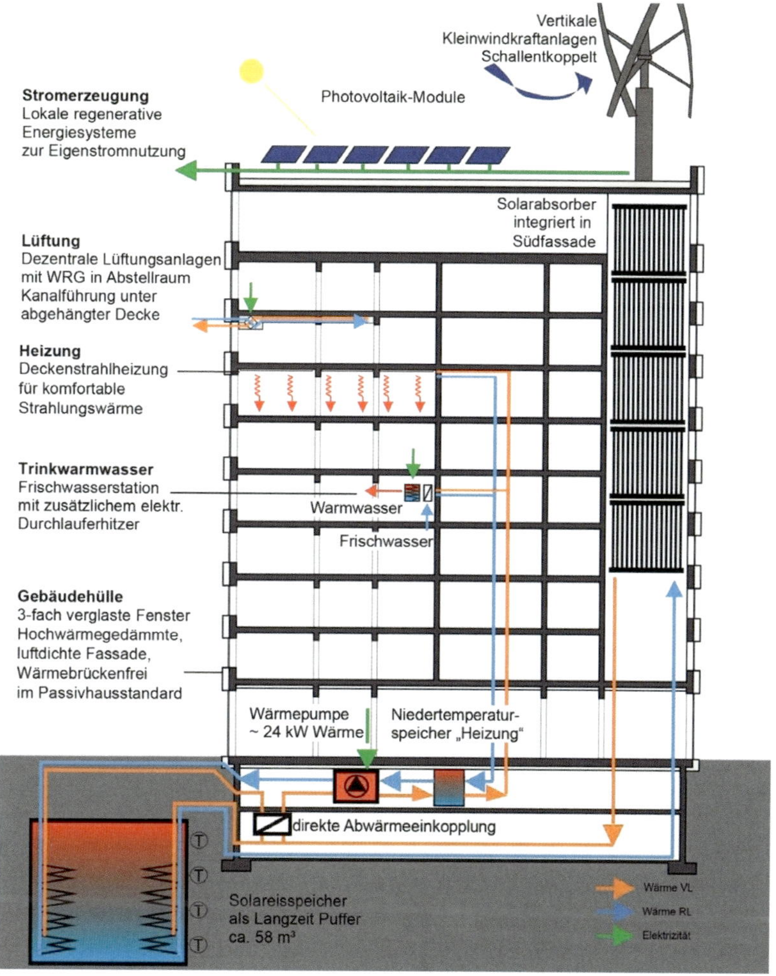

Energiekonzept | Energy concept

DAM Was war Ihnen bei der Erarbeitung des Projektes wichtig?
Freivogel Mayer Architekten Die signifikante Senkung des Energieverbrauchs und eine moderne, zeitlose Aufwertung des Stadtbildes.

DAM Was würden Sie beim nächsten Mal anders machen?
Freivogel Mayer Architekten Ein nächstes Mal würde das Projekt in dieser Form durch die kontinuierliche Zunahme an Bürokratie, Normen und Vorschriften wahrscheinlich wirtschaftlich unmöglich machen.

DAM What was important to you when developing the project?
Freivogel Mayer Architekten The significant reduction in energy consumption and the modern, timeless enhancement of the cityscape.

DAM What would you do differently next time?
Freivogel Mayer Architekten Due to the continuous increase in bureaucracy, standards, and regulations, it would probably be economically impossible to realise such a project a second time.

Nachdenken, bevor man anfängt

Interview mit | with Heinrich Bökamp

Bauingenieur und Präsident der Bundesingenieurkammer

Structural engineer and President of the German Federal Chamber of Engineers

Think before you act

DAM Energie ist ein zentrales Thema, besonders im Bauwesen, das erheblich zum Energieverbrauch und zu Treibhausgasemissionen beiträgt. Hat sich das Bewusstsein für Energiesparen gewandelt, und führt dies zu einem neuen Verständnis des Bauens?
Heinrich Bökamp Es gibt Fortschritte, das Bewusstsein entwickelt sich allmählich. Viele Menschen erkennen inzwischen, dass Handlungsbedarf besteht. Dennoch sind wir noch nicht so weit, dass jeder aktiv seinen Beitrag leistet. Ein umfassender Wandel im Verständnis und Handeln steht uns noch bevor.

DAM Energy is a central issue, especially in the construction sector, which contributes considerably to overall energy consumption and greenhouse gas emissions. Has the awareness of energy saving changed, and has this led to a new understanding of construction?
Heinrich Bökamp There is progress, and awareness is gradually evolving. Many people now realise that there is a need to act. Nevertheless, things have not yet reached the point where everyone actively plays their part. A comprehensive change in outlook and action has not yet materialised.

DAM Wie definieren Sie eine erfolgreiche Energiewende?
HB Eine Energiewende ist dann erfolgreich, wenn sie spürbare Fortschritte bringt – wenn wir tatsächlich vorwärtskommen und es nicht nur immer schwerer wird, die Ziele zu erreichen. Eine echte Wende bedeutet, dass die Situation messbar besser wird, anstatt weiterhin mit denselben Hindernissen zu kämpfen. Leider sind wir noch nicht an diesem Punkt.
DAM In den letzten Jahren lag der Fokus im Bauwesen stark auf Energieeffizienz. Haben wir dabei den Emissionen zu wenig Aufmerksamkeit geschenkt?
HB Ich denke, Effizienz und Emissionen wurden parallel berücksichtigt, da beide Themen im Bauwesen wichtig sind. Viele wissenschaftliche Untersuchungen und Diskussionen haben sich intensiv mit beiden Aspekten auseinandergesetzt. Die Herausforderungen liegen jetzt darin, diese Ziele in konkrete Maßnahmen umzusetzen und weiterzuentwickeln, anstatt nur über Lösungsansätze zu sprechen.
DAM Welche politischen Impulse wünschen Sie sich für den Bausektor?
HB Die Politik sollte stärker auf die praktischen Gegebenheiten eingehen. Häufig fehlt die Verbindung zur Realität des Baualltags. Entscheidungen, die ohne Rücksprache mit der Praxis getroffen werden, wie etwa beim „Heizungsgesetz" zeigen das Problem. Eine echte Verbesserung erreicht man nur, wenn alle Beteiligten, von der Planung bis zur Umsetzung, gemeinsam am Tisch sitzen. So kommen wir den Zielen näher und vermeiden Beschlüsse, die in der Praxis nicht umsetzbar sind.

DAM How would you define a successful energy transition?
HB An energy transition is successful if it yields tangible progress, if we actually make advances without it becoming ever harder to reach those goals. A genuine transition means that the situation becomes quantifiably better as opposed to our still having to face the same obstacles. Unfortunately, we have not yet reached that point.
DAM In recent years, the focus in the construction sector has been firmly on energy efficiency. Did we pay too little attention to emissions in the process?
HB I believe efficiency and emissions were considered alongside each other, as both topics are important in the construction sector. Many scientific studies and discussions have looked at both aspects closely. The challenges now are to translate these targets into actual measures and move them forward instead of only talking about possible solutions.
DAM As regards the construction sector, what political initiatives would you like to see?
HB Politicians should pay more attention to practical realities. Often, there's no link made between policies and the reality of everyday construction. Taking decisions without consulting the people involved, such as occurred with the Heating Act, highlight this problem. To make a genuine improvement, everyone concerned, from planning through to implementation, should be together at the table. That way, we'd be closer to achieving our goals and avoid impractical resolutions.

DAM Die sogenannten grauen Emissionen durch Bau und Abriss sind schwer zu messen, aber wichtig. Warum sollten sie stärker in den Fokus rücken?

HB „Graue Emissionen" bieten großes Einsparpotenzial und sind daher entscheidend für nachhaltiges Bauen. Ein bewusster Umgang mit Abriss und der Wiederverwendung von Materialien könnte einen erheblichen Beitrag leisten. Es geht darum, mehr Altbau statt Neubau zu fördern und zu prüfen, ob Abriss wirklich notwendig ist. Gerade beim Neubau sollten wir darauf achten, dass Materialien später wiederverwertbar sind. Das ist bei älteren Gebäuden oft schwierig, aber für die Zukunft wäre ein geschlossener Materialkreislauf eine wertvolle Lösung.

DAM Sollte der Fokus stärker auf Sanierungen liegen und weniger auf Neubauten?

HB Neubauten werden weiterhin notwendig sein, aber der Fokus muss stärker auf Bestandsbauten liegen. Viele bestehende Wohnungen sind nicht in einem bewohnbaren Zustand – hier muss zuerst angesetzt werden, bevor neu gebaut wird. Der Ressourcenverbrauch beim Neubau ist wesentlich höher, sodass eine Sanierung oft die umweltfreundlichere Option ist. Aber auch der Altbau hat Grenzen, und nicht jedes Gebäude kann erhalten werden. Deshalb brauchen wir ein Gleichgewicht, das beide Ansätze berücksichtigt. An einigen Stellen sehen wir bereits gelungene Quartiersanierungen, die zeigen, dass der Altbau durchaus Potenzial hat.

DAM It's hard to calculate so-called "grey emissions" caused by construction and demolition, but they are key. Why should the focus be more strongly on them?

HB "Grey emissions" offer great savings potential and are therefore decisive for sustainable construction. A conscious approach to demolition and the reuse of materials could make a considerable contribution here. The focus must be on greater support for existing buildings rather than new builds, and on a closer examination of whether demolition is really necessary. Precisely in the case of new builds, we should make certain that materials can later be reused. That is often far from the case with older buildings, but a closed material cycle would be a valuable solution for the future.

DAM Should there be a stronger focus on modernisation and less on new builds?

HB New builds will continue to be necessary, but there needs to be more focus on existing buildings. Many existing apartments are not in an inhabitable state, and that is what we should address first, and new builds second. Resource utilisation for a new build is far greater, meaning modernisation is often a more eco-friendly option. But relying on existing buildings also has its limits, and not every building can be salvaged. For that reason, we need a balance that factors in both approaches. In some places we have already witnessed successful modernisation of neighbourhoods, demonstrating the innate potential of existing buildings.

DAM Müssen Planungsprozesse zwischen Architekten und Ingenieuren enger verzahnt werden?

HB Absolut. In anderen Ländern sehen wir, wie gut interdisziplinäre Zusammenarbeit funktionieren kann. Hierzulande laufen viele Prozesse getrennt oder zeitlich versetzt ab, was oft zu unkoordinierten Ergebnissen führt. Eine enge Zusammenarbeit aller Disziplinen von Beginn an wäre entscheidend. Früher gab es den „Baumeister", der verschiedene Disziplinen in sich vereinte – davon könnte man sich einiges abschauen. Gerade in der frühen Planungsphase wäre es hilfreich, wenn Architekten und Ingenieure gemeinsam am Tisch sitzen würden.

„Im Architektur- und Ingenieurwesen werden unterschiedliche Ansätze verfolgt, und ein regelmäßiger Austausch würde das Verständnis und die Zusammenarbeit fördern"

DAM Sollte sich die Ausbildung im Architektur- und Ingenieurwesen anpassen?

HB Ja, mehr Verbindungen zwischen den Disziplinen wären hilfreich. Im Architektur- und Ingenieurwesen werden unterschiedliche Ansätze verfolgt, und ein regelmäßiger Austausch würde das Verständnis und die Zusammenarbeit fördern. Architekturschaffende bringen oft gestalterische Ideen ein, während Ingenieurinnen und Ingenieure die technische Machbarkeit sicherstellen. Junge Leute sind dafür offen und möchten gute Ergebnisse erreichen – das gelingt nur gemeinsam. In der

DAM Should architects and engineers interface more closely in the planning process?

HB Most definitely. Other countries have already shown how interdisciplinary cooperation can function really well. In Germany, many processes are still separate or staggered over time, resulting in uncoordinated outcomes. Close collaboration between all disciplines from the very outset is decisive in this regard. In the past, there were "master builders" who themselves covered several disciplines, and we could learn quite a bit from that. It would be helpful, precisely in the early phase of planning, if architecture planners and engineering experts sat down together at the same table.

DAM Should training in architecture and in engineering be adapted accordingly?

HB Yes, more interconnection of the disciplines would be helpful. Different approaches are taken in architecture and engineering respectively, and a regular exchange of opinions would foster mutual understanding and cooperation. Those active in architecture often contribute design ideas, while engineers ensure these are technically feasible. Young people are open-minded and want to achieve good results, something that can only be achieved together. In training, students should not only

"Different approaches are taken in architecture and engineering respectively, and a regular exchange of opinions would foster mutual understanding and cooperation"

Ausbildung sollten Studierende nicht nur ihren Bereich, sondern auch angrenzende Disziplinen kennenlernen, um später interdisziplinär zu arbeiten.
DAM **Was bedeutet klimaschonendes Bauen für Sie in einem Wort?**
HB Nachdenken, bevor man anfängt.
DAM **Was wünschen Sie sich von der nächsten Generation der Architekten und Ingenieure?**
HB Neugierde und die Bereitschaft, alternative Lösungen zu prüfen. Durch den Zeitdruck, der oft in Projekten herrscht, bleibt manchmal keine Gelegenheit, nachhaltige Lösungen zu erarbeiten. Mehr Zeit für die Planung und einen offenen Austausch halte ich daher für wichtig. Wir haben bereits das notwendige Wissen, um nachhaltiger zu bauen – jetzt gilt es, dieses Wissen konsequent umzusetzen.

get to know their own field but also be familiar with related disciplines in order to work in an interdisciplinary manner down the line.
DAM **In a nutshell, what does climate-friendly construction mean to you?**
HB Thinking before you act.
DAM **What would you like to see from the next generation of specialists in architecture and engineering?**
HB Curiosity and a willingness to explore alternative solutions. The time pressures that often characterise projects sometimes leave little opportunity to develop sustainable solutions. I therefore believe that more time for planning and an open exchange of views is crucial. We possess the necessary knowledge to build more sustainably—now we need to consistently implement what we already know.

Regine Leibinger

Energiewende – worauf es ankommt! Erfahrungen einer Architektin

Energy transition— what counts most! An architect's experiences

Wunsch und Wirklichkeit

Die Frage danach, ‚worauf es ankommt', ist nicht einfach zu beantworten, wenn man – wie ich – aus verschiedenen Blickwinkeln auf den Zusammenhang zwischen Klimakrise und Bausektor blickt. Aus Sicht der Hochschullehrerin ist die Sache klar, denn in der Lehre ist das Umdenken bereits mit voller Wucht angekommen: Klassische Neubauprojekte (mit denen ich mein eigenes Studium durchlaufen habe) sind in aktuellen Lehrangeboten kaum mehr zu finden. Revitalisierung, Transformation, Zirkularität, Selbstbau/Design Build lauten die großen neuen Überschriften. Der vertraute Baukonstruktions-Vierklang „Mauerwerk, Beton, Stahl, Holz" ist erweitert um Bambus und Pilze, Flachs und Hanf, Lehm und Algen. Studierende wollen heute wissen, wie sie mit nachwachsenden, biobasierten Materialien im Sinne der Kreislaufwirtschaft arbeiten können, welche neuen Verbundwerkstoffe mit natürlichen Komponenten welchen Beanspruchungen standhalten. Sie wollen wissen, wie ein Haus mit möglichst kleinem CO_2-Fußabdruck gebaut werden kann, um dann im Betrieb idealerweise mehr Energie zu erzeugen als es verbraucht und schließlich möglichst rückstandsfrei recycelt werden zu können.

Ganz ähnlich sieht das Bild aus, das sich mir als Gründerin der gemeinnützigen Organisation „Experimental" zeigt. Hier fördern wir in Zusammenarbeit mit „Bauhaus Erde" seit 2022 im Rahmen mehrmonatiger Fellowships praxisbezogene und forschungsorientierte Projekte für eine nachhaltige Architektur. Zum letzten Open Call haben 120 Bewerberinnen und Bewerber aus der ganzen Welt Projekte eingereicht; ausgewählt wurden schließlich zwei jeweils zweiköpfige Teams aus London und Lwiw in der Ukraine, die sich

Aspiration and reality

There is no simple answer to the question of "what counts most" if, like me, you look at the relationship between the climate crisis and the construction sector from different angles. From the viewpoint of a university teacher, things are abundantly clear, as the need to think differently has long since taken strong root in the classroom: Classic new-build projects (of the kind that I worked my way through as a student) are something you barely find in curricula today. Revitalisation, transformation, circularity, and self-construction/design-build are now the major topics. The familiar construction foursome of masonry, concrete, steel, and wood has been expanded to include bamboo and fungi, flax and hemp, clay and algae. Students today want to know how they can work with regenerative, bio-based materials in line with the notion of a circular economy, and what new composite materials using natural components withstand what stresses and loads. They want to know how a house can be built with the smallest possible carbon footprint and ideally produce more energy than it consumes, and how such a house could eventually be recycled, leaving an absolute minimum of residue.

I see a very similar picture in my role as founder of the non-profit organisation Experimental. In cooperation with Bauhaus Earth, since 2022 we have been supporting multi-month fellowships for research-oriented projects that chart new territory in sustainable architecture. The last open call attracted 120 project submissions from all over the world, with two duos ultimately selected: one team from London and another from Lviv in Ukraine, both of them exploring earth as a material. Past fellows investigated

mit dem Werkstoff Erde auseinandersetzen. Frühere Fellows hatten die Wiedervernässung von Mooren, die Wiederverwendung von Betonbauteilen oder das Potenzial mineralischer Materialien wie Muscheln und Eierschalen für kohlenstoffarme Bausysteme untersucht. Es gibt also eine neue Generation von Büros und Arbeitsgemeinschaften, die sich der Dringlichkeit der Lage bewusst ist und sich in Themen zur Bewältigung der Klimakrise einarbeitet. Sie nutzen die Freiheiten des akademischen Umfelds oder eines bewusst als „experimentell“ definierten Projektrahmens, und das ist auch gut so.

Nun blicke ich aber auch als praktizierende Architektin auf die Welt. Und hier stelle ich eine Diskrepanz fest zwischen dem, was den akademischen Diskurs bestimmt, und dem, was parallel Tag für Tag auf konventionelle Weise gebaut wird. Auch wir bei Barkow Leibinger planen und realisieren Projekte, die aufgrund der Zielsetzung, ihrer Budgets und Konstruktionsweisen weit entfernt von dem sind, was zum *state of the art* der Nachhaltigkeit auf Podien diskutiert und in Entwurfsstudios bearbeitet wird. Wir haben uns vielfältiges Wissen angeeignet, arbeiten außerdem mit den kompetentesten und innovativsten Fachplanern zusammen, um neue Konzepte zu entwickeln und unseren Bauherren vorschlagen zu können. Doch auf allzu großes Interesse stoßen wir selten – erst recht dann nicht mehr, wenn klar wird, dass wirklich nachhaltige Lösungen in der Regel größere Investitionen bedeuten, dass alternative Baustoffe oder die Wiederverwendung recycelter Materialien ein Abweichen von lange bewährten Standards und aufwendigere Genehmigungsverfahren mit sich bringen. Viele Projekte, an denen Architekten arbeiten, sind eher rendite- als weltverbesserungsorientiert. Stehen Zeit-

re-waterlogging peatlands, the reuse of concrete construction components, or the potential of mineral-based materials such as shells and eggshells as a basis for low-carbon construction systems. In other words, there is a new generation of practices and working groups that are well aware of the urgency of things and are closely examining topics relating to overcoming the crisis. They exploit the freedoms of an academic environment or a project context that is consciously defined as “experimental”, and that is a good thing.

However, I also look at the world as a practicing architect. And there I see a discrepancy between what defines the academic discourse and what is being built day-in, day-out in parallel to it. At Barkow Leibinger, we plan and realise projects which, given the goals and briefs, the budgets, and the forms of construction, are a far cry from what is discussed at the lectern as “state-of-the-art” sustainability and then gets worked on in design studios. We have onboarded a swath of knowledge, and we work with the most competent and innovative specialist planners on developing new concepts that we can propose to our clients. That said, rarely do we encounter much interest—and most certainly not once it is clear that, as a rule, truly sustainable solutions spell higher upfront investments, and that alternative construction materials or the reuse of recycled materials mark a departure from longstanding tried-and-true standards and therefore entail more effort when it comes to the approvals process. Many architectural projects are more focused on ROI than on improving the world. Idealism soon comes to nothing if it extends project lead times or increases costs.

verzögerungen oder höhere Kosten im Raum, ist es schnell vorbei mit dem Idealismus.

Was hingegen sicher auch in Zukunft als „nachhaltig" bezeichnet werden kann, sind die Robustheit und die Flexibilität eines Gebäudes. Es hat keinen Sinn, sämtliche Gebäude aus Beton zu verteufeln. Wenn sie materialeffizient sind, klug und vorausschauend geplant, wenn sie mit Blick auf eine möglichst „unendliche" Lebensdauer auf eine hohe Anpassbarkeit an künftige Nutzungen ausgelegt sind, dann ist schon viel gewonnen – selbst wenn kein Bambus oder gebrauchte Türen verbaut werden. So gehen wir an unsere aktuellen Bauvorhaben heran.

Erwähnen möchte ich allerdings den Sonderfall sogenannter Modellprojekte, die sich zwischen den beiden beschriebenen Welten bewegen, zwischen Utopie und „weiter so". Sie können zumindest in Teilen einlösen, was langfristig Standard werden muss. Ein Beispiel ist der „Frankfurt Prototype", an dem wir mit Planungs- und Beratungsleistungen beteiligt waren. Dieses Pilotprojekt basiert auf Entwürfen von Studierenden bei Niklas Maak an der Städelschule in Frankfurt am Main und bei Heinrich Lessing an der Frankfurt University of Applied Sciences. Das temporär bestehende Bauwerk sollte zeigen, wie ein neuer urbaner, bezahlbarer und nachhaltiger Bautypus aussehen könnte. Erklärtes Ziel war es, das Gebäude weitgehend aus zirkulären Materialien herzustellen. Aber selbst hier waren die Hürden hoch, die Materialbeschaffung aufwendig und sowohl eine Zusammenarbeit mit spezialisierten Unternehmen als auch viel Handarbeit nötig. Beispielsweise mussten alte sägeraue Bretterschalungen, die eigentlich gar nicht mehr

What will also be termed sustainable going forward are, without doubt, a building's robustness and flexibility. There is no point in simply damning all buildings made of concrete. If they are efficient in their use of materials, planned intelligently and with foresight, and designed with a view to having as "infinite" a service life as possible and thus highly adaptable to future usages, then that in itself is a great step forward, even if no bamboo or reused doors are deployed. That is how we tackle our current construction projects.

In all this, it would be amiss not to mention the special case of so-called model projects that move between the two worlds described above, between utopia and "business as usual". Such projects can, at least in part, come good on what must be the standard in the long term. One example is the "Frankfurt Prototype", for which we provided planning and advisory services. The pilot project was based on design proposals by students of Niklas Maak at Frankfurt's Städelschule and of Heinrich Lessing at the Frankfurt University of Applied Sciences. The temporary building was meant to demonstrate what a new urban, affordable, and sustainable structure could look like. The express goal was to construct the building mainly using circular materials. However, even here the hurdles were high: Procuring the materials involved much effort, and it was necessary both to collaborate with specialised companies and to invest a lot of labour. For example, the students had to devote considerable energy to cleaning and working up old rough-cut timber shuttering that should actually have never been recycled again in order to ready it for use as a façade material.(fig. 1)

A second lighthouse project is the Weissenhof Visitor and Information Centre that is set to be built to mark the hundredth anniversary of the Stuttgart

hätten wiederverwendet werden dürfen, von den Studierenden mühevoll gereinigt und aufgearbeitet werden, um als Fassadenmaterial zur Anwendung zu kommen.(Abb. 1)

Ein zweites „Leuchtturmprojekt" ist das Besucher- und Informationszentrum Weissenhof, das anlässlich des einhundertjährigen Bestehens der Stuttgarter Werkbundsiedlung von 1927 gebaut werden soll. Auch hier handelt es sich nicht um ein Developer-Projekt, bei dem kommerzielle Aspekte im Vordergrund stehen, sondern um einen Pionierbau, der vom Bauherrn und auch der Öffentlichkeit ausdrücklich mit höchsten Nachhaltigkeitsansprüchen gewünscht ist und damit Vorbildcharakter haben soll.(Abb. 2) Er soll den Innovationsanspruch, den die Weissenhofsiedlung schon zu ihrer Entstehungszeit verkörpert hat, einlösen und weiterführen. Daher haben wir eine Bauweise aus tragenden Lehmsteinen vorgeschlagen, die bisher in Deutschland bei einem Bauwerk dieser Größe noch nicht angewendet wurde. Dass große Ambitionen jedoch auch hier unsanft mit der Realität kollidieren, wenn eine prototypische Bauweise mit den baurechtlichen Auflagen für eine mehrgeschossige Versammlungsstätte in Einklang gebracht werden muss und die entsprechende DIN-Norm noch nicht in die technischen Baubestimmungen der Länder aufgenommen, folglich noch nicht bauaufsichtlich eingeführt ist, liegt auf der Hand. Wäre der Leuchtturmanspruch nicht, dann würden die Herausforderungen, die eine nachhaltige Bauweise aus Lehm in diesem Fall mit sich bringt, wahrscheinlich längst zu einer konventionellen Bauweise aus Stahlbeton geführt haben. So aber können wir unter viel Einsatz aller Beteiligten Wunsch und Wirklichkeit in der Waage halten. Auch darauf kommt es an.

Werkbund Housing Estate, which opened in 1927. It is likewise not a developer project, where commercial aspects are foregrounded, but a pioneering structure, which both the client and the public expressly want to see achieve the highest sustainability standards, and which is meant to function as a model for others to follow.(fig. 2) The building is intended to come good on innovation and advance the ideas that the Weissenhof Estate embodied back in its infancy. For this reason, we proposed a load-bearing structure of clay brick—something that to date has never been used on a structure of this size in Germany. Obviously, such great ambitions invariably collide harshly with reality, as a prototype structure has to be brought into line with the stipulations under building law for a multistorey meeting hall. What is more, the corresponding DIN norm has not yet been incorporated into the Federal States Technical Stipulations and is thus not yet covered by building approval regulations. If this was not about creating a lighthouse project, then the challenges innate in sustainable construction with clay would probably long since have led to the project switching to a conventional structure made of reinforced concrete. Fortunately, and thanks to much effort on the part of everyone involved, we have been able to strike a balance between aspiration and reality. And that is also of crucial importance.

Abb. 1 Modell Neubau Besucher- und Informationszentrum Weissenhof (BIZ), Stuttgart |
Fig. 1 Model for the new-build visitor and information centre at the Weissenhof Estate, Stuttgart

Abb. 2 | Fig. 2 **Axonometrie „Frankfurt Prototype"** | Axonometric diagram of the "Frankfurt Prototype"

Forschungshaus | Research house

Bad Aibling, Deutschland
Bad Aibling, Germany

Bauaufgabe | Task
Forschungshaus mit drei Wohnungen | Research house with three apartments

Entwurf Hochbau | Architects
Florian Nagler Architekten, München | Munich

Auftrag | Client
B&O Bau, Bad Aibling

Fertigstellung | Completion
2023

Finanzierung | Financing
Privat | Private

Energie / Emissionen
Reduzierung der Nutzung von Ressourcen; Minimierung des Einsatzes von Technik; Wiederverwendung von Materialien

Energy / Emissions
Reducing the use of ressources, minimising the use of technology, reusing materials

Die Frage, wie wir die Ökobilanz unserer Häuser verbessern können, hat uns zu einer zweiten Serie von Forschungshäusern mit deutlicher Reduzierung des Einsatzes von Zement und Beton angeregt. Die erforderliche Speichermasse in den Gebäuden wird durch das Material Lehm zur Verfügung gestellt. Das 2023 realisierte Forschungshaus 4 wurde als Kombination von tragenden Innenwänden aus Lehmsteinen und tragenden Außenwänden und Decken in Brettstapelbauweise ausgeführt. Als Besonderheit wurden die tragenden Innenwände mit einem Recyclingziegel errichtet. Die ersten drei Forschungshäuser in Bad Aibling, gebaut in monolithischer Bauweise aus Mauerwerk, Holzhybrid und Leichtbeton, erzielen in der Ökobilanz von Bauwerk und Technik mit Werten zwischen 8 und 12 kg CO_2Äq./2NRF*a [Treibhausgaspotenziale/Nettroraumfläche] überdurchschnittlich gute Ergebnisse. Dreigeschossige Mehrfamilienhäuser weisen üblicherweise Werte von 16 bis 18 kg CO_2Äq./2NRF*a auf. Das vierte Forschungsgebäude, Haus Halbholz, erreicht mit 7 kg CO_2Äq./2NRF*a sogar einen noch etwas besseren Wert, da der Einsatz von Beton reduziert und durch andere Materialien substituiert wurde. Für die Innenwände wurden hier Lehmstein und wiederverwendete Ziegel eingesetzt. Die Gestaltung der Forschungshäuser mit Satteldächern, durch tiefe Laibungen geschützten Fenstern und robusten, alterungsfähigen Oberflächen zeigt in der Betrachtung der Ökobilanz gute Ergebnisse.

Die Ökobilanzierung über den gesamten Lebenszyklus eines Gebäudes kann einen Beitrag dazu leisten, die notwendige Diskussion über nachhaltiges Bauen zu versachlichen und konkrete Optimierungspotenziale aufzuzeigen. Vor diesem Hintergrund sollen die nachfolgenden Forschungshäuser noch weiter optimiert werden.[1]

1 Vgl. Tilmann Jarmer, Innovation. Einfach Bauen: Material, Recyclingfähigkeit und Lebenszyklus (Technische Universität München), 1. Aufl. München 2024.

The question of how to improve the ecological balance of houses has led to a second series of research houses with a significant reduction in the use of cement and concrete. The required storage mass in the buildings is achieved by using clay. The fourth research house, built in 2023, was designed as a combination of load-bearing interior walls made of clay bricks and load-bearing exterior walls and ceilings in a board stack construction. As a special feature, the load-bearing internal walls were constructed with recycled brick. The first three research houses in Bad Aibling, built in monolithic construction methods using masonry, wood hybrid, and lightweight concrete, achieve above-average results in the life cycle assessment of construction and technology with values between 8 and 12 kg CO_2eq./2NRA*a. [greenhouse gas potential/net room area] Three-storey apartment buildings usually have values of 16–18 kg CO_2eq/2NRA*a. The fourth research house, Haus Halbholz, achieves an even better value of 7 kg CO_2eq/2NRA*a by reducing the use of concrete and substituting it with other materials. Half-timbered clay bricks and recycled bricks were used for the walls inside the house. The design of the research houses, with gabled roofs, windows protected by deep embrasures, and robust, durable surfaces, shows good results when considering the ecological balance of the construction and technology. The life cycle assessment of a building can help to objectify the necessary discussion about sustainable construction and to identify concrete optimisation potential. With this in mind, the next research houses will be further optimised.[1]

1 Cf. Tilmann Jarmer, *Innovation. Einfach Bauen: Material, Recyclingfähigkeit und Lebenszyklus*, 1st edition (Munich: Technische Universität München, 2024).

DAM Was war Ihnen bei der Erarbeitung des Projektes wichtig?
Florian Nagler Architekten Auf Beton zu verzichten und trotzdem genug thermisch träges Material zu verbauen: Lehmstein und Re-use-Ziegel.

DAM What was important to you when developing the project?
Florian Nagler Architekten To avoid concrete while still using enough thermally inert material: clay blocks and reused bricks.

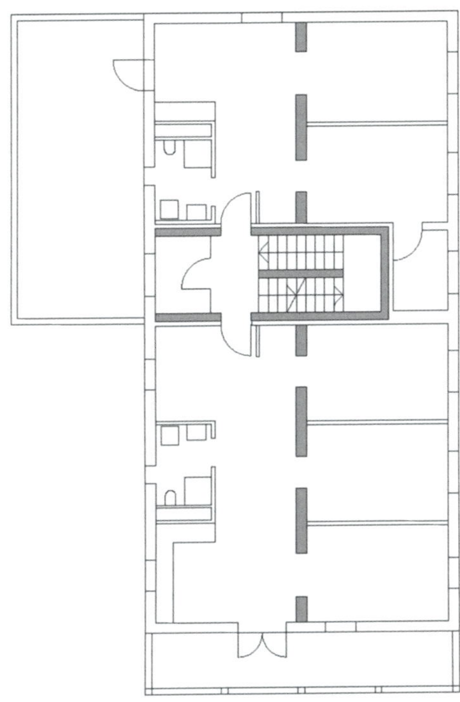

Grundriss 1. Obergeschoss | Floor plan—first floor

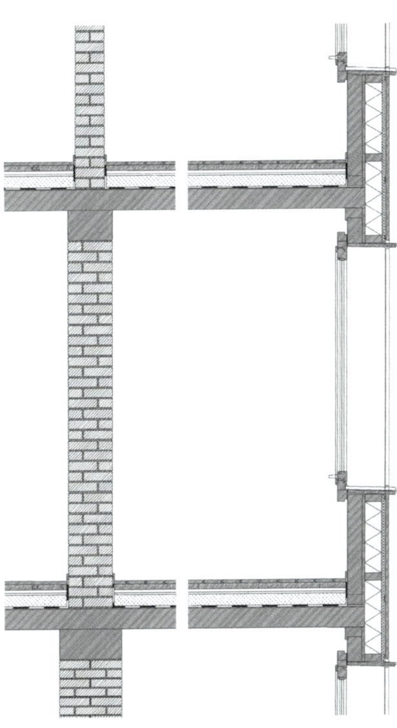

Fassadenschnitt | Sectional view of the façade

Lebensmittelmarkt | Food market

Wiesbaden, Deutschland
Wiesbaden, Germany

Bauaufgabe | Task
Neubau eines Lebensmittelmarkts mit Aquaponic-Farm |
New construction of a food market with aquaponic farm

Entwurf Hochbau | Architects
ACME, London

Entwurf Energiekonzept | Energy design
C4 engineers, Stuttgart

Auftrag | Client
REWE Group, Köln | Cologne

Fertigstellung | Completion
2021

Finanzierung | Financing
Privat | Private

Der REWE Green Farming Markt bedeutet ein anpassungsfähiges und nachhaltiges Marktkonzept, das sich an jede Standorttypologie anpassen kann. Er ist als großzügige Markthalle aus Holz konzipiert, in der lokal angebaute und vor Ort zubereitete Produkte durch die Architektur in Szene gesetzt werden. Im Gebäude ist eine aquaponische Fischzucht untergebracht, darüber ein modulares Gewächshaus. Große Glasfassaden auf der Vorder- und Rückseite schaffen eine Verbindung zur Landschaft und bringen Tageslicht ins Innere. Eine Reihe von Stützen wölbt sich über den Besuchern, schafft ein neues Einkaufserlebnis und gliedert den Raum in einen menschlichen Maßstab. Die Struktur ist leicht zu bauen und anzupassen, da viel schlichtes Holz mit einfachen Schraubverbindungen verwendet wird anstelle hochtechnisierter Elemente. Die Holzstruktur reicht über die Fassade hinaus und überformt einen geschützten Außenbereich.

Mit der Fertigstellung des Marktes in Wiesbaden entwickelte ACME gemeinsam mit dem Planungsteam eine Musterbaubeschreibung und -planung für die serielle Produktion. Ziel ist es insbesondere, die Herstellungs- und Bauprozesse weiter zu optimieren. Die Produktion in der aquaponischen Farm entspricht höchsten Ansprüchen an Umwelt- und Tierschutz, durch Ressourceneffizienz und Transparenz. In Wiesbaden werden jährlich rund 10 Tonnen Barsch/Tilapia und 800.000 Töpfe Basilikum produziert. Im Gewächshaus sorgen innovative Anbausysteme für eine sichere und ganzjährige Produktion. Es wurden vertikale Anbausysteme eingesetzt, bei denen die Pflanzen automatisch beleuchtet und bewässert werden. In einem Seitenflügel des Marktes, direkt unterhalb des Gewächshauses, befindet sich eine Fischzucht mit 13 Tanks. In der RAS-Kreislaufanlage können optimale Bedingungen im Einklang mit dem Tierschutz geschaffen werden, um ganzjährig gesunde Fische aufzuziehen. Zwei Wasserkreisläufe werden genutzt und gekoppelt betrieben: ein Aquakulturkreislauf für die Fischproduktion und ein Hydroponikkreislauf für die Pflanzenproduktion. Dies bietet drei entscheidende Vorteile: 1. Es können zwei verschiedene pH-Werte eingestellt werden, die für den jeweiligen Kreislauf optimiert sind; 2. In der Hydrokultur können für Pflanzen wichtige Mineralien als Ersatzdünger zugegeben werden, ohne den Fischen zu schaden; 3. Die Aquaponik kann das Wasser doppelt nutzen und die Fischausscheidungen als Dünger für die Pflanzen verwenden.

Energie / Emissionen
Kurze Transportwege reduzieren CO_2 und ermöglichen kunststofffreie Verpackungen; demontierbare Holzkonstruktion

Energy / Emissions
Short distances reduce CO_2 and enable plastic-free packaging, removable wooden construction

The REWE Green Farming Market is an adaptable and sustainable market concept that can be tailored to any type of location. It is designed as a spacious market hall built from wood where locally grown and prepared products are presented in an attractive setting. An aquaponic fish farm is housed in the building, with a modular greenhouse above it. Large glass façades at the front and back connect the building to the surroundings and bring daylight inside. A series of columns arches over visitors, creating a new shopping experience and putting the space on a human scale. The structure is easy to build and adapt, using lots of plain timber with regular screw connections, rather than ultra-technical elements. The timber structure extends beyond the façade to create a weather-protected outdoor area. Since the completion of the market in Wiesbaden, ACME has been working with the planning team to develop the design and plans for serial production. The aim is to further optimise the manufacturing and construction processes. The aquaponic farm meets the highest standards of environmental and animal protection through resource efficiency and transparency. The aquaponic farm in Wiesbaden produces around ten tonnes of tilapia per year, and 800,000 pots of basil. Innovative growing systems in the greenhouse ensure reliable production all year round. Vertical growing systems mean the plants are automatically exposed to light and watered. In a side wing of the market—directly below the greenhouse—there is a fish farm with thirteen tanks. Optimal conditions in line with animal welfare can be created in the RAS recirculation system to raise healthy fish all year round. Two water cycles are used and operated in tandem: an aquaculture cycle for fish production and a hydroponic cycle for plant production. This offers three key advantages: 1) two different pH values can be set, optimised for each individual cycle; 2) in hydroponics, important minerals can be added to the plants as a substitute fertiliser without harming the fish; and 3) aquaponics can use the water twice, using the fish excrement as fertiliser for the plants.

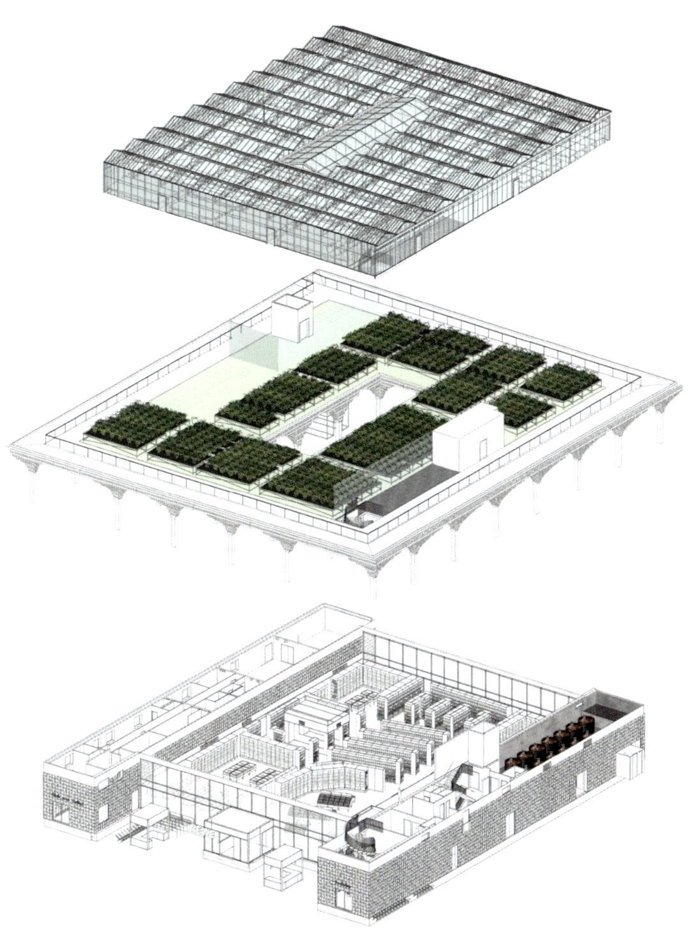

Isometrie | Isometric diagram

DAM **Was war Ihnen bei der Erarbeitung des Projektes wichtig?**
ACME Wir wollten einen Gebäudetyp schaffen, der als Bestandteil eines Netzwerks neuer Märkte das Thema Nachhaltigkeit neu betrachtet und erweitert. Daher haben wir ein Konzept entwickelt, das die Produktion der Lebensmittel in das Gebäude integriert, aber auch das Vertriebskonzept der REWE einbindet: Die Lieferwege können völlig neu organisiert werden, indem die ausliefernden LKW auf der Rückfahrt die Lebensmittel transportieren können, die im Markt produziert worden sind. Dadurch werden durch den Transport verursachte Emissionen um ein Vielfaches reduziert, zugleich werden den Kunden die Themen Regionalität und Produktion auf anschauliche Weise vermittelt.

DAM **What was important to you when developing the project?**
ACME We wanted to create a building type that, as part of a network of new markets, takes a fresh look at sustainability and further advances it. That is why we developed a concept that integrates food production into the building, while also incorporating the REWE retail concept: Delivery routes can be completely reorganised so that the delivery trucks are able to transport the food that has been produced in the store on their return journey. This will significantly reduce transport-related emissions and, for customers, will bring to life the value of regional food production.

Sozialer Wohnungsbau | Social housing

Brüssel, Belgien
Brussels, Belgium

Bauaufgabe | Task
Renovierung eines Sozialwohnungsbaus mit 80 Wohnungen und gewerblichem Erdgeschoss | Renovation of a social housing block with 80 apartments and a commercial ground floor

Entwurf Hochbau | Architects
51N4E, Brüssel | Brussels; Lacaton & Vassal, Montreuil

Auftrag | Client
Beliris (Belgian federal government), Sint-Joost-ten-Node

Fertigstellung | Completion
2024

Finanzierung | Financing
Öffentliche Mittel | Public funding

Der komplexe und mitunter schwierige soziale Kontext des Standorts unterstreicht die Dringlichkeit der Renovierung und Modernisierung. Angesichts der Fragilität des Kontextes war Bedingung des Projektes, die Renovierung bei bewohntem Gebäude durchzuführen, um eine vollständige Umsiedlung der Bewohner zu vermeiden. Alle Entscheidungen über Eingriffe innerhalb des Gebäudes wurden auf die Baustellensituation abgestimmt. Ziel des Projektes war es, die technische Ausstattung und die gemeinsam genutzten Innenräume des Bestandsgebäudes zu erneuern, um die Systeme des Gebäudes effizienter und langlebiger zu machen. Außerdem sollte an beiden Längsfassaden eine freistehende Konstruktion angebracht werden, durch welche die Wohnungen in den oberen Stockwerken einen Wintergarten erhielten – eine thermische „Filterschicht", die die Leistung des Gebäudes verbessert und den Bewohnern die Kontrolle über den Komfort überlässt. Der gezielte Eingriff in die Gebäudestrukturen erlaubte eine nachhaltige Renovierung mit großem Mehrwert, deren Kosten weit unter denen eines Neubaus liegen.

Ein solcher Ansatz strebt ein optimales Minimum an, indem so viele Qualitäten wie möglich innerhalb eines wirtschaftlich vertretbaren Rahmens realisiert werden. Dadurch kann dieses Projekt als Modell für andere Bauvorhaben dienen und letztlich zu einer umfassenden Verbesserung der Qualität dieser bestehenden Wohnbautypologie führen.

Energie / Emissionen
Erhaltung und Nutzung bestehender Strukturen; Reduzierung des Heizbedarfs durch Lowtech-Architektur

Energy / Emissions
Preservation and utilisation of existing structures, reduction of heating requirements through low-tech architecture

The complex and sometimes difficult social context of the site highlighted the urgency of renovating and upgrading. Given the fragility of the situation, the project required renovating an actively occupied site to avoid the need for relocating all residents. Decisions about interventions inside the building were aligned with this in mind. The goal was to renew the technical equipment and shared interior spaces of the existing building, making its systems more efficient and durable—and to introduce an independent structure on both long façades, a winter garden for each apartment located on the upper floors, thus adding a thermal "filter" layer that enhances the performance of the building and increases comfort for the inhabitants. Such an intervention allows for a sustainable renovation with great added value at a cost significantly lower than the cost of a new construction. This approach strives for an optimal minimum, realising as many qualities as possible within what is economically reasonable, thus creating a project that can serve as a model elsewhere, ultimately leading to an extensive improvement in this typology of housing.

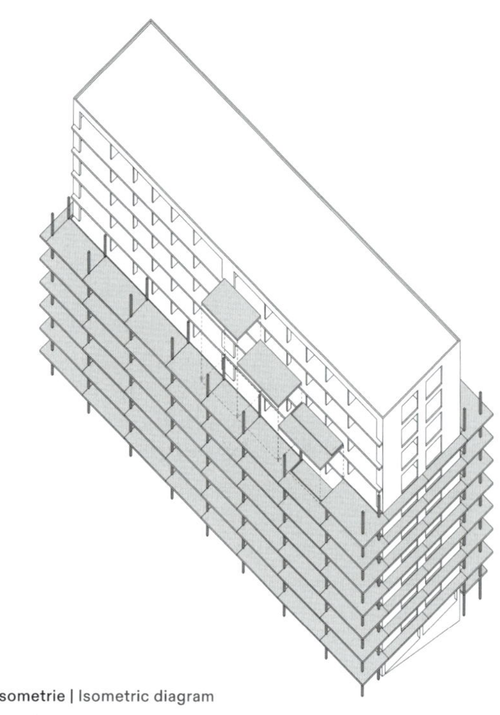

Isometrie | Isometric diagram

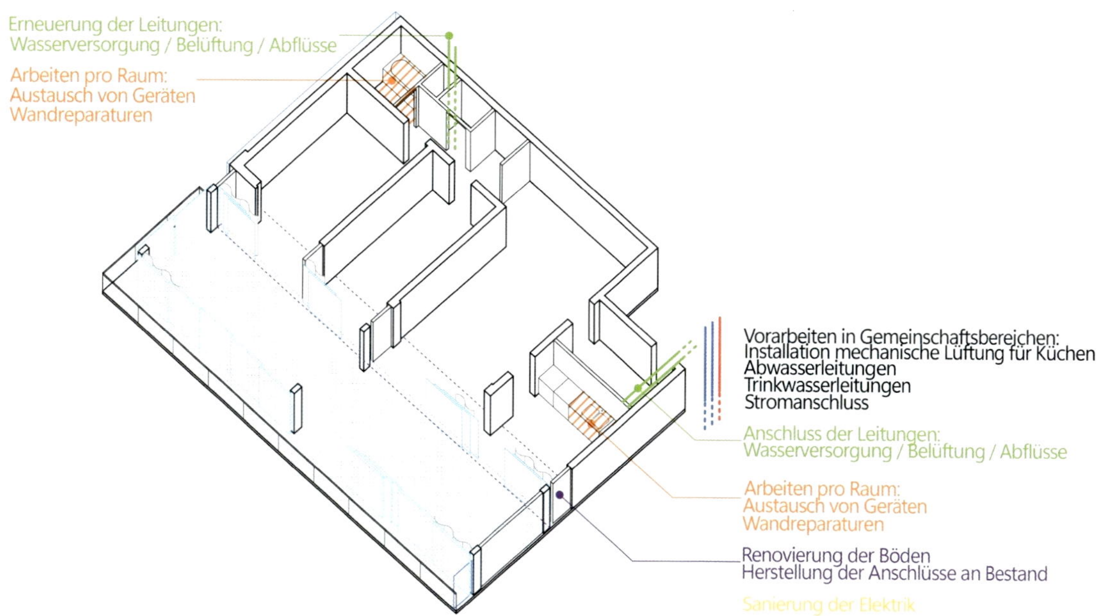

Technische Renovierungsarbeiten in den Wohnungen | Technical modernisation in the apartments

DAM **Was finden Sie an Ihrem Projekt besonders bemerkenswert?**
51N4E Die fast vollständige Renovierung (ausgenommen die Innenausstattung) zu bewerkstelligen, während die meisten Wohnungen bewohnt waren und alle bestehenden Systeme aktiv bleiben mussten. Hinzu kommt, dass alle Wohnungen um ca. 50 m² Wohnfläche erweitert wurden, bei Gesamtprojektkosten von ca. 1.250 €/m².

DAM **Welche Aspekte waren Ihnen bei der Entwicklung des Projektes wichtig?**
51N4E „Bewohnte" Baustelle, Großzügigkeit gegenüber den Bewohnern, aber auch gegenüber der Nachbarschaft; eine energetische Sanierung, die recht einfach ist und den Bewohnern die Kontrolle über ihren Komfort gibt.

DAM **What do you find particularly remarkable about your project?**
51N4E Managing the almost complete renovation (excluding apartment interiors) while most units remained inhabited, with all existing systems remaining active while renovating. This was accomplished while adding approximately 50 m² of liveable space to all apartments with a total project cost of approximately 1,250 €/m².

DAM **Which aspects were important to you when developing the project?**
51N4E Running an "inhabited" construction site, a benefit to the inhabitants but also the neighbourhood; achieving an energetic renovation that is quite basic and succeeds in giving the inhabitants control over their comfort.

Die Energiewende ist ein komplexes Puzzle

Interview mit | with Claudia Kemfert

Leiterin der Abteilung Energie, Verkehr, Umwelt am Deutschen Institut für Wirtschaftsforschung (DIW Berlin) und Professorin für Energiewirtschaft und Energiepolitik an der Leuphana Universität Lüneburg

Head of the Department of Energy, Transportation, and Environment at the German Institute for Economic Research in Berlin and Professor of Energy Economics and Energy Policy at Leuphana University Lüneburg

The energy transition is a complex puzzle

DAM Hat sich das Bewusstsein für Energiesparen tatsächlich gewandelt, und führt dieses Bewusstsein auch zu einem anderen Verständnis des Bauens?

Claudia Kemfert Pointiert gesagt ist der Gebäudesektor der größte Klimakiller in Deutschland: Bis zu 40 Prozent der energiebedingten Treibhausgasemissionen gehen auf das Konto von Gebäuden, und zwar nicht nur im Betrieb, sondern schon beim Bau. Die Studien dazu begleite ich als Wissenschaftlerin seit fast drei Jahrzehnten. Ich hätte nie gedacht, dass wir 2025 immer noch darüber diskutieren. Ein Trauerspiel.

DAM In Deutschland wird viel über die Energiewende diskutiert. Wie definieren Sie persönlich eine erfolgreiche Wende im Umgang mit Energie?

CK Die Energiewende ist ein komplexes Puzzle. Es gibt viele verschiedene Teile, die zuerst scheinbar nichts miteinander zu tun haben. Windräder, E-Fahrzeuge und Computerchips sind auf den ersten Blick völlig verschiedene Dinge. Aber nach und nach greifen sie ineinander und irgendwann ergibt sich ein klares Bild. Wenn wir den Anteil von Ökostrom steigern, in Gebäuden und auf der Straße mehr Energie sparen und den Energieverbrauch überall durch Digitalisierung und Speicher flexibilisieren, führt das in Summe zu einer erfolgreichen Energiewende. So erreichen wir die Klimaziele und sichern unsere Energieversorgung.

DAM Has public awareness on energy saving actually changed, and is this awareness now leading to a different understanding of construction?

Claudia Kemfert To put it perhaps over-bluntly, the construction sector is the single largest climate-killer in Germany: Up to 40% of energy-driven greenhouse gas emissions are attributable to buildings, and not just their operations, but their construction, too. As a scientist, I have been following the relevant studies for almost three decades. I would never have thought we would still be discussing this in 2025. A tragedy.

DAM In Germany, there's a lot of discussion around the energy transition. How would you personally define a successful transition in our approach to energy?

CK The energy transition is a complex puzzle. There are many different parts that seem at first to have nothing to do with each other. Wind turbines, e-vehicles, and computer chips can easily be seen as completely different things. However, they gradually interlock and, at some point, a clear picture emerges. If we boost the proportion of eco-electricity in the mix, save more energy in buildings and on the roads, and render energy consumption flexible through digitisation and storage systems, then this will lead to a successful energy transition overall. In this way we achieve our climate goals and secure our energy supplies.

DAM Welche politischen Impulse und Initiativen wünschen Sie sich?
CK Die Politik hat zu lange darauf gesetzt, dass der Markt das allein regelt. Aber jetzt braucht es endlich klare Rahmenbedingungen. Zum Glück passiert da auch was, aber bei Weitem nicht genug. Das Ziel ist klar: Gebäude energetisch sanieren und fossile Energiesysteme durch emissionsfreie Technologien austauschen. Dafür braucht es ambitionierte Ziele, klare Richtlinien und ausreichende finanzielle Mittel. Hier stattdessen auf die Schulden- oder Investitionsbremse zu treten, ist in jeder Hinsicht kontraproduktiv. Der Bausektor ist eine zentrale Größe für die gesamte Volkswirtschaft. Je mehr dort investiert wird, desto mehr profitieren wir. Zudem wird das regionale Handwerk gestärkt. Mehr Win-Win-Win geht nicht!
DAM Kann die Bauindustrie Klimaneutralität erreichen und ausschließlich mit nicht-fossilen Energieträgern versorgt werden?
CK Sie kann! Und es ist gar nicht so schwer. Bessere Dämmung, effiziente Heiz- und Kühlsysteme und energieeffiziente Geräte – das ist alles schon erfunden und alles schon da. Solarpaneele auf Dächern und Wärmepumpen sind im Handel und amortisieren sich schnell. Auch der Einsatz von erneuerbaren Energiequellen, Smart-Home-Technologien und Gebäudemanagementsystemen ist kein Hexenwerk. Man kann nachhaltige Baumaterialien verwenden, die über ihren gesamten Lebenszyklus eine geringere Umweltbelastung aufweisen. Und wenn die Politik obendrein den Fokus auf eine nachhaltige Stadtplanung legt, fügt sich das große Klimapuzzle fast von selbst zusammen. Technisch jedenfalls ist das kein Problem.

DAM What political initiatives would you like to see?
CK The politicians have insisted for far too long that the market alone can regulate things. What we now need is to impose well-defined framework conditions at long last. Fortunately, something is happening on that front, too, but by no means enough. The objective is clear: to modernise buildings in terms of their energy consumption and replace fossil energy systems with emission-free technologies. To this end we need ambitious targets, clear guidelines, and sufficient financial resources. However you look at it, it is counterproductive to insist simply on upholding the cap on national debt and thus stop investments. The construction sector is a central variable for the entire economy. The more that is invested there, the more we benefit. Moreover, it boosts the regional trades. Hard to imagine a greater win-win-win situation!
DAM Can the construction industry achieve climate neutrality and be powered exclusively from non-fossil energy sources?
CK Yes, it can! And it's really not that difficult. Better insulation, efficient heating and cooling systems, and energy-efficient appliances: They have all long since been invented and are available. Solar panels on roofs and heat pumps can be bought from retailers, and the purchase swiftly pays off. The use of renewable energy sources, smart-home technologies, and building management systems are all fairly straightforward. You can use sustainable construction materials that place less of a burden on the environment across their entire lifecycle. And if, to top it all, the politicians were to focus on sustainable urban planning,

DAM Unsere Klimaziele für den Ausbau der nicht-fossilen Energien werden in Sektoren aufgeteilt. Im Gebäudesektor wird der Energiebedarf für die Gebäudenutzung erfasst, nicht aber die Energie, die für die Errichtung des Gebäudes aufgewendet wird, die sogenannte graue Energie. Halten Sie diese sektorale Aufteilung für problematisch?
CK Ja, absolut. Bau und Nutzung von Gebäuden gehören gedanklich zusammen. Die Umweltökonomie betrachtet immer den gesamten Lebenszyklus, berücksichtigt also alle Energie, die für den Bau, die Nutzung, die Instandhaltung, den Umbau und irgendwann den Abriss benötigt wird. Architektur- und Planungsbüros versuchen richtigerweise zunehmend, Gebäude zu entwerfen, die mit geringerem Energiebedarf gebaut und mit wenig Energie genutzt werden können. Im Sinne einer klimabewussten Kreislaufwirtschaft ist auch die Verwendung von Recycling- und nachhaltigen Materialien, die sich beim Rückbau wieder sortenrein trennen lassen.
DAM In der Diskussion um die notwendige Energie- bzw. Wärmewende haben wir im letzten Jahr viel Unsicherheit und mangelnde Kommunikation seitens der politischen Entscheidungsträger erlebt. Welche Strategien empfehlen Sie, um auch Eigenheimbesitzer von der Sinnhaftigkeit der Energiewende zu überzeugen?
CK Die Lobbyisten der Vergangenheit wenden leider enorme Ressourcen auf, um die fossilen Geschäftsmodelle zu verlängern. Sie verbreiten durch aggressive Störkommunikation Unsicherheiten und Zweifel in die Sinnhaftigkeit des Tuns. Das macht eine sachliche

then the pieces of the big climate puzzle as good as come together on their own. At any rate, technically speaking, it's not a problem at all.
DAM Our climate goals for expanding non-fossil energy sources are spread across sectors. In the building sector, the energy requirement is logged for operating the buildings, but the energy required to construct the buildings, the so-called "grey energy", is not. Do you find this distinction problematic?
CK Yes, most definitely. We need to think of construction and operation of the building as two sides of the same coin. Environmental economics always considers the entire lifecycle, meaning all the energy required to build, operate, maintain, convert, and, at some point, demolish the building. Architecture and planning practices are correctly and increasingly attempting to design buildings that require less energy inputs for their construction and can be operated using less energy. With a view to a climate-conscious circular economy, the utilisation of recycling and sustainable materials that can be separated cleanly from one another when a building is torn down is to be welcomed.
DAM In the debates on the energy and/or heat transition that society requires, last year we saw a lot of uncertainty and a lack of communication on the part of the political decision-makers. What strategies would you recommend in order to convince owner-occupiers of the meaningfulness of the energy transition?
CK The lobbyists of yesterday sadly deploy a massive amount of resources in order to prolong the fossil business models. With their

„Dabei gäbe es so viele wunderbare Storys über die positiven Auswirkungen der Energiewende auf die Lebensqualität und die Umwelt“

Aufklärung und Information nicht gerade leicht. Trotzdem lohnt es sich dagegenzuhalten. Zunächst braucht es leicht verständliche Informationen über die ökologischen und vor allen die ökonomischen Vorteile der Energiewende. Die Energiewende spart langfristig irre viel Geld. Das haben die wenigsten verstanden.

DAM Ist das alles?

CK Jedenfalls alles, was Staat und Baubranche tun können. Obendrein könnte sich allerdings auch die Medienbranche fragen, inwieweit sie sich von der fossilen Industrie instrumentalisieren lassen will. Allzu oft berichtet sie – auf der Suche nach schnellen Klicks – lieber über Streitereien und nebensächliche Probleme statt über positive Erfahrungen und Erfolgsgeschichten, die es überall im Land gibt. Dabei gäbe es so viele wunderbare Storys über die positiven Auswirkungen der Energiewende auf die Lebensqualität und die Umwelt. Die Luftqualität verbessert sich durch energieeffiziente Heizsysteme. Der Lärm reduziert sich durch Elektromobilität. Eine klimagerechte Welt wäre nur für die fossile Gas- und Ölindustrie schlechter. Alle anderen profitieren: Menschen, Tiere, Pflanzen, der ganze Planet.

aggressive and disruptive communications, they spread uncertainty and sow doubts as to the meaningfulness of acting. As a result, it is not exactly easy to put the objective case and provide objective information. Nevertheless, it is worth our while to resist them. What we need first and foremost is readily comprehensible information on the ecological and above all the economic advantages of the energy transition. The energy transition saves a shedload of money in the long term. Only a very few people have really understood this.

DAM Is that all?

CK This is, at any rate, everything that the state and the construction sector can do. Added to which, however, the media industry could ask itself to what extent it wishes to let itself be instrumentalised by the fossil industry. In the media's hunt for clickbait, they all too often prefer reporting on quarrels and side-issues instead of favourable experiences and success stories that exist up and down the country. And believe me, there are so many wonderful stories to tell about the positive impacts of the energy transition on quality of life and the environment. Energy-efficient heating systems improve the quality of our air. Electromobility reduces noise levels.

“There are so many wonderful stories to tell about the positive impacts of the energy transition on quality of life and the environment”

DAM Was bedeutet klimaschonendes Bauen für Sie in einem Wort?
CK In einem einzigen Wort? Vielleicht „Puzzle-Stück". Denn klimaschonendes Bauen ist ein Puzzlestück im Gesamtkunstwerk der erfolgreichen Energiewende, allerdings ein zentrales!
DAM Was wünschen Sie sich von der nächsten Generation der Architekten und Ingenieure im Hinblick auf klimaschonendes Bauen?
CK Ich wünsche mir, dass die nächste Generation sich mit den früheren Generationen zusammentut und gemeinsam politisch durchsetzt, was seit mindestens zwanzig Jahren an Hochschulen und Universitäten gelehrt wird: nachhaltiges und klimaschonendes Bauen! Das ist doch keine Zukunftsmusik, das ist vielerorts längst Wirklichkeit. Ich wünsche mir, dass immer mehr Menschen den Mut und die Kraft haben, sich an diesem Wandel aktiv zu beteiligen – egal welcher Generation sie angehören.

A climate-appropriate world would only be worse for the fossil oil and gas industry. Everyone else benefits: people, animals, plants, the whole planet.
DAM To your mind, in a nutshell, what does "climate-friendly construction" mean?
CK In a nutshell? Well, maybe "piece of a jigsaw puzzle". Because climate-friendly construction is a piece of the larger puzzle of a successful energy transition, albeit a critical piece!
DAM What would you like to see from the next generation of architects and engineers as regards climate-friendly building?
CK I would hope that the next generation sits down with earlier generations and together they get political approval for what has been taught at colleges and universities for at least the last twenty years: sustainable and climate-friendly construction! This is definitely not pie in the sky but has long since been a reality in many places. I would like ever more people to find the courage and energy to play an active part in this process of change, irrespective of the generation to which they belong.

Gemischter Quartiersblock
Mixed neighbourhood block

Wuppertal, Deutschland
Wuppertal, Germany

Energie / Emissionen
Nutzung und Sanierung bestehender Gebäude; Verzicht auf konventionelle Wärmedämmung; Beheizung und Kühlung durch intelligente Wärmedämmung als Luftschicht hinter Polycarbonatfassade; Photovoltaikanlage

Energy / Emissions
Use and renovation of existing buildings, no conventional thermal insolation, heating and cooling through intelligent thermal insulation as an air layer behind a polycarbonate façade, photovoltaic system

Bauaufgabe | Task
Umbau einer ehemaligen Textilfabrik zu einem gemischten Quartierbaustein | Conversion of a former textile factory into a mixed neighbourhood block

Entwurf Hochbau | Architects
raumwerk.architekten, Hübert und Klußmann PartGmbB, Köln | Cologne

Entwurf Energiekonzept | Energy design
Delzer Kybernetik, Lörrach; energiebüro vom Stein, Köln | Cologne

Auftrag | Client
Urbane Nachbarschaft BOB, Bonn

Fertigstellung | Completion
2022

Finanzierung | Financing
Montag Stiftung Urbane Räume

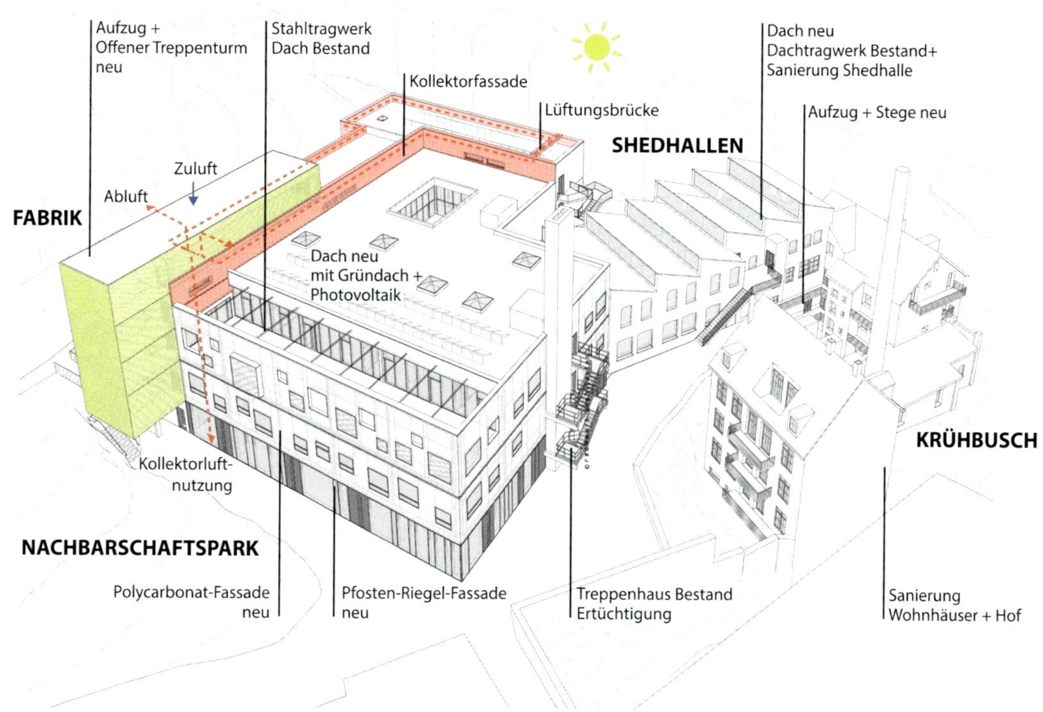

Übersichtsplan | Master plan

Bereits zu Beginn der Planung stand das Ziel einer kostengünstigen Bauweise im Mittelpunkt – eine Grundbedingung für die Gemeinwohlentwicklung. Gleichzeitig war aufgrund der Gebäudetiefe von bis zu 40 Metern die maximal mögliche Tageslichtausnutzung im Vordergrund. Als Alternative zu einer teuren Glasfassade erwies sich eine Kombination aus einer komplett über die Bestandshülle gezogenen kostengünstigen Polycarbonatfassade mit einzelnen Fensteröffnungen, welche zugleich Lüftung und transparente Blickbeziehungen nach außen ermöglichen.

Hinter der Polycarbonatfassade als Außenhaut besteht vor den geschlossenen Wandabschnitten eine 20 Zentimeter dicke Luftschicht, die von der Sonneneinstrahlung erwärmt wird. Eine zusätzliche Dämmung gibt es hier nicht. Die vorgewärmte Luft wirkt als sogenannte intelligente Wärmedämmung und bringt die solaren Gewinne je nach Bedarf über die Betonaußenwand in die Innenräume. Die Kollektorfassade besteht aus einem ununterbrochenen Luftvolumen, das mit mechanischer Unterstützung einer kleinen Lüftungsanlage horizontal um das Gebäude bewegt wird: Morgens wird die erwärmte Luft von der Ostseite auf die übrigen Fassadenseiten geführt und wärmt dort die Außenwände vor. Wenn an warmen Tagen im Süden eher gekühlt werden soll, kann die solar erwärmte Luft in die kühle untere Ebene 3 geführt werden, um dort die Raumluft zu erwärmen. An heißen Tagen wird die Kollektorluft aus dem Fassadenzwischenraum herausgezogen und durch Umgebungsluft ersetzt.

Right from the start of the planning process, the focus was on cost-effective construction—a basic requirement for the development of this community. At the same time, the building's depth of up to 40 metres meant that the focus was on maximising the use of daylight. As an alternative to an expensive glass façade, a cost-effective polycarbonate façade that covers the entire existing shell was used in combination with individual window openings to allow ventilation and views to the outside.

Behind the polycarbonate façade, there is a 20-centimetre layer of air in front of the closed wall sections. This air is heated by the direct sunlight, and there is no additional insulation here. The preheated air acts as "intelligent thermal insulation" and brings the solar gains into the interior via the external concrete wall. The collector façade consists of an uninterrupted volume of air, which is pushed laterally around the building by a small ventilation system: In the morning, the heated air is directed from the east side to the other sides, where it preheats the outer walls. If cooling is required in the south on warm days, solar-heated air can be fed into the cool lower third to preheat the indoor air there. On very warm days, the collector air is drawn out of the space between the façades and replaced with ambient air.

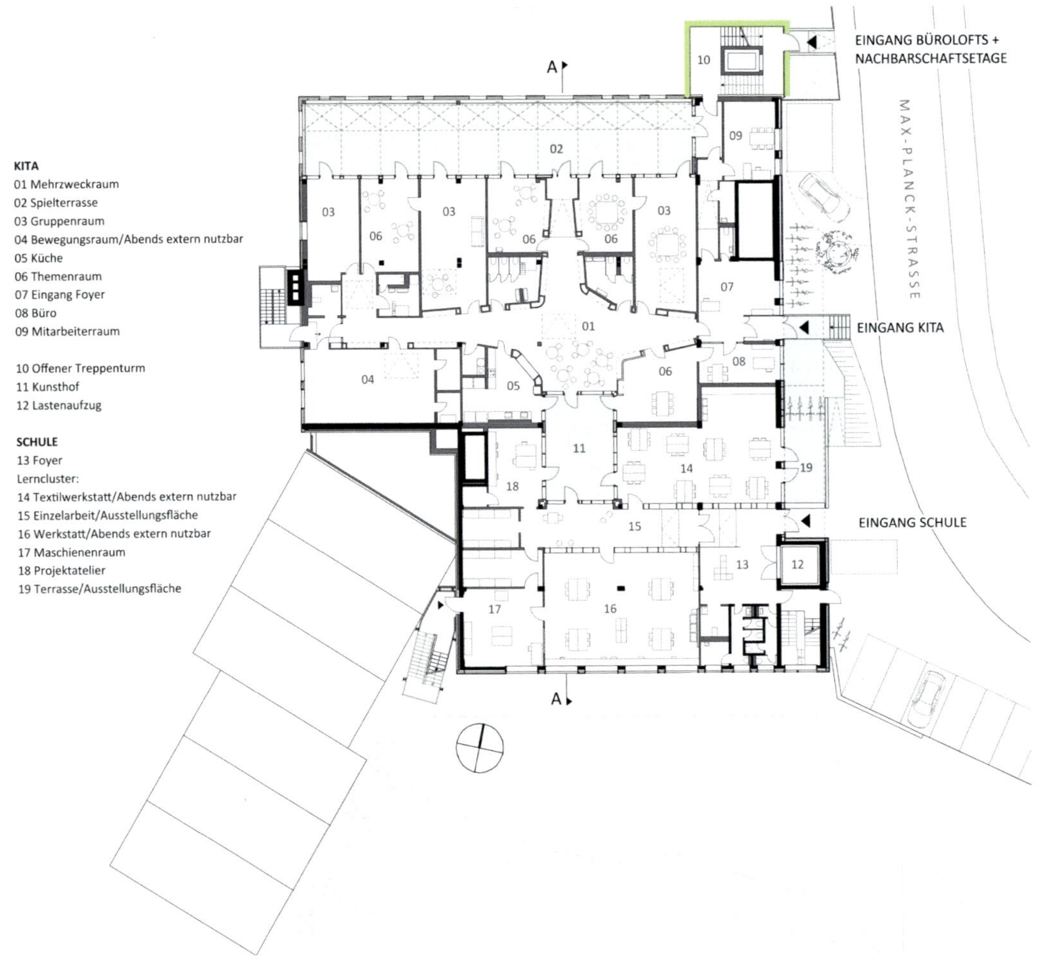

Grundriss Ebene 5 Kita + Schule |
Childcare centre and school: floor plan—fifth floor

DAM Was finden Sie besonders gelungen an Ihrem Projekt?
raumwerk.architekten Die neue Gebäudehülle und den umfangreichen Erhalt der alten Bausubstanz.

DAM Was war Ihnen bei der Erarbeitung des Projektes wichtig?
raumwerk.architekten Einfache und unkonventionelle Lösungen für komplizierte Gegebenheiten vor Ort zu finden.

DAM Was würden Sie beim nächsten Mal anders machen?
raumwerk.architekten Noch mehr auf die Nachhaltigkeit der einzelnen Materialien achten.

DAM What do you find particularly remarkable about your project?
raumwerk.architekten The new building façade and the large-scale preservation of the old building fabric.

DAM Which aspects were important to you when developing the project?
raumwerk.architekten Finding simple and unconventional solutions for complex local conditions.

DAM What would you do differently next time?
raumwerk.architekten Pay even more attention to the sustainability of materials.

BOB
CAMPUS

Plusenergie-Kindertagesstätte
Plus-energy daycare centre

Marburg, Deutschland
Marburg, Germany

Energie / Emissionen
Plusenergiehaus als vorgefertigter Holzbau; Südwestfassade und Dach als PV-Faltwerk; Wärmerückgewinnung; Luft-Wasser-Wärmepumpe

Energy / Emissions
Plus-energy house, prefabricated timber construction, southwest façade and roof with a photovoltaic folding system, heat recovery, air-to-water heat pump

Bauaufgabe | Task
Neubau einer fünfgruppigen Plusenergie-/Solar-Kindertagesstätte | New construction of a plus-energy/solar daycare centre in five groups

Entwurf Hochbau | Architects
opus Architekten, Darmstadt

Entwurf Energiekonzept | Energy design
ee-concept, Darmstadt

Auftrag | Client
Universitätsstadt Marburg

Fertigstellung | Completion
2015

Finanzierung | Financing
Universitätsstadt Marburg und öffentliche Förderprogramme | City of Marburg and public-funding programmes

Ähnlich einem Pavillon im Park bezieht sich der Entwurf in erster Linie auf die umgebende Landschaft und tritt nicht in Konkurrenz zum historischen Gebäudebestand. Im Erdgeschoss orientieren sich die Gruppen nach Westen zur Wiese, im Obergeschoss nach Osten zur Kapelle. Um den Plusenergiestandard zu erreichen, wurden die Dachflächen und die südwestliche Fassade im Obergeschoss aktiv auf Photovoltaik ausgerichtet. Diese Bauteile wurden im Gegensatz zum Erdgeschoss als Faltwerk in leichter Holzbauweise ausgeführt. Durch die Faltung wird zugleich die Ausrichtung der Solarmodule optimiert und die solaraktive Oberfläche vergrößert. Die zweigeschossige Bauweise ergibt darüber hinaus einen kompakten Baukörper sowie eine höher liegende und somit weniger verschattete Dachfläche. Die Solarmodule wurden nicht additiv verwendet, sondern sind integraler und gestaltbildender Bestandteil der Gebäudehülle. Die zentrale Lüftung ist mit einer hocheffizienten Wärmerückgewinnung ausgestattet und dient die Räume über Weitwurfdüsen an. Die Wärmeabgabe erfolgt über eine Fußbodenheizung – so ist beim Spielen auf dem Boden auch bei kleinen Kindern keine erhöhte Auskühlung zu befürchten. Zwei Luft-Wasser-Wärmepumpen liefern die für den Gebäudebetrieb notwendige Energie.

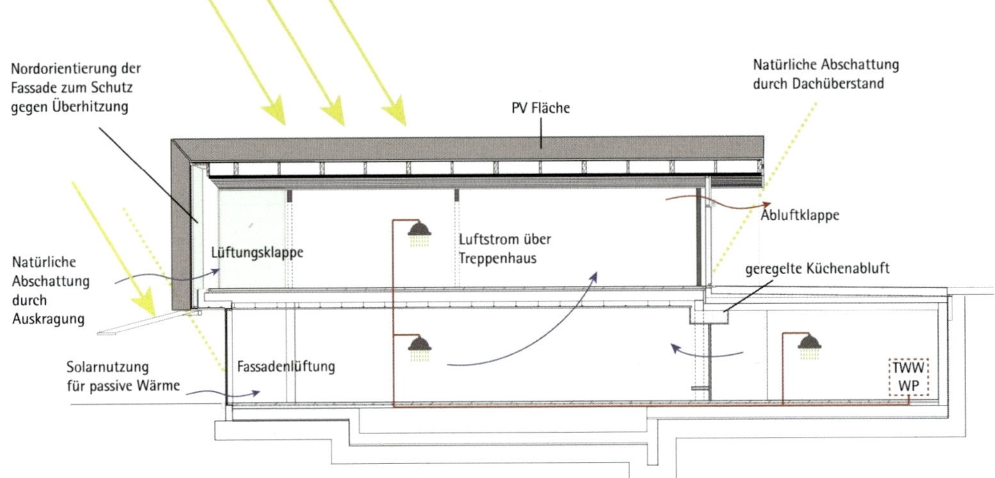

Energieversorgung im Sommer | Energy supply in summer

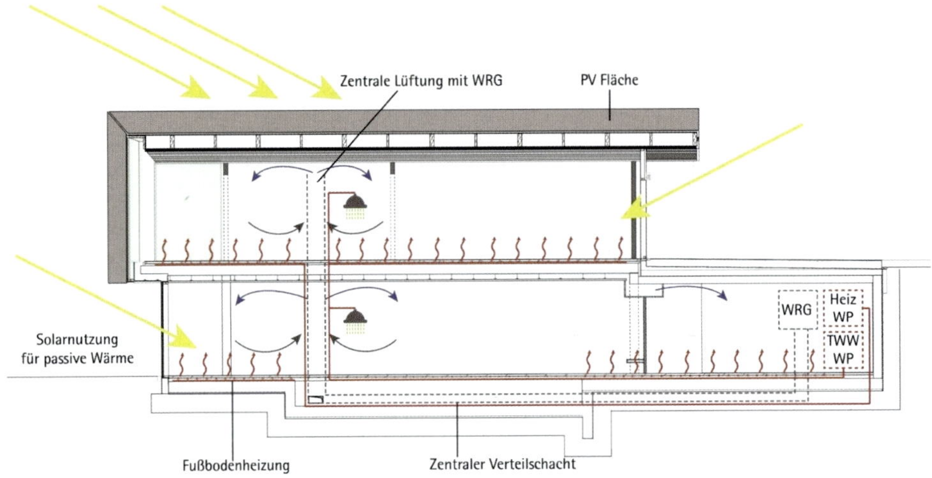

Energieversorgung im Winter | Energy supply in winter

Similar to a pavilion in a park, the design primarily engages with the landscape and therefore does not compete with the historic buildings. On the ground floor, the groups face west towards the meadow; on the upper floor, they face east towards the chapel. To achieve the plus-energy standard, the roof surfaces and the southwestern façade on the upper floor are used for solar panels. In contrast to the first floor, these components were designed as a folding structure in lightweight timber construction. The folding also optimises the orientation of the solar modules and increases the solar-active surface area. The two-storey design also results in a compact structure and a higher, and therefore less shaded, roof area. The solar modules are not used additively, but as an integral and design-forming component of the building envelope. The central ventilation system is equipped with a highly efficient heat-recovery system and serves the rooms via jet nozzles. Heat is transferred via underfloor heating—there is no risk of increased cooling when playing on the floor, even with small children. Two air-to-water heat pumps generate the energy required to operate the building.

DAM **Was finden Sie besonders gelungen an Ihrem Projekt?**
opus Architekten Dass das Gebäude – über das Jahr gerechnet – mehr Energie erzeugt als es selbst verbraucht und die Integration der Photovoltaik als gestaltbildender Bestandteil der Gebäudehülle.

DAM **Was war Ihnen bei der Erarbeitung des Projektes wichtig?**
opus Architekten Die Nutzung als Kita sowie die Beteiligung von Auftraggeber und Nutzern am Planungsprozess.

DAM **Was würden Sie beim nächsten Mal anders machen?**
opus Architekten Weniger Hightech, mehr Lowtech, wobei wir die PV nicht zur Hightech zählen.

DAM **What do you consider to be the highlights of your project?**
opus Architekten Calculated over the course of a year, the building generates more energy than it consumes. The integration of photovoltaics as a design element of the building envelope.

DAM **What was important to you when developing the project?**
opus Architekten The use as a children's daycare centre and the participation of the client and users in the planning process.

DAM **What would you do differently next time?**
opus Architekten Less "high-tech", more "low-tech", although we wouldn't count photovoltaics as "high-tech".

Klimagerechtes Bauen bedeutet für mich Zukunft

Interview mit | with Angèle Tersluisen

Professorin an der Technischen Universität Berlin, Institut für Architektur, Fachgebiet Architektur, Gebäudetechnik und -systeme

Professor at the Technical University in Berlin, Institute of Architecture, Department of Architecture, Facilities Technology and Systems

Climate-friendly construction— for me, that means the future

DAM Die Nutzung von Gebäuden trägt erheblich zu unserem Energieverbrauch und damit auch zu den Treibhausgasemissionen bei. Hat sich das Bewusstsein für Energiesparen in den letzten Jahren gewandelt? Führt das zu einem neuen Verständnis von Baukultur?
Angèle Tersluisen Ja, das Bewusstsein hat sich gewandelt, und das war auch dringend nötig. Seit dem Bericht des Club of Rome 1972 wissen wir um die Grenzen des Wachstums. Jetzt, fünfzig Jahre später, sprechen wir endlich über Baukultur, Klimaschutz und Ressourcenschutz. Das ist eine wichtige Entwicklung.

DAM The use of buildings contributes greatly to our energy consumption levels and thus also to greenhouse gas emissions. Has an awareness of energy saving changed in recent years? And has that contributed to a new understanding of our built culture?
Angèle Tersluisen Yes, awareness has grown, which was absolutely necessary. Ever since the Club of Rome report in 1972, we have known there are limits to growth. Now, fifty years later, we are at long last talking about built culture, climate protection, and protecting resources. This is an important development.

„Bei Architekturwettbewerben zeigen sich zwischen den energetisch optimierten und nicht-optimierten Entwürfen Unterschiede von bis zu 30 Prozent im Energiebedarf“

DAM In den letzten zwanzig Jahren lag der Fokus im Bauwesen stark auf Energieeffizienz. Haben wir dabei die Emissionen in der Herstellung vernachlässigt?
AT Ja und nein. Früher machten die Emissionen im Betrieb den allergrößten Teil der Gesamtemissionen eines Gebäudes aus, daher lag der Fokus auf dem Energieverbrauch. Heute haben wir effizientere Wärmeversorgungssysteme; das Verhältnis zwischen Herstellung und Betrieb liegt bei etwa 50:50. Damit erweitert sich auch folgerichtig der Fokus.
DAM Die sogenannten grauen Emissionen durch Bau und Abriss sind schwer zu quantifizieren, aber genauso relevant. Warum ist es so wichtig, diese zu beachten?
AT Der Baubereich ist für ca. 40 Prozent der Treibhausgasemissionen in Deutschland verantwortlich, bindet ca. 90 Prozent der inländischen mineralischen Rohstoffe und verursacht ca. 50 Prozent des

DAM Over the last twenty years, the focus in the construction sector has mainly been on energy efficiency. As a consequence, have we lost track of emissions caused by producing building materials and the construction process itself?
AT Yes and no. In the past, operational emissions accounted for about three quarters of a building's total emissions, which is why the focus was on energy consumption. Today, we have more efficient heat supply systems, and the relationship between production and operation is about fifty-fifty.
DAM It is hard to quantify the so-called grey emissions innate in construction and demolition, but they are equally relevant. Why is it so important to consider them?
AT Because in the case of energy-optimised construction about 50% of emissions arise during production, maintenance, and demolition. We need to calculate very precisely what emissions and resources are hidden there in order to reduce them.
DAM A large part of the energy consumed by buildings is attributable to heating. How can construction methods and planning be adapted in order to reduce the emissions caused by heating?
AT Today, thanks to heat pump systems we have fewer problems with heating. Nevertheless, the architecture, choice of materials, and design of the building enable us to control the energy requirement for operating the building. In architecture competitions, there are differences of as much as 30% in the energy requirements between the worst designs and the best.

gewichtsbezogenen Abfallaufkommens. Die Zahlen verdeutlichen, wie relevant die Berechnung der Auswirkungen des Bauens ist. Die planungsbegleitende Berechnung ermöglicht eine Optimierung.

DAM Ein Großteil des Energieverbrauchs von Gebäuden entfällt auf das Heizen. Wie können Bauweise und Planung angepasst werden, um es emissionsärmer zu gestalten?

AT Uns stehen heute deutlich effizientere Heizsysteme zur Verfügung als noch vor ein paar Jahren. Das führt dazu, dass das Heizen heute eigentlich nicht mehr im alleinigen Fokus steht. Dennoch können wir durch Architektur, Konstruktions- und Materialwahl, also den Gebäudeentwurf, den Energiebedarf im Betrieb steuern. Bei Architekturwettbewerben zeigen sich zwischen den energetisch optimierten und nicht-optimierten Entwürfen Unterschiede von bis zu 30 Prozent im Energiebedarf.

DAM Energieeffizientes Bauen wird oft mit komplexer Technik verbunden. Wie können architektonische Prinzipien den Einsatz von Technik und Ressourcen minimieren?

AT Architektur definiert den Energiebedarf eines Gebäudes. Der Gebäudeentwurf, die Fensterflächen, Ausrichtung und thermische Zonierung beeinflussen stark, wie viel Energie im Betrieb benötigt wird. Deshalb beginnen wir bei der Energieplanung immer mit der Optimierung der Architektur, der Konstruktion und der Materialwahl, bevor wir uns um die technische Versorgung kümmern.

“In architecture competitions, there are differences of as much as 30% in the energy requirements between the worst designs and the best”

DAM Energy-efficient construction often involves complex technology. How can architectural principles minimise the use of technology and resources?

AT Architecture defines the energy requirement of a building. The design of the building, its alignment to the cardinal points, and thermal zoning strongly impact how much energy is required to operate it. That is why, when it comes to energy planning, we always start with optimisation of the architecture, the structure, and the choice of materials before we address the facilities technology.

DAM How must the planning process be changed in order to enable climate-appropriate construction?

AT The customary methodology whereby everybody prepares their own reports independently is no longer fit for purpose. In future, we must plan in an interdisciplinary and integrated manner in order to develop

„Zukünftig müssen wir interdisziplinär und integrativ planen, um energieoptimierte, ressourcenschonende und klimagerechte Gebäude zu entwickeln“

DAM Wie muss sich der Planungsprozess verändern, um klimagerechtes Bauen zu ermöglichen?
AT Die herkömmliche Arbeitsweise, bei der die Fachplanenden parallel und nicht untereinander verzahnt arbeiten, ist nicht mehr zeitgemäß. Zukünftig müssen wir interdisziplinär und integrativ planen, um energieoptimierte, ressourcenschonende und klimagerechte Gebäude zu entwickeln. Zu dieser Arbeitsweise gehören auch interdisziplinär erstellte Entscheidungsvorlagen, die die Grundlage für eine ganzheitliche Planung bieten.
DAM Was bedeutet klimaschonendes Bauen für Sie in einem Wort?
AT Ich würde die Frage gern ändern in „klimagerechtes“ Bauen. Das bedeutet für mich: Zukunft.

energy-optimised, resource-conserving, and climate-appropriate buildings.
DAM What does climate-friendly construction mean for you in a nutshell?
AT I would like to change that question to “climate-appropriate” construction. To my mind that means: the future.
DAM Do you have a tip for architects and developers on how they can build in a way that causes fewer emissions and is more energy efficient?
AT They should optimise the building’s design and integrate passive strategies from old architecture into contemporary designs. It is also important to consider a building’s lifecycle if you want to conserve resources and develop a form of architecture that does justice to the notion of circularity.
DAM What would you like to see from the next generation of architects and engineers as regards climate-appropriate building?
AT I would wish for it to be courageous, cast established forms of building into question, and find new solutions. That is crucial if we are to advance climate protection and conserve resources.

DAM Haben Sie einen Tipp für Architekten und Bauende, die emissionsärmer und energieeffizienter bauen wollen?
AT Sie sollten den Gebäudeentwurf optimieren und passive Strategien, die bereits in der Architektur unserer Vorfahren funktioniert haben, wieder mehr in zeitgemäße Entwürfe integrieren. Nur so schaffen wir es, robustere Häuser zu entwerfen, die auch unabhängig von der Gebäudetechnik gut funktionieren. Wichtig ist auch, den Lebenszyklus des Gebäudes zu bedenken, um Ressourcen zu schonen und kreislaufgerechte Architektur zu entwickeln.
DAM Was wünschen Sie sich von der nächsten Generation der Architekten und Ingenieure im Hinblick auf klimagerechtes Bauen?
AT Ich wünsche mir, dass sie mutig ist, genau hinschaut, etablierte Bauformen hinterfragt und wissensbasiert neue Lösungen findet. Das ist entscheidend, um Klimaschutz und Ressourcenschonung voranzutreiben.

"In future, we must plan in an interdisciplinary and integrated manner in order to develop energy-optimised, resource-conserving, and climate-appropriate buildings"

Ganztagsschule | All-day school

Bretenoux, Frankreich
Bretenoux, France

Bauaufgabe | Task
Neubau einer Ganztagsschule aus Holz mit 21 Klassen, für 450 Schüler | New construction from wood of an all-day school with 21 classes for 450 pupils

Entwurf Hochbau | Architects
Dietrich Untertrifaller Architectes, Paris

Auftrag | Client
Département du Lot, Cahors

Fertigstellung | Completion
2023

Finanzierung | Financing
Öffentliche Mittel | Public funding

Am Ortsrand von Bretenoux ist Holz allgegenwärtig, mit dem für das Collège d'Orlinde eine helle und warme Atmosphäre erreicht wurde, die das Lernen und Zusammenleben fördert. Der horizontale Monolith ist harmonisch in die ländliche Umgebung eingebettet und setzt einen urbanen Akzent am Eingang des Ortes. Das Collège ist die erste Schule im Département du Lot, die mehr Energie erzeugt als sie verbraucht. Die räumliche Komposition des Gebäudes um zwei Höfe ist inspiriert von den mittelalterlichen Bastiden der Region, wozu auch Bretenoux gehört. Das Ensemble knüpft an die historische Bauweise an, die durch Fachwerk, Steinsockel und dunkle Dächer charakterisiert ist. Ein umlaufendes auskragendes Vordach aus dunklem karbonisierten Holz schützt vor zu starker Sonneneinstrahlung. Dieses Material garantiert Langlebigkeit ohne jegliche Wartung. Die äußerlich zurückhaltende, geschlossene Form steht im Kontrast zu den großzügigen, kommunikativen Innenräumen, bei denen helles Holz dominiert. Einige Trennwände zwischen den Klassenräumen wurden aus Lehmziegeln errichtet, um die Akustik und den hygrothermischen Komfort zu verbessern. Energieautarkie, bioklimatische Planung, Verwendung von biobasierten und lokalen Materialien, maximale Nutzung des natürlichen Lichtes: Alles dient dazu, den CO_2-Fußabdruck der Schule zu reduzieren und ihren hohen ökologischen Ansprüchen gerecht zu werden. Auf dem Dach befindet sich eine 1.200 m² große Photovoltaikanlage mit einer Kapazität von 250 Kilowattpeak. Im Winter wird das Gebäude mittels einer Erdwärmesonde beheizt.

Energie/Emissionen
Verwendung von biobasierten und regionalen Materialien; Deckung Strombedarf über Photovoltaikanlage; Heizung mittels Erdwärmesonde

Energy/Emissions
Use of bio-based and local materials, electricity needs covered by photovoltaic system, heating provided by geothermal probe

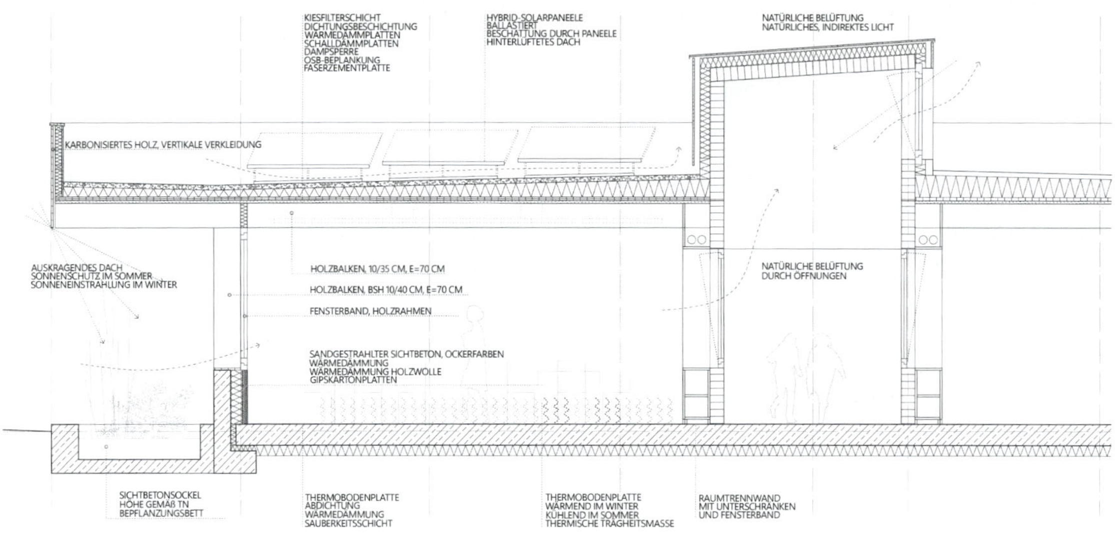

Gebäudeschnitt | Sectional view of the building

At Collège d'Orlinde on the outskirts of Bretenoux, wood is used throughout to create a bright and warm atmosphere that promotes learning and living together. The horizontal monolith is harmoniously embedded in its rural surroundings and adds an urban touch to the town's entrance. The college is the first school in the Lot region to generate more energy than it consumes. The spatial composition of the school around two courtyards is inspired by the medieval fortified towns of the region, of which Bretenoux is one. The ensemble ties in with the historical building style, which is characterised by half-timbering, stone bases, and dark roofs. A canopy made of dark, charred wood running around the entire building protects against strong sunlight. This material guarantees a long service life without any maintenance. The restrained, closed form contrasts with the spacious, communicative interiors, where light-coloured wood dominates. Some of the partition walls between the classrooms were built from adobe bricks to improve the acoustics and the hygrothermal comfort. Energy self-sufficiency, bioclimatic planning, use of bio-based and local materials, maximum use of natural light: Everything was done to reduce the school's carbon footprint and to meet its high ecological standards. The roof is equipped with a 1,200 m² photovoltaic system with a peak capacity of 250 kilowatts. In winter, the building is heated with a geothermal probe.

DAM Was finden Sie besonders gelungen an Ihrem Projekt?
Dietrich Untertrifaller Architectes Analogie zur mittelalterlichen Bastide, die Qualität der räumlichen Sequenzen, das Materialisierungskonzept und den Plusenergie-Status.

DAM Was war Ihnen bei der Erarbeitung des Projektes wichtig?
Dietrich Untertrifaller Architectes Einen identitätsstiftenden, atmosphärisch dichten, inspirierenden Lernort entstehen zu lassen, dabei eine vorbildliche Materialisierung und Energiebilanz zu garantieren und somit die Zukunftsfähigkeit sicherzustellen.

DAM Was würden Sie beim nächsten Mal anders machen?
Dietrich Untertrifaller Architectes Weniger versiegelte Flächen im Außenbereich.

DAM What do you think is particularly successful about your project?
Dietrich Untertrifaller Architectes The analogy to a medieval fortified village (*bastide*), the quality of the spatial sequences, the materialisation concept, and the Plus Energy status.

DAM What was important to you when developing the project?
Dietrich Untertrifaller Architectes To create an inspiring place for learning that fosters a sense of identity and has a rich atmosphere, to guarantee exemplary materialisation and energy balance, and to ensure future sustainability.

DAM What would you do differently next time?
Dietrich Untertrifaller Architectes Fewer sealed surfaces in the outdoor areas.

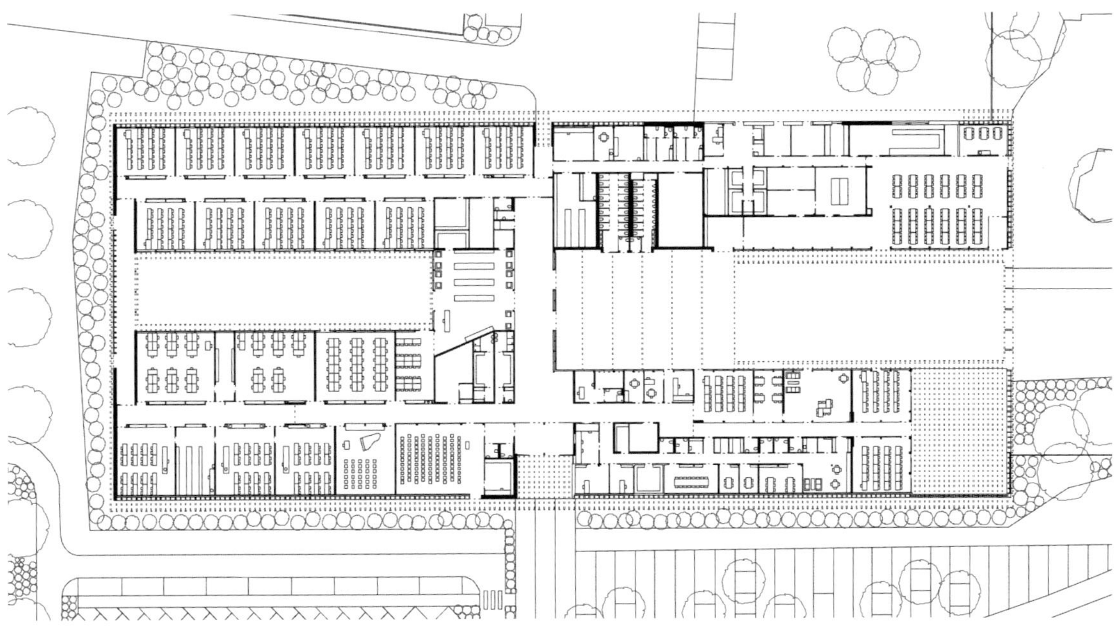

Grundriss Erdgeschoss | Floor plan—ground floor

Kindertagesstätte | Daycare centre

Memmingen, Deutschland
Memmingen, Germany

Energie / Emissionen
Erhalt bestehender Ressourcen; Sanierung ohne konventionelle Dämmmaßnahmen; Fassade als eine Art Sonnenkollektor für den Wärmehaushalt; Photovoltaikanlage; Wärmepumpe

Energy / Emissions
Preservation of existing resources, renovation without conventional insulation, façade as a kind of solar collector for heat balance, photovoltaic system, heat pump

Bauaufgabe | Task
Umbau eines bestehenden Wohnhauses aus den 1960er-Jahren in eine Kindertagesstätte | Conversion of an existing residential building from the 1960s into a daycare centre

Entwurf Hochbau | Architects
heilergeiger architekten und stadtplaner, Kempten

Entwurf Energiekonzept | Energy design
Güttinger Ingenieure, Kempten; Ifes Institut für angewandte Energiesimulation, Köln | Cologne

Entwurf Freianlagen | Landscape Architects
LATZ+PARTNER, LandschaftsArchitektur Stadtplanung, Kranzberg

Auftrag | Client
Alois Goldhofer Stiftung, Memmingen

Fertigstellung | Completion
2019

Finanzierung | Financing
Stiftungsmittel | Foundation funds

Das Konzept für die Kita entspringt der darin angewendeten Reggio-Pädagogik. Hier ist Wiederverwenden des Gebrauchten ein wesentlicher Wert. Dieser wird für die Kinder in der Architektur der Kita erfahrbar. Dafür wird das alte Wohnhaus der Stifterfamilie weitergenutzt und sein Bestand aktiviert. Die drei bestehenden Gebäudeteile des alten Gebäudes wurden erhalten, freigestellt und unter eine neue Hülle aus recycelbaren Polycarbonatstegplatten gestellt. Die entstandenen Zwischenräume sind gleichermaßen Raumerweiterung für die Kita-Funktionen und Element des nachhaltigen Energiekonzepts. Die neue Hülle ist zugleich Kollektor von Licht und Energie und erlaubt es, die Bestandswände ungedämmt und als historische Schicht zu erhalten. Das Energiekonzept ist ein kybernetisches Zusammenwirken von Raum, Konstruktion und Nutzung. Dank dieser Lösung konnte die energetische Sanierung ohne konventionelle Dämmung an den Außenwänden, etwa das Anbringen eines Wärmedämmverbundsystems, durchgeführt werden. In den Wintermonaten dient die Fassade als eine Art Sonnenkollektor; die gewonnene passive Solarenergie wird für den Wärmehaushalt und die kontrollierte Be- und Entlüftung genutzt. Die über eine Photovoltaikanlage erzeugte Energie wird für den Betrieb der Wärmepumpe und der Beleuchtung verwendet. Die Kita suchte nach architektonischen Antworten auf die relevanten Fragen des Bauens: Wie nutzen wir Bestand und schonen Ressourcen? Wie reduzieren wir CO_2 und gewinnen Raum? Wie wird Klimaschutz als Bereicherung erfahrbar?

The concept for this daycare centre is based on the Reggio pedagogical method that is practiced there. A key value lies in the reuse of materials. Through the architecture of the daycare centre, children can experience and learn about this value. The old residential building of the founding family is still in use, and its existing structure remains present. The three existing building sections of the old residential building are preserved, detached, and placed under a new shell made of recyclable polycarbonate web plates. The resulting spaces expand the room for the daycare functions and are an element of the sustainable energy concept. The new shell collects light and energy. It allows the existing walls to be preserved without insulation as a historical layer. The energy concept is a cybernetic interaction of space, construction, and use. Thanks to this solution, the energy-efficient renovation could be carried out without conventional insulation measures on the exterior walls, such as the application of a thermal insulation composite system. In the winter months, the façade serves as a kind of solar collector, and the passive solar energy obtained is used for the heating system and the controlled ventilation. The energy generated by a photovoltaic system is used to operate the heat pump and the lighting. The daycare centre seeks architectural answers to the relevant questions of construction: How do we use existing structures and conserve resources? How do we reduce CO_2 and gain space? How can climate protection be experienced as an enrichment?

Schema Entwurfskonzept | Outline of the design concept

Gebäude vor dem Umbau. Obwohl 75 Prozent des Bestandsbaus erhalten wurden, ist er nach dem Umbau kaum wiederzuerkennen. | Building pre-conversion: Although 75% of the existing building was retained, after the conversion work it looks almost completely different.

gegenüber | opposite page: **Grundriss Erdgeschoss** | Floor plan—ground floor

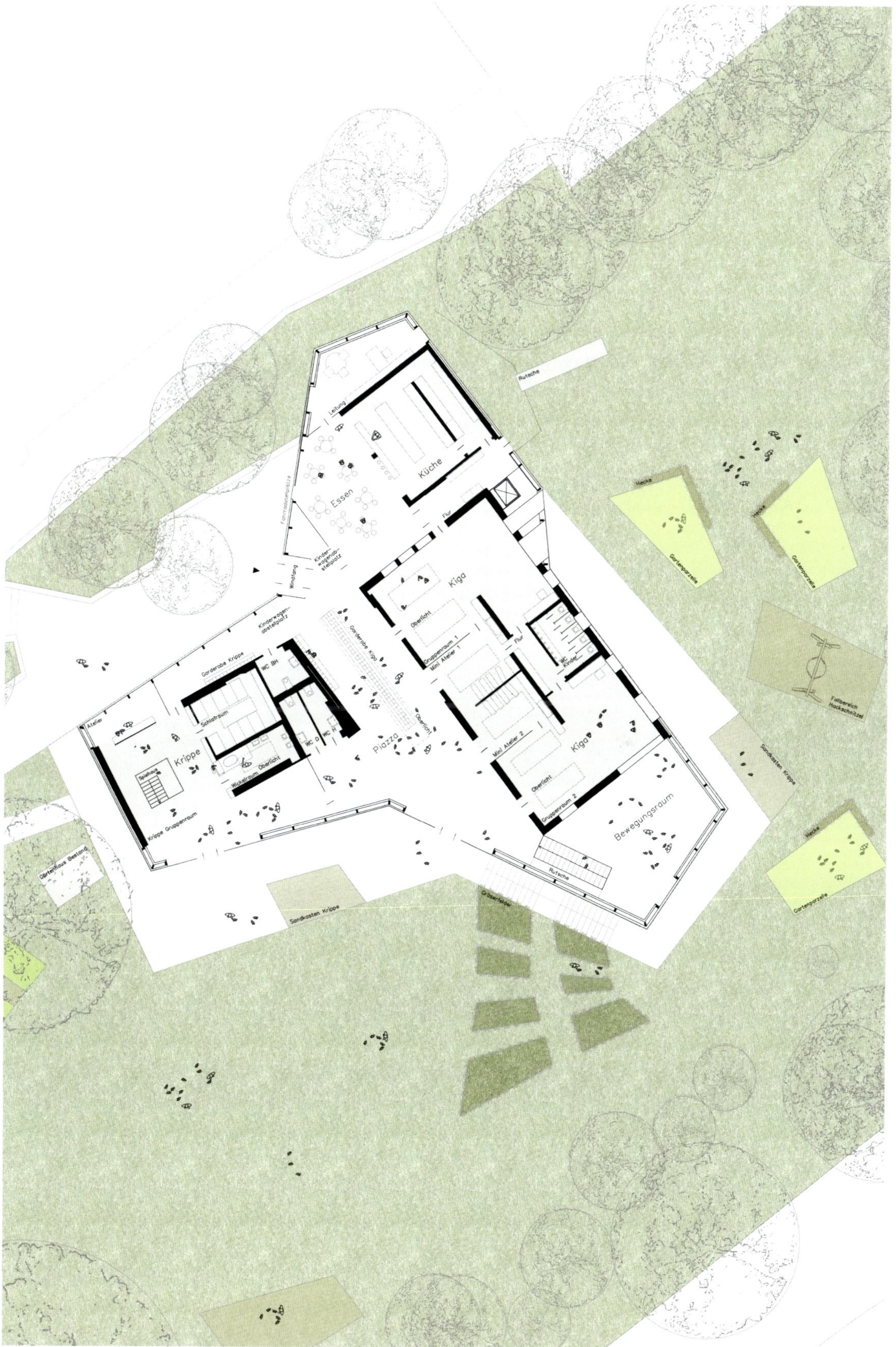
Rutsche
Leitung
Küche
Essen
Flur
Kinderwagenabstellplatz
Windfang
Kiga
Oberlicht
Gruppenraum 1
Mini Atelier 1
Garderobe Kiga
Piazza
Oberlicht
Garderobe Krippe
WC BH
Schlafraum
Krippe
Atelier
Wickelraum
Oberlicht
Krippe Gruppenraum
Mini Atelier 2
Kiga
Oberlicht
Gruppenraum 2
Bewegungsraum
Rutsche
Hecke
Gartenparzelle
Fallbereich Hackschnitzel
Sandkasten Krippe
Gartenhaus Bestand
Sandkasten Krippe

DAM **Was finden Sie besonders gelungen an Ihrem Projekt?**
heilergeiger architekten Anstelle eines konventionellen ‚Dämmpullovers' gewinnt die Hülle aus recycelbarem Polycarbonat solare Energie, schafft neuen Raum und erhält den Bestand als Ressource, graue Energie und Zeitzeugnis. Klimaschutz und das natürliche Gewinnen von Energie werden für die Kinder in ihrem Kita-Alltag erfahrbar.

DAM **Was war Ihnen bei der Erarbeitung des Projektes wichtig?**
heilergeiger architekten Uns war wichtig, ganzheitlich das pädagogische Konzept, die Wiederverwendung des Bestands, den erforderlichen Raumgewinn für die Kita und energetische Sanierung in einer nachhaltigen Architektur zu vereinen.

DAM **Was würden Sie beim nächsten Mal anders machen?**
heilergeiger architekten Die Fragestellungen blieben dieselben: Um beim ökologischen Wandel in der Architektur noch mehr voranzukommen, würden wir versuchen, bei neuen Bauteilen 100 Prozent zirkuläre Materialien einzusetzen. Auch würden wir mit unserer Bauherrin sowie den Nutzerinnen und Nutzern diskutieren, wie sich andere, durchmischte Nutzungen in das Raumprogramm integrieren lassen.

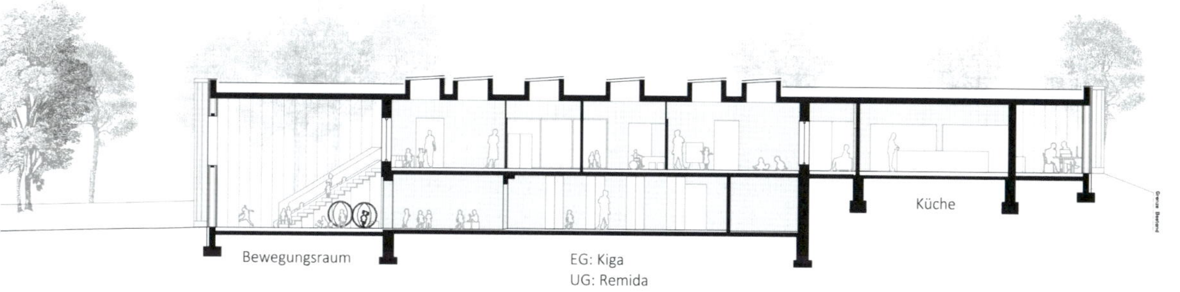

Schnitt | Sectional view

DAM What do you think is particularly positive about your project?
heilergeiger architekten Instead of a conventional "Dämmpullover" (insulating jumper), the recyclable polycarbonate shell captures solar energy, creates new space, and preserves the existing building as a resource—a testimony to the past. Climate protection and natural energy generation are brought to life for children in their everyday experience at the daycare centre.

DAM What was important to you when developing the project?
heilergeiger architekten For us it was important to find a holistic combination of the educational concept, the reuse of the existing building, the necessary space gain for the daycare centre, and the energy-efficient renovation in a sustainable architecture.

DAM What would you do differently next time?
heilergeiger architekten The questions remain the same: To make even more progress in the ecological transformation of architecture, we would try to use 100% circular materials in new components. We would also discuss with our client and the users how additional mixed uses could be integrated into the space allocation plan.

Schulerweiterung | Extension of a school

Rønde, Dänemark
Rønde, Denmark

Bauaufgabe | Task
Erweiterung einer Schule um einen Klassenraum und Physiklabor | Extension of a school with a classroom and physics laboratory

Entwurf Hochbau | Architects
Henning Larsen, Kopenhagen | Copenhagen

Entwurf Energiekonzept | Energy design
Reeholm & Bredahl, Randers, Dänemark | Denmark

Auftrag | Client
Feldballe School, Rønde

Fertigstellung | Completion
2022

Finanzierung | Financing
Mittel der Realdania | Funds from Realdania

Energie / Emissionen
Emissionseinsparung durch regionale und biobasierte Materialien, die CO_2 binden; Energieeinsparung durch effektive Isolierung und ein innovatives passives Belüftungssystem mit Seegrasfilterung

Energy / Emissions
Emission reductions through local and bio-based materials that bind CO_2 and energy savings through high insulation and an innovative passive ventilation system with sea-grass filtration.

Der Entwurf für die Feldballe-Schule basiert auf fünf Hauptprinzipien, die dem Kreislaufgedanken folgen. Ein Effekt ist die Verwendung regionaler, biobasierter Materialien wie Holz, Stroh und Seegras als Alternativen zu herkömmlichen Systemen aus Beton, Ziegel und Stahl. Ziel war es, Materialien zu nutzen, die CO_2 binden und damit die Gesamtbelastung verringern, sodass nicht nur dieser Gebäudeteil, sondern die

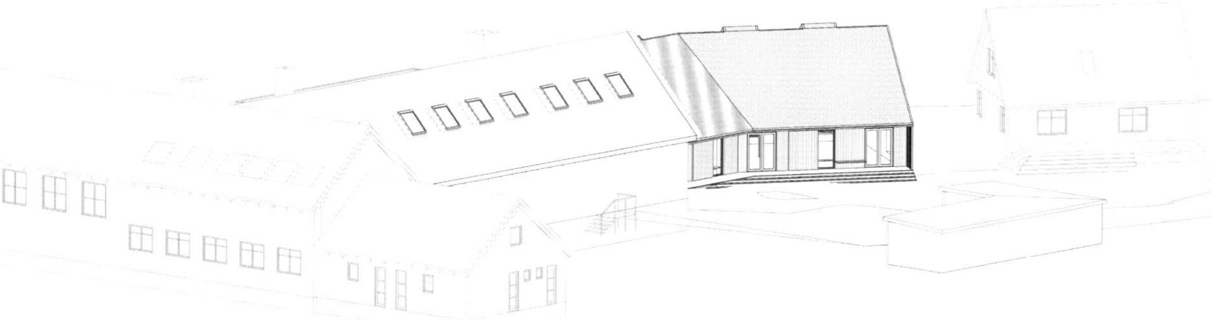

Isometrie | Isometric diagram

gesamte Schule CO_2 einspart. Das Projekt wurde zudem so konzipiert, dass es vollständig aus schadstofffreien Materialien bestehen kann, um ein gesundes Innenraumklima zu schaffen. Durch die Verwendung von Wandpaneelen aus gepresstem Stroh, Massivholz und Lehmputz konnten das Ziel erreicht und gleichzeitig die Brandschutzanforderungen erfüllt werden. Das Planungsteam war dabei bestrebt, den Energieverbrauch durch aktive Komfortsysteme praktisch zu eliminieren. Erreicht wurde dies durch die Verwendung hochisolierender Bausysteme in Verbindung mit einem innovativen passiven Belüftungssystem mit Seegrasfilterung. Das Gebäude wurde von Anfang an so angelegt, dass es eine lange Lebensdauer hat, leicht umgestaltet und gewartet werden kann und am Ende der Nutzbarkeit seine Bestandteile demontierbar und wiederverwendbar sind.

The design for the Feldballe School is based on five main principles, ensuring circularity. This resulted in the use of local, bio-based materials like wood, straw, and seagrass, as alternatives to the conventional systems of concrete, brick, and steel. The goal was to use materials that hold CO_2, and thereby subtract from carbon-impact, creating carbon-savings for not just this one building, but carbon-sequestering for the entire school. In addition, the project was designed to be built completely of toxin-free materials to provide for a healthy indoor environment. Using compressed-straw wall panels, solid timber, and clay plaster helped us achieve this objective while meeting fire-safety requirements. The design team also sought to virtually eliminate energy consumption by active comfort systems. This was accomplished through the use of highly insulative building systems in conjunction with an innovative passive ventilation system using seagrass filtration. From the outset, the building was designed to have an extended lifespan, ease of reconfiguration and maintenance, and means for disassembly and reuse.

DAM **Was finden Sie besonders gelungen an Ihrem Projekt?**
Henning Larsen Der Erfolg des Feldballe-Projekts liegt in der Harmonie zwischen der Natur und der Schaffung widerstandsfähiger, anpassungsfähiger Räume, die sowohl den Menschen als auch der Umwelt zugutekommen. Durch die durchgängige Integration natürlicher Elemente kann der Entwurf als Modell für alternative Entwurfsprozesse dienen: Er fördert die Gemeinschaft und stellt gleichzeitig die Umweltverträglichkeit in den Mittelpunkt unserer Arbeit.

DAM **Was war Ihnen bei der Erarbeitung des Projektes wichtig?**
Henning Larsen Ziel war es, ein Gebäude im Einklang mit dem Kohlenstoffkreislauf zu errichten und dabei Konstruktionsstrategien und Materialien zu verwenden, die über die gesamte Lebensdauer des Gebäudes CO_2 speichern. Das Projekt ist zugleich eine Möglichkeit für die Schüler und weitere Nutzer, das Potenzial kohlenstoffkreislauffähiger Gebäude kennenzulernen und zu erleben, die innerhalb der begrenzten Ressourcen des Planeten bestehen können.

DAM **What do you consider to be the highlights of your project?**
Henning Larsen The success of the Feldballe project lies in the harmony between nature and the creation of resilient, adaptable spaces beneficial to both people and the environment. Through the integrated incorporation of natural elements, the design serves as a model for alternative design processes—it fosters communities while placing environmental sustainability at the core of our work.

DAM **What was important to you when developing the project?**
Henning Larsen The goal was to create a building in harmony with the carbon cycle, using construction strategies and materials that store carbon over the building's entire lifespan. The building is also a way for students and others to learn about and experience the potential of carbon-cyclable buildings that can exist within the limits of the planet's resources.

Oliver Geden

Die Minderung von Emissionen im Gebäudesektor als globale Herausforderung

Reducing emissions in the building sector as a global challenge

Der letzte Bericht des Weltklimarats IPCC[1] hat gezeigt, dass die Errichtung und Nutzung von Gebäuden für einen sehr großen Anteil der globalen Emissionen an Treibhausgasen (THG) mitverantwortlich ist – je nach Zählweise bis zu einem Fünftel. Der weitaus größere Teil ergibt sich aus dem Energieverbrauch. Zunehmend geraten aber auch Emissionen in den Blick, die bei der Produktion von Baumaterialien anfallen, etwa Zement und Stahl. Seit 1990 ist der Anteil des Gebäudesektors weltweit um etwa 50 Prozent gestiegen, ähnlich wie auch die globalen Emissionen insgesamt. Anzeichen einer Trendwende sind bislang allenfalls in einigen vornehmlich europäischen Industrieländern zu erkennen. Ob der Rest der Welt den Vorreitern folgen wird, ist indes noch längst nicht ausgemacht.

Die Weltgemeinschaft hat sich 2015 in Paris dazu verpflichtet, den globalen Temperaturanstieg im Vergleich zum vorindustriellen Niveau auf deutlich unter 2 Grad Celsius und möglichst auf unter 1,5 Grad zu begrenzen. Zudem sieht das Pariser Abkommen vor, dass die THG-Emissionen in der zweiten Jahrhunderthälfte den Stand von „Netto-Null" erreichen, also alle verbleibenden Emissionen von Kohlendioxid, Methan und Lachgas durch die Entfernung von CO_2 aus der Atmosphäre ausgeglichen werden, entweder durch Wiederaufforstungsmaßnahmen oder ingenieurtechnische Lösungen. Beim Erreichen von Netto-Null-Treibhausgasen würde die globale Erwärmung mindestens gestoppt; wahrscheinlich könnte die Durchschnittstemperatur leicht zu sinken beginnen.

Diese Netto-Null hat sich – häufig unter dem Begriff „Klimaneutralität" – inzwischen als klimapolitisches Leitbild etabliert. Zwar schreibt das Pariser Klimaabkommen einzelnen Ländern nicht exakt vor, welche nationalen Ziele

1 Vgl. 6. IPCC-Sachstandsbericht (AR6), 2021–2023, abrufbar: https://www.de-ipcc.de/250.php.

The last report by the Intergovernmental Panel on Climate Change[1] shows that construction and the use of buildings is responsible for a very large portion of global greenhouse gas (GHG) emissions—as much as one fifth, depending on the calculation method. Most of these emissions stem from energy consumption, yet increasingly the spotlight is turning to emissions that arise during the production of construction materials such as cement and steel. Since 1990, the emissions generated by the building sector worldwide have risen by about 50%, an increase comparable to global emissions as a whole. Signs that an inflection point has been reached is discernible in, at best, a few industrial nations, primarily in Europe. Whether the rest of the world will follow these pioneers is by no means clear.

In Paris in 2015, the community of nations committed to limiting the global temperature rise to significantly below 2°C compared to pre-industrial levels, and if possible to below 1.5°C. Furthermore, the Paris Agreement envisages GHG emissions reaching net zero in the second half of the century, meaning that all remaining emissions of carbon dioxide (CO_2), methane, and nitrous oxide will be offset through removal of CO_2 from the atmosphere by means of either reforestation measures or engineering technology. Reaching net-zero GHGs would at least stop global warming, and the average temperature may even then start falling slightly.

This "net zero" has meanwhile established itself as the guideline for climate policy—frequently under the heading of "climate neutrality". The Paris Climate Agreement does not exactly specify what national targets each individual country needs to set itself. However, since the European Union and

1 Cf. 6th IPCC-Sachstandsbericht (AR6), 2021–2023; access: https://www.de-ipcc.de/250.php.

sie zu setzen haben. Aber da sich die Europäische Union und Deutschland als internationale Vorreiter im Klimaschutz begreifen, haben sie sich ambitionierte Klimaneutralitätsziele gesetzt: für 2050 bzw. 2045.

In einer Region oder einem Land Netto-Null-Emissionen erreichen zu wollen, bedeutet aber nicht zwingend, dass auch alle Sektoren diesen Stand schaffen oder jedenfalls nicht bis zur Jahrhundertmitte. Der Gebäudesektor zählt zu jenen Bereichen, in denen das Erreichen dieses Zieles sehr herausfordernd sein wird – nicht nur global, sondern je nach Berechnungsweise selbst in Europa.

Sofern man nur die energiebedingten Emissionen in den Blick nimmt, ist die Klimaneutralität des Gebäudebestands in der EU bereits Teil aller klimapolitischen Planungen und erscheint realisierbar, auf der Basis von Energieeffizienzmaßnahmen wie einer verbesserten Wärmedämmung sowie der schrittweisen Umstellung von fossilen auf erneuerbare Energieträger, also etwa von Gasheizungen auf Wärmepumpen. Das theoretische Wissen darüber, wie dies technisch zu erreichen ist, bedeutet jedoch nicht, dass es in der Praxis leicht umzusetzen wäre, zumal im Wohngebäudebestand, also mit spürbaren Interventionen in den Alltag der Bevölkerung. Wie wir hierzulande in den vergangenen Jahren gesehen haben, ist dazu ein politischer Grundkonsens und eine sozialverträgliche Umsetzung notwendig, aber allein längst nicht ausreichend. Zugleich müssen Investitionen mobilisiert werden, sowohl im Bau- als auch im Energiesektor. Überdies werden Fachkräfte benötigt, insbesondere um die notwendigen Effizienzverbesserungen im heterogenen Bestand zu erreichen. Dies alles im Zeitraum von 20 bis 25 Jahren zu schaffen, bedeutet eine Herausforderung, ist im Prinzip aber durchaus zu bewältigen.

Germany consider themselves international trailblazers in climate protection, they have set themselves ambitious climate neutrality targets for 2050, and in Germany's case for 2045.

Trying to achieve net-zero emissions in a region or a country does not necessarily mean that all sectors achieve net-zero emissions, or at any rate not by the middle of the century. The building sector is one of those sectors where achieving net zero will be a massive challenge, not just globally but, depending on how the calculations are made, even in Europe.

If we consider only the energy-related emissions, then the climate neutrality of existing buildings within the EU is already part of all climate-policy planning and also seems to be a target that can be achieved on the basis of energy-efficiency measures, such as improved heat insulation and the gradual switch from fossil to renewable energy sources, for example from gas-fired heating to heat pumps. The fact that we have the theoretical knowledge necessary to achieve this in technical terms does not mean that it is easy to implement it in practice, specifically in the field of existing housing, where appreciable intervention will be necessary in the everyday lives of the electorate. As we have seen in recent years here in Germany, making this a reality requires a basic political consensus as well as a way of accomplishing things in a socially equitable manner, although this alone is by no means sufficient. Investments also need to be mobilised in both the construction and energy sectors. Added to which, there is a need for skilled labour, above all in order to achieve the necessary efficiency improvements in the heterogeneous existing building stock. All of this is challenging,

Bezieht man allerdings die Baumaterialien selbst in die Betrachtung der Klimaneutralität mit ein, wird es komplizierter. Zwar lässt sich auch der Energiebedarf der Stahl- und Zementproduktion dekarbonisieren, etwa über Elektrifizierung oder den Einsatz von Biomasse. Das eigentliche Problem aber liegt bei den „prozessbedingten" Emissionen, etwa aufgrund chemischer Reaktionen bei der Herstellung von Klinker, dem Kernbestandteil von Zement. Hier sind bislang keine entscheidenden Fortschritte zu verzeichnen, mit dem Ergebnis, dass die Zementproduktion derzeit für 8 Prozent des globalen CO_2-Ausstoßes verantwortlich ist. Selbst wenn man, wie auf EU-Ebene und in Deutschland geplant, einen Großteil des prozessbedingten CO_2 in den Zementwerken einfängt und in unterirdischen geologischen Speichern einlagert, werden sich die Emissionen nicht ganz auf Null verringern lassen. Höhere Recyclingquoten von Baumaterial sowie die vermehrte Verwendung von Holz als Baustoff können hilfreich sein, aber auch hier ist das Potenzial nicht unendlich groß.

Am Ende werden in jedem Fall „schwer vermeidbare Restemissionen" bleiben, die durch das gezielte Entfernen von CO_2 aus der Atmosphäre ausgeglichen werden müssen. Das ist im Kern das „Netto" in Netto-Null. Schon heute entziehen wir der Atmosphäre CO_2 durch Maßnahmen zur (Wieder-) Aufforstung; die Emissionen der EU sind im Sektor Landnutzung und Forstwirtschaft schon seit Jahrzehnten „Netto-Negativ". Allerdings wird es mit fortschreitendem Klimawandel immer schwerer werden, diesen Status aufrecht zu erhalten, beispielsweise wegen Extremwetterereignissen oder Schädlingsbefall. Deshalb planen viele Länder, darunter auch Deutschland, schon heute mit dem zukünftigen Einsatz neuartiger technologischer Methoden zur

especially over a period of twenty to twenty-five years, but in principle it can be achieved.

However, if one factors only the construction materials themselves into the calculation of climate neutrality, then things are more complicated. The energy requirement for producing steel and cement can be decarbonised, for example through electrification or the use of biomass. But the real problem is the so-called "process-related" emissions, as for example result from the chemical reactions used to produce clinker, the core element of cement. Here, no noteworthy decarbonisation progress has been made to date, with the result that cement production at present accounts for 8% of the global CO_2 emissions. Even if—and this is the plan at both the EU level and in Germany—a large proportion of the process-related CO_2 is captured in the cement factories and deposited in subterranean geological stores, it will still not be possible to reduce these emissions to zero. Higher recycling quotas for construction materials as well as an increased use of timber as a building material can help, but here, again, the potential is not infinitely great.

At the end of the day, "residual emissions that are hard to avoid" will remain, and these can then be offset by deliberate removal of CO_2 from the atmosphere. That is, essentially, the "net" in "net zero". Today, we already remove CO_2 from the atmosphere through (re-)forestation; the EU's emissions in fields of land usage and forestry have for decades been "net negative". However, as climate change gains pace it will become ever harder to maintain this status, for example through extreme weather events or pest infestation. This is why many countries, including Germany, are already developing innovative

CO_2-Entfernung aus der Atmosphäre, etwa der beschleunigten Verwitterung von Gesteinsmehl, dem Einbringen von Pflanzenkohle in Böden oder Baumaterial sowie der Direktabscheidung von CO_2 aus der Umgebungsluft mit anschließender geologischer Speicherung. Es wäre allerdings riskant, sich heute schon auf den großflächigen Einsatz von längst noch nicht ausgereiften Methoden zu verlassen. Insofern muss das Vermeiden von Emissionen immer Vorrang haben. Und selbst wenn die neuartigen CO_2-Entnahmemethoden effizient funktionieren sollten: Eine nicht emittierte Tonne CO_2 ist einer nachträglich entfernten Tonne grundsätzlich vorzuziehen, da bei letzterer beträchtlicher technischer und regulatorischer Aufwand betrieben werden muss, damit das CO_2 nicht doch wieder in die Atmosphäre gelangt.

Solche Überlegungen zur „letzten Meile" auf dem Weg zu Netto-Null-Emissionen des Gebäudesektors in der EU und in Deutschland dürfen nicht den Blick darauf verstellen, dass von den sehr ernsthaften Dekarbonisierungsplänen auf unserem Kontinent bislang noch keine großen Nachahmungseffekte in andere Industrie-, Schwellen- und Entwicklungsländer ausgehen. Eine über einzelne Vorzeige-Neubauprojekte hinausreichende, breit angelegte Effizienzregulierung im Altbestand ist selbst in Industrieländern wie den USA oder Australien bislang nicht zu beobachten, von einer begleitenden Dekarbonisierung des gesamten Energiesektors ganz zu schweigen. Zugleich haben mehr als 120 Länder weltweit ein nationales Netto-Null-Ziel beschlossen. Wenn es ihnen damit ernst ist, werden sie sich früher oder später mit dem Gebäudesektor beschäftigen müssen – tendenziell früher, da der Umbau erfahrungsgemäß viel Zeit in Anspruch nehmen wird. Einmal mehr sollte Europa als

technological methods for extracting CO_2 from the atmosphere, for example the accelerated weathering of powdered rock, the introduction of vegetable carbon into soil or building materials, or the direct capture of CO_2 from the ambient air with subsequent geological storage. It would, however, be risky to rely today on the large-scale deployment of methods that are by no means mature. To this extent, avoiding emissions must always be the priority. And even these novel CO_2-extraction methods should function efficiently: A non-emitted ton of CO_2 is fundamentally preferable to a ton subsequently extracted, because for the latter you have to put in massive technical and regulatory inputs to prevent the CO_2 from landing back in the atmosphere.

Such deliberations on the "last mile" down the path to "net-zero" emissions in the buildings sector in the EU and in Germany must not mar our view of the fact that the very serious decarbonisation plans on our continent have not to date caused broad "us too" effects in the building sectors in other industrial nations, emerging markets, and developing countries. At present, even in industrialised nations such as the United States or Australia, other than individual showcase new-build projects there is not yet any evidence of broad efficiency regulations for existing buildings, let alone of any accompanying decarbonisation of the entire energy sector. At the same time, over 120 countries around the world have set national "net-zero" goals. If they are indeed serious about this, they will sooner or later have to concern themselves with the building sector, presumably sooner, as experience shows that conversion requires more time. Once again, Europe will have to act as the trailblazer in climate policy, as a laboratory for profound and, in the final instance,

klimapolitischer Vorreiter agieren, als Labor für tiefgreifende, aber letztlich notwendige Veränderungen. Um auch andere Weltregionen von der Machbarkeit einer Dekarbonisierung des Gebäudesektors zu überzeugen, wird es letztlich aber nicht nur auf das „Was" – sich verbessernde Stoffströme und die Formen der architektonischen Umsetzung – ankommen. Entscheidend wird zudem das „Wie" des Transformationsprozesses sein, also die gewählten Regularien und die Akzeptanz in der breiten Bevölkerung.

imperative changes. To convince other regions of the feasibility of building-sector decarbonisation, ultimately what will count is not just the "what"—meaning improving material flows and the ways in which the objectives are realised in architecture—what will truly be decisive is the "how" of the transformation process, meaning the regulatory regimes chosen and their acceptance by the population as a whole.

Insel Samsø, Dänemark

Die dänische Gemeinde Samsø hat ihr Energiesystem vollständig von fossilen Brennstoffen abgekoppelt und ist damit die weltweit erste Insel. Zu den wichtigsten Ergebnissen gehören Kohlenstoffnegativität, 100 Prozent lokale Beteiligung an Investitionen in erneuerbare Energien und erhebliche sozioökonomische Vorteile durch die Energiewende.

Die Reduktion der CO_2-Emissionen auf nahezu Null wurde durch eine Reihe von Investitionen in erneuerbare Energien erreicht: 11 Onshore- und 10 Offshore-Windturbinen, 4 lokale Fernheizwerke, die mit Biomasse betrieben werden, Sonnenkollektoren und Elektrofahrzeuge.

Samsø will bis 2030 komplett kohlenstofffrei werden. Damit ist man dem nationalen Ziel Dänemarks und den EU-Klimazielen für das Jahr 2030 weit voraus.

Im Mittelpunkt des Finanzierungsmodells standen die Beteiligung der Bürger und Interessengruppen sowie die lokale Eigenverantwortung bei den Investitionen in erneuerbare Energien. Das führte zu erheblichen Vorteilen für die Inselgemeinschaft und die Wirtschaft, zu neuen Arbeitsplätzen und lokalem Wachstum. Samsø zeigt damit, wie erneuerbare Energien als Katalysator für die Verbesserung der Zukunftsperspektiven einer Gemeinde und gleichzeitig für wirksame Klimaschutzmaßnahmen wirken können.

Die Erkenntnis, dass dieser Übergang andere ebenso betrifft und viele Gemeinden daran interessiert sind, von den gemachten Erfahrungen zu lernen, führte zur Gründung der Samsø Energy Academy mit einem Mandat der Gemeinde. Die Akademie stellt Ressourcen für den Aufbau von Kapazitäten für die kommunale Entwicklung und die internationale Zusammenarbeit in Dänemark, Europa und darüber hinaus bereit. Sie nimmt an Programmen zu Kooperation und Wissensaustausch teil, berät zu nachhaltiger Kommunalentwicklung und organisiert auf der Insel Studienbesuche, Workshops und Führungsprogramme, um lokale Führungskräfte, Interessenvertreter und politische Entscheidungsträger aus der ganzen Welt zu inspirieren.[1]

1 https://unfccc.int/climate-action/un-global-climate-action-awards/climate-leaders/samso; UNFCCC secretariat (UN Climate Change), Bonn.

Island of Samsø, Denmark

The municipality of the Danish island of Samsø has completely transformed its energy system from being powered by fossil fuels to renewable energy, becoming the first Sustainable Energy Island. Key outcomes include: becoming carbon net-negative, 100% local ownership of renewable energy investments, and significant socio-economic benefits from the energy transition.

The reduction of CO_2 emissions to almost zero was achieved through a series of investments in renewable energies, namely eleven on-shore and ten off-shore wind turbines, four local biomass-fuelled district-heating plants, solar panels, and electric vehicles.

Samsø has renewed its ambition and aims to become completely carbon-free by 2030. This is far ahead of both Denmark's national goals for 2030 and the EU climate goals for the same year.

At the core of the financing model was the participation of citizens and stakeholders as well as local ownership of the renewable energy investments. This led to significant benefits for the island community and economy, new jobs, and local growth.

Samsø demonstrated how renewable energy can be a catalyst for improving the future outlook of the community, generating business, and achieving effective climate action, all at the same time.

Samsø realised that it is not alone in this transition and that many other communities would be interested in learning from its experience. This led to the establishment of the Samsø Energy Academy with a mandate from the municipality. The Samsø Energy Academy provides resources for capacity building to community developments and international partnerships in Denmark, Europe, and beyond. It also participates in joint-projects and knowledge-exchange programmes, provides advice on sustainable community development, and organises study visits, workshops, and leadership programmes to inspire local leaders and stakeholders as well as policymakers from around the world.[1]

1 https://unfccc.int/climate-action/un-global-climate-action-awards/climate-leaders/samso; UNFCCC secretariat (UN Climate Change), Bonn.

Jeder Mensch hat eine globale Verantwortung

Interview mit | with Werner Sobek

Architekt und Ingenieur. Gründer des Instituts für Leichtbau Entwerfen und Konstruieren ILEK sowie Gründer der heutigen Werner Sobek AG

Architect and engineer. Founder of the Institute for Lightweight Structures and Conceptual Design at Stuttgart University and of Werner Sobek AG

Everyone has a global responsibility

DAM **Energie spielt eine zentrale Rolle, und Gebäude tragen erheblich zum Energieverbrauch und zu Treibhausgasemissionen bei. Hat sich das Bewusstsein für Emissionen und damit für die Bedeutung der gebauten Umwelt wirklich verändert?**
Werner Sobek In der Bevölkerung gibt es zwar ein größeres Bewusstsein, doch das Verhalten hat sich nicht grundlegend geändert. Der Boom bei Öl- und Gasheizungen und die immer schwereren, PS-stärkeren Autos zeigen, dass zwischen Verstehen und Handeln noch eine große Lücke klafft.
DAM **Wie definieren Sie eine erfolgreiche Energiewende?**
WS Die Definition ist klar: Ein Ausstieg aus der Energieerzeugung durch Verbrennung und Kernkraft und der konsequente Umstieg auf die sogenannten erneuerbaren Energien. Anmerkung am Rande: Das Wort „erneuerbare" nutze ich ungern, denn Energie ist bekanntlich nicht erneuerbar.
DAM **Bei Ihren Projekten haben Sie früh den Fokus auf innovative Energiesysteme und neue Konstruktionsmethoden gelegt. Würden Sie sagen, dass das Emissionsthema im Bauwesen generell bislang zu kurz gekommen ist?**
WS Ja. Die bundesdeutsche Energieeffizienzpolitik entstand nach der ersten Ölkrise aus wirtschaftsstrategischen Gründen. Als Ende der 1990er-Jahre klar wurde, dass die Erderwärmung nur durch eine Reduktion der Emission klimaschädlicher Gase beschränkt werden kann, setzte der Gesetzgeber die Emissionsreduktion im Bauwesen mit

DAM **Energy plays a central role in everyday life, and buildings contribute significantly to energy consumption and greenhouse gas emissions. Has the awareness of emissions—and therefore of the significance of our built world—really changed?**
Werner Sobek There is greater awareness among the population, but our behaviour has not fundamentally changed. The boom in oil and gas heating along with ever larger and more powerful cars show that there is still a huge gap between understanding and action.
DAM **How would you define a successful energy reform?**
WS The definition is obvious: an exit from energy generated by combustion and/or nuclear power and a committed transition to so-called renewable energies. Incidentally, I don't like using the word "renewable" because, as we know, energy cannot be renewed.
DAM **From early on, your projects have focused on innovative energy systems and new construction methods. Would you say that insufficient attention has been paid so far to the issue of construction industry emissions?**
WS Yes. In terms of economic strategy, the German energy efficiency policy was developed after the first Oil Crisis. When it became clear at the end of the 1990s that we would only be able to limit global warming by reducing greenhouse gas emissions, the government equated the reduction of construction industry emissions with energy efficiency in the heating and hot water supply. However, the combustion of fossil fuels is only responsible for about 60% of building emissions.

der Energieeffizienz bei der Bereitstellung von Raumwärme und Warmwasser gleich. Das Verbrennen fossiler Energieträger ist aber nur für ca. 60 Prozent der Emissionen von Gebäuden verantwortlich. Die verbleibenden 40 Prozent entstehen bei der Herstellung der Baustoffe, deren Transport sowie dem Bau, dem Umbau und dem Rückbau der Häuser selbst. Diese grauen Emissionen werden bis heute außer Acht gelassen.

DAM Was für politische Impulse braucht es, um die Emissionspolitik wirklich voranzubringen?

WS Wir benötigen ein starkes Klimaschutzgesetz, das auch einen Emissionsreduktionspfad beinhaltet. Wir hatten seit 2021 ein solches Gesetz, es wurde allerdings vom Gesetzgeber selbst nicht beachtet, teilweise verstieß die Bundesregierung gegen ihre eigenen Vorgaben. Das Gesetz wurde schließlich im Jahr 2023 neu gefasst in einer Weise, die es nahezu bedeutungslos gemacht hat. Wir haben also heute keine verbindliche und umfassende Regelung für die Reduktion der Emissionen, die wir innerhalb der kommenden zwanzig Jahre auf nahezu Null bringen müssen.

DAM Die graue Energie und die damit verbundenen Emissionen sind für viele abstrakt. Warum sind diese Emissionen dennoch so relevant, vielleicht sogar relevanter als die, die beim Betrieb eines Gebäudes anfallen?

WS Die in der Prozesskette Ressource–Baustoff–Bauteil–Bauwerk entstehenden grauen Emissionen sind für viele Menschen wenig greifbar, auch weil hierüber zu wenig bekannt ist. Graue Emissionen sind

The remaining 40% stem from the production of the building materials, their transport, and the construction, conversion, and demolition of the houses themselves. To this day, we ignore these grey emissions.

DAM What political stimuli are needed to really make progress in emissions-reduction policy?

WS We need a strong climate protection law that also includes an emissions-reduction path. We've had such a law since 2021, but it was not respected by the legislature itself; in some cases, the German government actually broke its own law. The law was eventually rewritten in 2023 in a way that made it almost meaningless. As a result, we currently have no binding and comprehensive regulation for the reduction of emissions, and over the next twenty years we effectively need to reduce emissions to zero.

DAM For many people, grey energy and the associated emissions are abstract ideas. Why are these emissions still so relevant, perhaps even more relevant than those associated with the operation of a building?

WS The grey emissions that arise in the resource–material–component–building process chain are not very tangible for many people, partly because they know too little about them. On the one hand, grey emissions are the energy-related emissions that arise when providing heat generated by combustion, e.g., when drying bricks. But grey emissions also arise as process-related emissions, e.g., as a result of chemical reactions. And they arise as transport-related emissions

einerseits die energiebedingten Emissionen bei der Bereitstellung von Wärme durch Verbrennung, beispielsweise beim Trocknen von Ziegelsteinen. Graue Emissionen entstehen aber auch als prozessbedingte Emissionen, also beispielsweise infolge chemischer Reaktionen. Und sie entstehen als transportbedingte Emissionen durch die Fahrzeuge, welche die Materialien und Bauteile zu den Baustellen transportieren.

DAM Sie gelten als Vordenker eines Perspektivwechsels von Energie- zu Emissionseinsparung. Diese Forderungen haben auch soziale Dimensionen. Wie fließt diese in Ihre Überlegungen ein? Ist emissionsarmes Bauen für alle erschwinglich?

WS Das ist eine extrem wichtige Frage. Die soziale Komponente wurde viel zu oft ignoriert, dabei ist sie zentral. Zum ersten Mal in der Geschichte der Menschheit haben wir die Situation, dass das Emissionsverhalten eines Menschen in Australien oder Kanada meine persönlichen Lebensbedingungen in Deutschland beeinflusst, vielleicht sogar beeinträchtigt. Und umgekehrt. Jeder hat also ab sofort eine globale Verantwortung. Damit diese von jedem verstanden und angenommen wird, bedarf es einer weltweiten, quasi gesamtgesellschaftlichen Übereinkunft. Dies aber ist etwas, was unsere politischen Führungskräfte derzeit offensichtlich nicht bewältigen können. Wir müssen deshalb auf der Ebene der Bürgerinnen und Bürger anfangen – und uns dabei der Tatsache bewusst sein, dass Personen mit niedrigem Einkommen deutlich weniger emittieren als Personen mit hohem Einkommen. In einer gerechten Gesellschaft darf aber jeder Mensch nur so viel emittieren wie

from the vehicles that carry the materials and components to the construction sites.

DAM You're seen as a trailblazer in shifting attention away from saving energy to preventing emissions. There is a social dimension to this change. How does it affect your way of thinking? Is low-emission construction affordable for everyone?

WS That is an extremely important question. The social component has been ignored all too often, even though it's crucial. For the first time in human history, the emissions behaviour of a person in Australia or Canada influences, perhaps even impairs, my personal living conditions in Germany—and vice versa. Meaning, as of now, everyone has a global responsibility. In order for this to be understood and accepted by all of us, we need a worldwide, social consensus. However, this is something that our political leaders clearly can't achieve at the moment. So we must start at the citizen level and remember that people with low incomes emit significantly less than people with high incomes. In a just world, however, no one should be allowed to emit more than anyone else. Thus, reducing emissions will have a much greater impact on people with high incomes. This would ease the burden on people with low incomes compared to the current energy efficiency regulations.

DAM The housing and construction industry plays a key role because everyone needs a roof over their heads. If we want to reduce emissions, should we stop building new homes?

der andere. Emissionsreduktion wird also bei den Menschen mit hohem Einkommen viel stärker greifen. Wodurch Menschen mit geringem Einkommen im Vergleich zu den heutigen Regelungen auf der Ebene der Energieeffizienz entlastet werden würden.

DAM Die Wohnungs- und Baubranche spielt eine Schlüsselrolle, denn Wohnen ist für jeden essenziell. Sollten wir uns angesichts des Ziels, die Emissionen zu senken, vom Neubau verabschieden?

WS Sanierung und Neubau sollte man nicht in Kategorien wie „gut" oder „schlecht" einteilen, sondern unter wissenschaftlich eindeutigen Kriterien wie dem Materialverbrauch, dem Abfallaufkommen oder den mit baulichen Maßnahmen verbundenen Emissionen bewerten. Bislang war der finanzielle Aspekt das Hauptkriterium bei der Entscheidung „Abriss und Neubau" oder „Erhaltung". Das Finanzargument wird bald durch die Betrachtung der Schädigungswirkung auf die Atmosphäre abgelöst werden. Ein Neubau muss nicht automatisch mit höheren Emissionen verbunden sein als eine Sanierung oder der Umbau eines Bestandsgebäudes. Teilweise kann man die entstandenen Emissionen zudem im Sinne von Net-Zero kompensieren. Wir müssen also immer das ganze Bild betrachten.

DAM Das Thema Heizen ist zentral, da es einen Großteil des Energieverbrauchs in Haushalten ausmacht. Wie muss sich unsere Bauweise ändern, um das Heizen emissionsärmer zu gestalten?

WS Raumwärme macht etwa 70 Prozent des Energieverbrauchs im Haushalt aus. Sie wird noch zu oft durch Verbrennungsprozesse bereit-

WS Rather than classifying modernisation and new builds as "good" or "bad", they should be evaluated according to clear scientific criteria such as material consumption, waste generation, or emissions associated with construction measures. To date, the financial aspect has been the main criterion in decisions on "demolition and new build" as opposed to "preservation". The financial argument will soon give way to a different benchmark: the damaging effect on the atmosphere. A new build does not automatically have to be associated with higher emissions than modernising or partially converting an old building. In some cases, the resulting emissions can also be offset in the sense of "net zero". Meaning, we must always consider the big picture.

DAM The topic of heating is key here, as it accounts for around 70% of household energy consumption. How should we change the way we build in order to make heating less emissions-intensive?

WS Heating accounts for around 70% of household energy consumption. It is still too often generated by burning fossil fuels. We need to replace this with emissions-free systems, which means ensuring an adequate electricity supply. We've known this for quite some time. Nevertheless, Germany has failed to push forward in providing electrical energy, expanding the grid networks accordingly, and ensuring storage capacity to bridge periods of low sunlight and wind. This is not

> "We need a strong climate protection law that also includes an emissions-reduction path"

„Wir benötigen ein starkes Klimaschutzgesetz, das auch einen Emissionsreduktionspfad beinhaltet“

gestellt. Diese müssen wir durch emissionsfreie Systeme ersetzen. Dafür ist eine ausreichende Stromversorgung erforderlich. Das ist seit Langem bekannt. Trotzdem hat man es in Deutschland nicht geschafft, die Bereitstellung von elektrischer Energie rapide zu forcieren, die Leitungsnetze entsprechend auszubauen und für Speicherkapazität zu sorgen, um beispielsweise die sogenannte Dunkelflaute zu überbrücken. Die Gründe hierfür sind nicht allein bei der politischen Führung oder den Genehmigungsbehörden zu suchen, sondern auch und in hohem Umfang bei der Bevölkerung selbst, die sich allzu oft massiv gegen den Ausbau der Erneuerbaren wehrt.

Mit dem Umstieg auf strombasierte Systeme stellt sich die Frage, ob stets genügend Strom zur Verfügung steht und ob dieser bezahlbar bleibt. Für den Fall, dass ausreichend günstiger Strom aus erneuerbaren Quellen verfügbar ist, können wir die Emissionsziele allein durch den Umstieg auf alternative Heizsysteme erreichen. Dort wo dies nicht der Fall ist, kommen mehrere Optionen ins Spiel, die kombiniert werden können: Man kann den Verbrauch senken oder ihn zeitlich verschieben, man kann Strom oder Wärme speichern oder man kann gezielte bauliche Maßnahmen vornehmen, um den Heizbedarf zu senken.

DAM Sie haben erwähnt, dass Quartiersplanung für Energieeffizienz und Emissionsminderung im Bausektor entscheidend ist. Können Sie näher erläutern, welche Rolle dabei die quartiersweite Planung spielt?

just the result of our political leadership or the regulatory authorities, but also, to a large extent, in the population itself, which all too often opposes the expansion of renewable energies. When switching to electricity-based systems, the question is whether there will always be enough electricity available and whether it will remain affordable. Assuming there is sufficient cheap electricity from renewable sources, we can achieve the emissions targets simply by switching to alternative heating systems. Where this is not the case, several options come into play that can be combined: You can reduce consumption, you can store electricity or heat, or you can take specific construction measures to reduce the need for heating.

DAM You have gone on the record as saying that neighbourhood planning is crucial for energy efficiency and emissions reduction in the construction sector. Can you explain in more detail how neighbourhood planning can help?

WS Neighbourhood planning is key because it expands the systemic limits from the individual building to the neighbourhood as a whole. This enables cities and municipalities to coordinate the joint generation, storage, and use of energy. Crucial here is the storage of heat and cold, rather than just electricity. Not every household has to have its own complex unit in the basement; we could instead rely on shared neighbourhood infrastructure—for example, for storing heat or using local or remote heating. Such shared solutions significantly boost efficiency levels and pave the way for climate-neutral construction at the neighbourhood level.

WS Quartiersplanung ist essenziell, weil sie die Systemgrenze vom einzelnen Gebäude auf das gesamte Quartier erweitert. Das ermöglicht es Städten und Kommunen, die gemeinsame Erzeugung, Speicherung und Nutzung von Energie zu koordinieren oder koordinieren zu lassen. Besonders wichtig ist dabei die Speicherung von Wärme und Kälte, nicht nur von Strom. Es muss nicht jeder Haushalt eigenständig eine komplexe Anlage im Keller vorhalten, sondern er kann auf eine im Quartier gemeinsam genutzte Infrastruktur zugreifen, beispielsweise zur Speicherung von Wärme oder zur Nutzung von Nah- oder Fernwärme. Solche gemeinschaftlichen Lösungen steigern die Effizienz erheblich und erleichtern den Weg zu klimaneutralem Bauen auf Quartiersebene.

DAM Oft wird energieeffizientes Bauen mit komplexer Gebäudetechnik assoziiert. Können architektonische Prinzipien den Technikeinsatz reduzieren?

WS Ja. Übermäßige Technik entsteht häufig aus unrealistischen Komfortansprüchen, etwa bei übermäßig eingeschränkten Schwankungen der Raumtemperatur. In Frankreich ist gesetzlich geregelt, dass an wenigen Tagen im Jahr eine Mindesttemperatur unterschritten werden darf. Dies hat einen wichtigen (und positiven) Einfluss auf die Entwicklung der Gesamtkosten. Unsere Gesellschaft muss klären, welche Komfortstandards künftig als sinnvoll erachtet werden sollen und welche Umweltschäden wir dafür in Kauf nehmen wollen.

DAM Was bedeutet für Sie persönlich klimaschonendes Bauen, gerne in einem Satz oder einem kurzen Statement?

DAM Energy-efficient construction is often associated with extensive facilities technology. Can architectural principles reduce the use of technology?

WS Yes. Excessive technology often results from demands for unrealistic comfort levels, e.g., overly restricted fluctuations in room temperature. In France, there are legal regulations that stipulate that room temperature can drop below a certain level on a few days of the year. This has an important (and positive) impact on overall costs. Our society must clarify which comfort standards should be considered reasonable in the future and what environmental damage we are willing to accept in return.

DAM What does climate-friendly construction mean to you? Please give a one-sentence answer or a short statement.

WS For me, climate-friendly construction means that every building is designed to be as resource-efficient and low-emission as possible, not only in terms of how it is built but also across all phases of its life—from the extraction of raw materials to construction and demolition.

DAM What do you hope to see from the next generation of architecture and engineering professionals?

WS I would hope that the next generation approaches things fundamentally differently and is not satisfied with the status quo. We need young people who act with a clear sense of their global responsibility. They should question all conventional wisdom. My hope is that the next generation will critically and courageously examine the standards that

WS Klimaschonendes Bauen bedeutet für mich, dass jedes Gebäude nicht nur in seiner Bauweise, sondern in all seinen Lebensphasen – von der Rohstoffgewinnung über den Bau bis hin zum Rückbau – so ressourcenschonend und emissionsarm wie möglich gestaltet wird.

DAM Was wünschen Sie sich von der nächsten Generation der Architekten und Ingenieure?

WS Ich wünsche mir, dass die kommende Generation die Dinge grundlegend anders anpackt und sich nicht mit dem Status quo zufriedengibt. Wir brauchen junge Menschen, die mit einem klaren Bewusstsein für ihre globale Verantwortung agieren. Sie sollten jede Wahrheit hinterfragen, die ihnen vermittelt wird. Meine Hoffnung ist, dass sich die kommende Generation kritisch und mutig mit den Standards auseinandersetzt, die in unserer Branche gelten – und dabei keine Angst hat, eigene Lösungen zu entwickeln. Die jungen Menschen müssen verstehen, dass die Forderung nach Netto-Null-Emissionen kein vages Ziel oder leeres Ideal ist, sondern eine echte Notwendigkeit – und sie müssen lernen, dieses Ziel durch technische, ökologische und architektonische Maßnahmen umzusetzen. Unsere Welt steht vor großen Herausforderungen, die wir nur gemeinsam bewältigen können. Wir brauchen dafür Personen im Architektur- und Ingenieurwesen, die verstehen, dass wir in einer Welt leben, in der Individualismus zwar Platz hat, in der aber gemeinsames Handeln unverzichtbar ist. Mein Wunsch ist, dass diese Generation erkennt: Wir sind eine Weltbürgergemeinschaft. Entweder wir kommen gemeinsam ans Ziel oder wir gehen gemeinsam unter. Aussteigen kann keiner.

apply in our industry—and not be afraid to develop their own solutions. Young people need to understand that the call for net-zero emissions is not a vague goal or an empty ideal, but a compelling necessity—and that they must learn to implement it by technological, environmental, and architectural means. Our world faces major challenges that we can only overcome by working together. To this end, we need architects and engineers who understand that we live in a world where individualism may have its place, but joint action is essential. My hope is that the new generation recognises that we are a global community. Either we achieve our goals together or we fail together. Nobody can avoid this fact.

Bürogebäude | Office building

München, Deutschland
Munich, Germany

Bauaufgabe | Task
Sanierung eines Bürogebäudes und Aufstocken in Holzbauweise | Renovation of an office building plus an extension in timber construction

Entwurf Hochbau | Architects
Element A Architekten, München | Munich

Entwurf Energiekonzept | Energy design
Transsolar, Stuttgart

Auftrag | Client
Deutscher Alpenverein e.V., München | Munich

Fertigstellung | Completion
2021

Finanzierung | Financing
Private und öffentliche Fördermittel | Private and public funding

Energie/Emissionen
Revitalisierung eines Bürogebäudes durch Holzgerüst; mechanische Klimatisierung entfällt durch Nachströmung; Bauwerk bindet CO_2 langfristig in der Konstruktion

Energy/Emissions
Renovation of an office building using a wooden frame, mechanical air conditioning is no longer necessary due to air circulation, the building stores CO_2 within its construction in the long term

Ein ausgedientes Bürogebäude wurde revitalisiert und aufgestockt, der Betonkern des Altbaus ressourcenschonend erhalten. Zwei neue Stockwerke, ein vorgebautes Atrium und der Konferenzbereich sind als Holzmassivbau ausgeführt, bis hin zum Brandschutz schwerer Stahlträger durch Holz. Das längsseitig angefügte Holzgerüst sorgt für Begrünung und Schatten. Für das Klimakonzept war Lowtech gefragt; eine konventionelle Sanierung schied schon wegen der Geschosshöhe von 2,68 Meter aus. Element A und Transsolar haben gemeinsam eine Lösung entwickelt, die die vorhandene Substanz einbezieht, äußeren Lärm ausgrenzt und eine hervorragende Arbeitsatmosphäre schafft. Spezielle Fassadenbrüstungen stellen Konditionierung und Luftführung sicher. Zwei zentrale Luftschächte organisieren die Nachströmung, was auch für eine sommerliche Nachtauskühlung sorgt; eine mechanische Klimatisierung konnte somit entfallen. Das Bauwerk emittiert weniger Treibhausgase und bindet CO_2 langfristig in der Konstruktion.

A former office building was refurbished and extended, preserving the concrete core of the old building in a resource-efficient manner. Two new floors, a built-on atrium, and the conference area are designed in a solid timber construction, including the fire protection made of heavy steel girders. The timber structure attached to the long side of the building provides greenery and shade. The climate concept had to be low-tech, as a conventional renovation was out of the question due to the 2.68-metre height of each storey. Element A and Transsolar developed a solution that incorporates the existing structure, blocks out external noise, and creates an excellent working atmosphere. Special façade balustrades ensure optimal ventilation and air circulation. Two central air shafts regulate the air supply, including nighttime cooling in summer, making mechanical air conditioning unnecessary. The building emits fewer greenhouse gases and binds CO_2 in the structure in the long term.

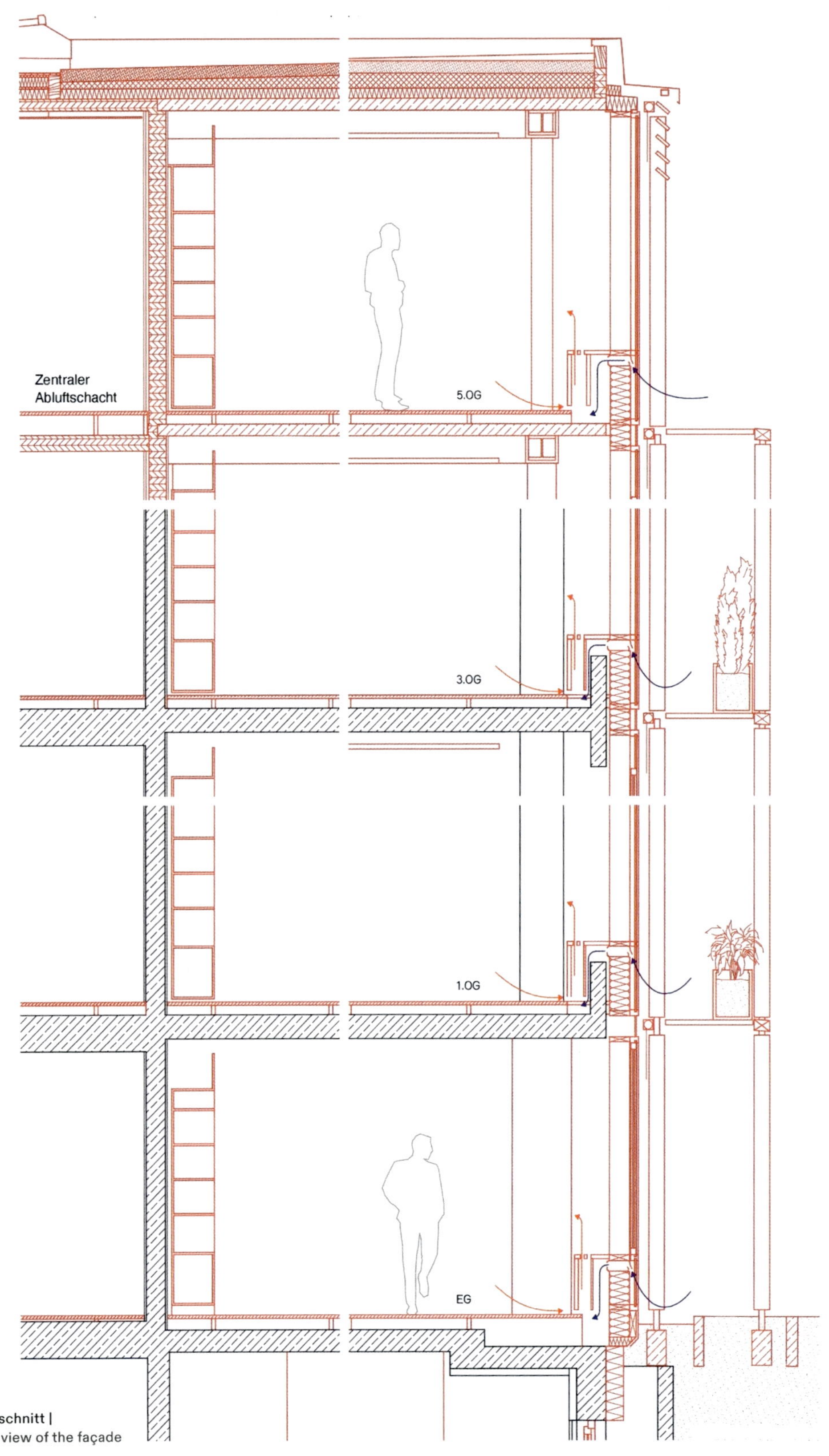

Fassadenschnitt |
Sectional view of the façade

DAM Was finden Sie besonders gelungen an Ihrem Projekt?
Element A Jeder hatte erwartet, dass dieses aus der Zeit gefallene Gebäude nicht revitalisiert, sondern abgerissen würde. Das nun entstandene Bürogebäude weist nach, dass es anders geht: für tausende ausrangierte Bürobauten, bei überzeugenden Kosten!

DAM Was war Ihnen bei der Erarbeitung des Projektes wichtig?
Element A Bester Komfort bei Achtung der Suffizienz war das Motto des Umbauprojekts: keine Klimatisierung, Verwendung natürlicher Materialien (Holz, Merinowolle, Pflanzen), und zugleich Weglassen alles Überflüssigen: keine PV auf meist beschattetem Dach, kein Sonnenschutz an immer beschatteten Fenstern, keine Wärmerückgewinnung, deren CO_2-Einsatz sich laut Berechnungen erst nach vierzig Jahren amortisiert hätte.

DAM What do you find particularly successful about your project?
Element A Everyone expected this outdated building to be demolished rather than restored. The result is an office building that proves there is another way, at a cost that's convincing, thus opening up new possibilities for thousands of abandoned office buildings.

DAM What was important to you when developing the project?
Element A The aim of the conversion was to achieve the highest possible level of comfort while ensuring sufficiency. There is no air conditioning, natural materials (wood, merino wool, plants) have been used, and everything unnecessary has been eliminated: no photovoltaics on the mostly shaded roof, no sun protection on the always shaded windows, and no heat recovery, as the calculations showed that its use would only pay off after forty years.

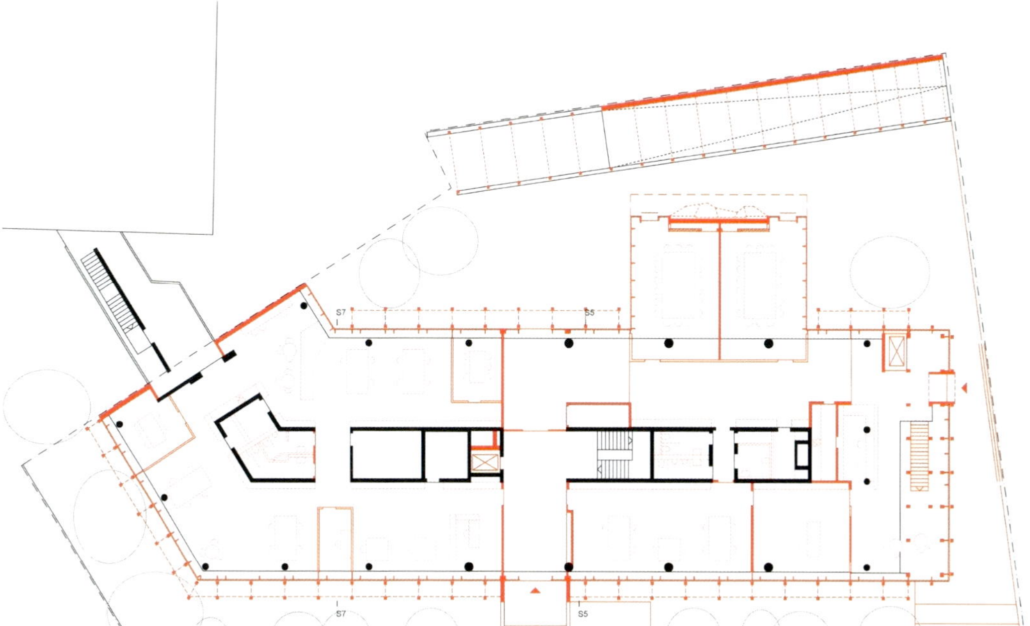

Grundriss Erdgeschoss | Floor plan—ground floor

Büro- und Laborgebäude
Office and laboratory building

Schlieren, Schweiz
Schlieren, Switzerland

Bauaufgabe | Task
Neubau eines Büro- und Laborgebäudes mit hoher Nutzungsflexibilität |
New construction of an office and laboratory building with high flexibility of use

Entwurf Hochbau | Architects
Baumschlager Eberle Architekten, Zürich | Zurich

Entwurf Energiekonzept | Energy design
EK Energiekonzepte, Zürich | Zurich

Auftrag | Client
Swiss Prime Site Immobilien, Olten

Fertigstellung | Completion
2024

Finanzierung | Financing
Privat | Private

Energie / Emissionen
Lowtech-Ansatz; massive Wände reduzieren den Wärmeaustausch; Verzicht auf Heizung, Lüftung und Kühlung sowie Zuführung von Fremdenergie

Energy / Emissions
Low-tech approach, solid walls reduce heat loss, no heating, ventilation, or cooling, and no external energy supply

Auf dem Gelände einer ehemaligen Druckerei in Schlieren sollte ein autarker Neubau entstehen. Dabei galt der Anspruch des Areals JED (Join.Explore.Dare), ein Zentrum für Innovation und Wissenstransfer zu sein, auch hinsichtlich der Architektur. Der Neubau setzt neue Maßstäbe in der Kosten-, Energie- und Flächeneffizienz – und beim Komfort. Es entstand ein qualitativ hochwertiges Gebäude, das ohne Heizung, Lüftung und Kühlung sowie Zuführung von Fremdenergie auskommt. Dies entspricht dem innovativen Prinzip 22·26, das sich auf die genuinen Möglichkeiten ressourcenschonender Architektur konzentriert. Ein möglichst stimmiges Verhältnis von Volumen und Oberfläche ist Basis für die Umsetzung eines Gebäudes ohne technische Klimatisierung.

Mit rund 17.000 m² Geschossfläche steht in Schlieren die bisher größte Immobilie nach dem Prinzip 22·26. Der Baukomplex erhielt seine Passung und die räumlichen Qualitäten durch die rhythmisierte Abfolge unterschiedlich dimensionierter Volumina in einer funktionierenden Synthese aus Architektur und Gebäudekonzept. Massive Wände reduzieren den Wärmeaustausch, bis zu 3,79 Meter hohe Räume sorgen für Wohlbefinden und passend dimensionierte Fenster bringen das notwendige Licht. Sensoren steuern die Lüftungsflügel. Damit entstand ein optimales Arbeitsklima mit optimalen Temperaturen zwischen 22 und 26 Grad Celsius.

A self-sufficient new building has been constructed on the site of a former printing company in Schlieren. The JED (Join.Explore.Dare) area's ambition to become a centre for innovation and knowledge transfer also applies to the architecture. The building sets new standards in cost, energy, and space efficiency—and in comfort: The result is a high-quality structure that does not require heating, ventilation, or cooling, nor a supply of external energy. This is in line with the innovative principle 22·26, which focuses on the genuine possibilities of resource-saving architecture. The most harmonious possible ratio between volume and surface area is the basis for implementing a building without mechanical air conditioning. The new building complex gets its fit and spatial qualities from the rhythmic sequence of differently dimensioned volumes. The synthesis of architecture and building concept works. With around 17,000 m² of floor space, the Schlieren property is the largest building to date to be based on the 22·26 principle. Thick walls reduce heat loss, rooms up to 3.79 metres high ensure a sense of well-being, and correctly dimensioned windows provide the necessary light. Sensors control the ventilation flaps. This creates an optimal working environment with optimal temperatures between 22 and 26°C.

DAM Was finden Sie besonders gelungen an Ihrem Projekt?
Baumschlager Eberle Durch den Verzicht auf konventionelle Haustechnik entfällt der Aufwand für deren Planung, Beschaffung und Wartung. Der Energieverbrauch wurde deutlich reduziert. Technikräume und Steigzonen konnten substanziell minimiert werden.

DAM Was war Ihnen bei der Erarbeitung des Projektes wichtig?
Baumschlager Eberle Es geht um Komfort. Energieersparnis und damit auch ökonomische Vorteile sind lediglich die willkommenen Folgen unseres Konzepts, das ressourcenarm funktioniert.

DAM What do you find particularly successful about your project?
Baumschlager Eberle Avoiding conventional building technology eliminates the need for planning, procurement, and maintenance. Energy consumption is significantly reduced. Technical rooms and riser zones can be substantially minimised.

DAM What was important to you when developing the project?
Baumschlager Eberle It's about comfort. Conserving energy and the economic advantages that come with it are simply welcome consequences of our concept, which works with few resources.

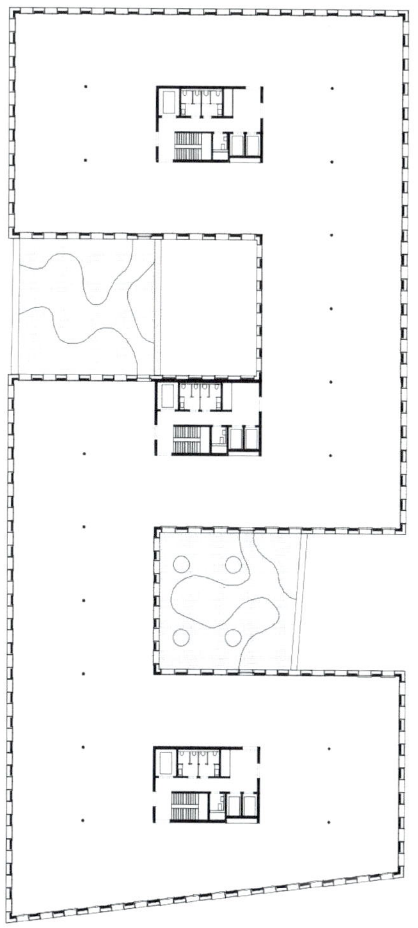

Regelgeschoss | Standard floor

Andres Herzog

Eine Chance für eine vielfältigere Architektur: Klimagerechtes Bauen vermitteln

An opportunity for a more diverse architecture: Enabling climate-friendly construction

Wer die Treibhausgase reduzieren will, muss von der emissionsarmen Ausnahme zu einer Klimabaukultur finden und die Kreativität für die Durchschnittsarchitektur wecken. Dafür braucht es positive Narrative.

Anyone wishing to reduce greenhouse gas emissions must transition from low-emission exceptions to a climate-driven construction culture and stimulate creativity in the field of everyday architecture. To this end, favourable narratives are needed.

Klimaschutz ist in der Bevölkerung als wichtiges Thema fest verankert. Das zeigen Umfragen, das machen die Nachrichten fast wöchentlich klar. Und doch sind die politischen Debatten festgefahren, die CO_2-Zahlen zeigen nicht wie erhofft nach unten, gebaut wird in den meisten Ländern wie eh und je. Derweil macht sich in der Bevölkerung „Klimamüdigkeit" breit – die Menschen können nicht die nächsten Jahrzehnte im Krisenmodus verbringen. Das merken selbst die Aktivisten auf der Straße, deren Aktionen bei vielen Verdruss auslösen, die eigentlich für die Sache sind.

Auch emissionsarmes Bauen braucht ein Umdenken. Der Fokus sollte von den Klimaklebern zu Klimamachern wechseln. Die Erderwärmung ist ernsthaft und dringlich, aber sie ist nicht der Weltuntergang. Die Apokalypse-Rhetorik versagt, die Wirkung bleibt aus, die Leute wenden sich ab. Nötig sind stattdessen positive Geschichten und Lösungen, auch wo sie erst in Ansätzen vorhanden sind. Die „Umweltverweigerer" kann man mit Mindestanforderungen in den Baugesetzen zwingen; Leuchtturmprojekte strahlen aus und spornen an. Von ihnen aus muss der Blick in die Breite gehen. Die dringlichste Aufgabe besteht darin, den gebauten Mittelstand auf ein gutes CO_2-Niveau zu bringen. Wir müssen von der emissionsarmen Ausnahme zu einer Klimabaukultur finden, zu einer ressourcenschonenden Durchschnittsarchitektur. Doch was heißt das? Und wie vermittelt man es?

Das CO_2-Zahlenrechnen ist eine trockene Angelegenheit. Der Vorteil: Die Rechnung ist unideologisch. Unterm Strich geht es um weniger Treibhausgasemissionen, egal wie man dies erreicht. Die Dekarbonisierung ist zu komplex und zu groß für ein Entweder-oder-Denken im Entwurf. Es gibt

The population as a whole has accepted that climate protection is an important issue. This can be seen both from opinion surveys and from the news almost every week. Yet political debate is stuck in a rut, carbon emission figures are not decreasing as hoped, and, in most countries, construction follows the business-as-usual pattern. In the meantime, the population is growing tired of the focus on climate. People cannot spend the next decades lodged in crisis mode. Even the activists out in the streets are noticing this, and their actions are annoying many of those who are essentially in favour of the cause.

We need to rethink low-emission construction. The focus must shift from the climate protesters to the climate makers. Global warming is a serious and urgent issue, but it is not the end of the world. The apocalyptical rhetoric fails: It has no impact, and people turn their backs on it. What we need instead are positive stories and solutions, even if they are still in their infancy. The climate-change refuseniks can be forced to act through the inclusion of minimum standards in the construction codes. Lighthouse projects can have a far-reaching influence and encourage emulation, so we must look from them to the broad mass of projects. The main task consists in ensuring that "middle-class" buildings have a better carbon footprint. We must transition from the low-emission exceptions to a culture of climate-conscious construction, to everyday architecture that preserves resources. But what does that mean? And how do we get the message across?

Totting up the CO_2 numbers is a dull matter, but it does have an advantage: The tally is not ideological. The goal is fewer greenhouse gas emissions, irrespective of how one achieves this. Decarbonisation is too complex and

Konstruktionen aus Holz, Beton, Lehm, aus Naturstein. Kein Material ist des Teufels – es kommt darauf an, wie man es einsetzt. Die Zukunft gehört den hybriden Konzepten. Jeder Baustoff, jede Technologie, jeder räumliche Kniff soll möglichst viel erreichen. Der Eklektizismus, die Methoden der Postmoderne und die Vielfalt werden damit wichtiger. Doch wohin genau sich die Architektur entwickeln wird, bleibt abzuwarten.

Die Klimabaukultur ist offen und generalistisch. Wir sollten weder dem Technofuturismus verfallen, der die technische Innovation als Heilsversprechen verkündet. Noch sollten wir einseitig Verzichtskultur predigen, die allen Komfort für überflüssig hält und in der Vergangenheit die rosige Zukunft sieht. Am weitesten kommt, wer alt und neu, Low- und Hightech, digitale Vorfabrikation und lokales Handwerk miteinander verbindet. Manche Start-ups wollen die traditionelle Lehmbauweise für den Massenmarkt verfügbar machen. Andere entwickeln materialsparende Tragstrukturen aus Beton, die wesentlich weniger CO_2 verursachen.

Die Planung wird wichtiger, wenn mit weniger Ressourcen mehr erreicht werden soll. Neben bautechnischen Neuerungen geht es um Entwurfsansätze, die aus der Netto-Null-Herausforderung gute Architektur machen. Die Baukultur darf ob der CO_2-Frage nicht zu kurz kommen. Sie ist voller gestalterischen Potenzials, räumlicher Ausdruckskraft und konstruktiver Entdeckungen. Und wenn wir die Klimakreativität wecken, wirkt sie doppelt: Eine starke Klimabaukultur spart nicht nur Emissionen ein, sie wird auch Nachahmer anregen, weil sie architektonisch überzeugt.

too large an issue for an either/or approach in the design. There are structures made of timber, concrete, clay, and natural stone: No material is wicked per se; it is a matter of how it is used. The future belongs to hybrid concepts. Every building material, every technology, every spatial trick should try and achieve as much as possible. Eclecticism, postmodernist methods, and diversity thus become all the more important, yet it remains to be seen exactly in what direction architecture will evolve.

A climate-driven construction culture needs to be open and generalist. We should make certain we neither succumb to Technofuturism, which proclaims that technological innovation promises salvation, nor unilaterally preach a culture of self-denial that considers all comfort superfluous and sees the past as a rosy future. Those who will get furthest are the ones who combine old and new, low-tech and high-tech, digital prefabrication and local craftsmanship. Some startups seek to employ traditional building techniques that use clay for the mass market, while others develop concrete load-bearing structures that save materials and cause far fewer carbon emissions.

Planning is especially important if more is to be achieved with fewer resources. Alongside innovations in construction technology, the focus here must be on design approaches that make good architecture on the back of the net-zero challenge. Architectural culture must not be thrown under the bus of carbon emissions. It is full of design potential, spatial expression, and constructive discoveries. And if we nurture that climate creativity, it will have a dual impact: A strong climate-driven construction culture not only saves emissions but will also persuade others to follow suit simply by virtue of being architecturally persuasive.

Die Mühen der Ebene

Nahezu jede Firma will heute CO_2-neutral sein. Trotzdem ist das Problem bei Weitem nicht gelöst. Es gibt einen Performance-Gap zwischen Wort und Tat. Gefragt sind mehr realistische Vorschläge und weniger lautes Marketing. Die schrille Weckrufphase ist vorbei, nun kommen „die Mühen der Ebenen", wie Bertolt Brecht schrieb. Gemeint sind also nicht die großen Versprechen, sondern die kleinen Erfolge: das gebaute Beispiel, die anwendbare Technologie, das wiederholbare Element, der kluge Praxistipp, das Experiment, von dem man lernen kann.

Dazu müssen wir über die Sprache reden, mit der wir kommunizieren. Der Begriff „nachhaltig" prangt heute auf fast jedem Produkt, Projekt oder Service, sodass er seine Bedeutung verloren hat. Wir sollten unsere Worte präziser wählen, wenn wir effektiv sein wollen. Klimaneutral oder gar klimafreundlich bauen wird man noch lange nicht können. Jedes Haus hat seinen CO_2-Rucksack; ein Netto-Null-Gebäude ist bis heute nicht möglich. Aber emissionsarm oder klimabewusst, vielleicht dereinst „klimagerecht" sollte die Planung sein.

In der Umsetzungsphase ändert sich die Tonlage im Diskurs. Statt von der Klimakrise, sollten wir besser von einer „Klimachance" sprechen. Das Wort macht uns handlungsfähig. Trotz der immensen Aufgabe können wir optimistisch in die Zukunft blicken: Wir können neue Konstruktionen testen, der Architektur eine andere Wendung geben, die Städte weiterdenken. Es wird eine aufregende Zeit für die Baukultur. Vor einer so umfassenden Neujustierung stand die

The labours of the plains

Today, every company would like to be carbon-neutral. Nevertheless, the problem is by no means solved. There is a performance gap between words and deeds. What is needed are more realistic proposals and less brash marketing. The strident call to wake up and change has come and gone, and we now face what Bertolt Brecht called "the labours of the plains"—meaning it is no longer about the big promise of the mountains, but instead all about the small successes of the even terrain ahead: the built example, the usable technology, the iterative element, the smart practical tip, the experiment from which we can learn.

In this context, we need to discuss the language with which we communicate. The term "sustainable" is boasted on all products, projects, and services today, to the extent that it has lost any meaning. We should choose our words with greater precision if we wish to be effective. It will be a long time until we can build in a climate-neutral, let alone climate-friendly, way. Every building at present comes with a tally of CO_2 emissions; a net-zero building is still not possible. But planning should at least try and keep emissions low and be climate-conscious, and possibly soon align with climate justice.

When it comes to the implementation phase, the tone of the discourse should change. Here, we should stop talking about a climate crisis and instead discuss a climate opportunity. That label should give us scope to act. Despite the immensity of the task, we can look to the future with optimism: We can road-test new structures, give architecture a new thrust, and make advances in how we think about our cities. It will be an exciting time for our built culture. Architecture last faced such a comprehensive recalibration during Modernism,

Architektur zuletzt in der Moderne, als man mit der Tradition brach. Heute lösen wir das fossile Bauzeitalter ab.

Anders als die Moderne damals sollten wir jedoch die Geschichte nicht ausblenden. Sie hält viele Lösungsansätze bereit, die wir vergessen haben. Bauteile hat man während Jahrtausenden wiederverwendet. Alle Kulturen haben mit dem lokalen Klima gebaut und nicht dagegen. Jede Stadt war vor der Mobilitätsrevolution eine Stadt der kurzen Wege. Auch der Blick zurück in die jüngere Geschichte hilft. Das ressourcenschonende Bauen ist keine Erfindung des 21. Jahrhunderts. Doch die ökologischen Bestrebungen der 1970er- und 1980er-Jahre in der Architektur – angetrieben durch die Ölkrisen – verfehlten ihre Breitenwirkung, weil sie in der Nische blieben und zum Teil vergessen wurden. Wir sollten von ihnen lernen. Die Architektur hat schon damals mit Photovoltaik oder Stroh experimentiert. Nun müssen wir die Ideen weiterspinnen und mehrheitsfähig machen. Das heißt auch: Wir sollten keine plakative Öko-ästhetik anstreben, sondern eine ansprechende Architektur in all ihren Facetten.

Pragmatismus und Beharrlichkeit – das sind die Stichworte der Klimabaukultur. Die Ära der Stararchitekten ist vorbei, heute werden die Projekte stärker im Kollektiv und interdisziplinär entwickelt. Architektinnen und Architekten tragen große Verantwortung, gleichzeitig sollten sie ihre Rolle nicht überstilisieren. Man kann mit Architektur die Welt nicht retten. Aber mit jedem Gebäude kann man einen kleinen Teil dazu beitragen.

when it broke with tradition. Today we are busy bidding farewell to the fossil construction age.

Unlike Modernism did back then, however, we should not ignore history. It offers many possible approaches that we have since forgotten: Components were reused for thousands of years. All cultures built in line with their local climate and not by ignoring it. In every city prior to the mobility revolution, things were close by.

A glance back to more recent history also helps. Building in a way that conserves resources is not a twenty-first-century invention, but the ecological currents in architecture in the 1970s and 1980s, spurred on by the Oil Crisis, failed to have a broad impact because they remained a niche affair and were in part forgotten. We should learn from them. Back then, architecture experimented with photovoltaic systems and with straw. We now need to advance those ideas and lend them a shape that is acceptable to the majority. In other words, we should not seek to create in-your-face eco-aesthetics but rather architecture that is appealing in all its facets.

Pragmatism and tenacity: Those are the buzzwords for a culture of climate-proofed construction. The era of "starchitects" has come and gone, and today projects are to a greater extent developed collectively and in an interdisciplinary manner. Architects bear a great responsibility, but they should not overemphasise the importance of their role. As an architect, you cannot save the world. But with each new building, you can make a small contribution to that effort.

Die globale Perspektive

Die Klimabaukultur muss der Realität in die Augen schauen. Und das heißt auch: Wir müssen über die Kosten reden. Die Dekarbonisierung kann kein elitäres Projekt sein. Wer die Ökonomie außer Acht lässt, kann keine breitenwirksamen Strategien entwickeln, schon gar nicht in globalem Maßstab. Die gute Neuigkeit: Die Preise für Technologien wie zum Beispiel Solarpaneele sind stärker gefallen als angenommen, was neue Anwendungen in der Architektur ermöglicht.

Die Bauwirtschaft ist wenig veränderungsfreudig. Sie sollte mehr in Forschung und Entwicklung investieren – insbesondere die großen Bauunternehmen, die im Unterschied zu anderen in der kleinteiligen Branche über das nötige Kapital für Investitionen in Forschung und Entwicklung verfügen. Die Zentralheizung, der Lift und der Stahlbeton haben die Architektur revolutioniert. Heute wendet die ganze Welt diese bautechnischen Errungenschaften an. Auch die klimabewussten Erneuerungen können global Fuß fassen, angepasst an die lokalen Bedingungen.

Je wohlhabender ein Land ist, desto höher ist sein ökologischer Fußabdruck. Desto mehr Ressourcen kann es aber auch für die Entwicklung von CO_2-optimierten Lösungen verwenden. Reiche Länder wie Deutschland oder die Schweiz haben die Mittel für die teure Grundlagenforschung, und an ihnen orientieren sich viele andere Länder. Das soll jedoch nicht heißen, dass die Industrienationen der Welt das emissionsarme Bauen erklären. Im Gegenteil: Die Bauwirtschaft, eine lokale Branche, sollte die Ideen globaler teilen und mehr voneinander lernen. Bei diesem Austausch wird wertvolles Wissen aus allen

The global perspective

The culture of climate-proofed construction must look reality square in the eye. And that also means we need to talk about money. Decarbonisation must not be an elitist project. Anyone ignoring economic reality cannot field a strategy that appeals to many, and most certainly not on a global scale. The good news is that the prices for technologies such as solar panels have fallen further than expected, and this gives rise to new applications in architecture.

The construction industry is fairly change-averse. It should invest more in research and development, with the lead taken particularly by the major construction corporations which, unlike others in the fragmented sector, have the capital resources to shoulder such investments. Central heating, elevators, and reinforced concrete revolutionised architecture. Today, the whole world uses these achievements in construction technology. Climate-conscious innovations can also gain a global foothold once they are adapted to local conditions.

The more affluent a country is, the larger its ecological footprint, and yet at the same time the greater the resources it can commit to developing carbon-optimised solutions. Rich countries like Germany or Switzerland have the means to undertake the expensive basic research. And many other countries take their cues from that research. That is not to say that the industrialised nations of this world should explain to everyone how low-emissions construction works. On the contrary. The construction industry, which is a local sector, should share its ideas globally so its players learn from one another. That exchange can link up invaluable knowledge from all the different regions

Weltregionen vernetzt, von der neuesten Photovoltaikzelle aus China bis hin zu vernakulären Bauweisen mit Bambus in Indonesien.

Der Architekturdiskurs funktioniert seit Bestehen des Internets global. Im Schlechten bedeutet das: Viele Konstruktionen werden von der ‚Konfektionsstange' übernommen und sind oft weder orts- noch klimagerecht. Hingegen profitiert das lokal verankerte Bauen von einer internationalen Zusammenarbeit. Die Schweiz kann vom Lehmbau in Niger lernen, Australien orientiert sich an der Solararchitektur in Deutschland. Globale Ideen lokal anzuwenden, ist ein Schlüssel für eine Klimabaukultur. Diese Architektur ist – ähnlich wie die Treibhausgase – weltweit wirksam, entsteht aber unter spezifischen Bedingungen vor Ort.

of the world, from the latest photovoltaic cell in China to vernacular construction methods using bamboo in Indonesia.

Since the advent of the internet, the architectural discourse has functioned globally. The downside to this is that many structures are simply taken off the peg and so do justice neither to local conditions nor to the climate. By contrast, construction with local roots benefits from international cooperation. Switzerland can learn from the way Niger builds with clay. Australia can reflect solar architecture in Germany. Applying global ideas locally is a key to a culture of climate-proofed construction. This form of architecture—which in this regard resembles greenhouse gases—has an impact the world over, but arises under specifically local conditions.

Wohnen im ehemaligen Weinlager
Conversion of warehouse building

Basel, Schweiz
Basel, Switzerland

Energie / Emissionen
Nutzung des Bestandes und vorhandener Ressourcen; Photovoltaikanlage; Grundwasser-Wärmepumpe

Energy / Emissions
Use of existing buildings and resources, photovoltaic system, groundwater heat pump

Bauaufgabe | Task
Umnutzung eines Lagergebäudes zum Wohnhaus mit 64 Wohnungen, Café-Bar, Gewerberaum, Joker- und Gästezimmer oder Gemeinschaftsraum | Conversion of warehouse building into residential building with 64 apartments, café-bar, commercial space, guest rooms, and common room

Entwurf Hochbau | Architects
Esch Sintzel Architekten, Zürich | Zurich

Entwurf Energiekonzept | Energy design
Gartenmann Engineering, Zürich | Zurich

Auftrag | Client
Stiftung Habitat, Basel

Fertigstellung | Completion
2023

Finanzierung | Financing
Stiftung | Foundation

Die mächtigen Pilzstützen des ehemaligen coop-Weinlagers im Baseler Lysbüchel-Quartier erzählen auf eindrucksvolle Weise die Geschichte des Hauses. Sie sind die prägnantesten Elemente des Bestandsbaus und bilden den wichtigsten Ausgangspunkt für den Entwurf. Um ihre Wirkung trotz der Kleinteiligkeit der neuen Wohnnutzung erlebbar zu halten, wurden sie in verschiedener Weise freigespielt und in Szene gesetzt: In den quer zur Gebäuderichtung liegenden Wohnungen ist ihre sperrige Monumentalität an sich ein Erlebnis – in der Sequenz sind sie spürbar in den beiden *Rues intérieures* (inneren Straßen), die das Haus in Längsrichtung durchziehen. So bilden die Stützen auch den Ausgangspunkt für die innere Organisation des Hauses: Der eigentliche Städtebau ist zwar durch den Bestand gesetzt, doch entlang der inneren Straßen entstand gewissermaßen eine Stadt im Haus. Diese erschließen nicht nur die Treppenhäuser, die gemeinschaftlich genutzten Räume und die Waschküchen, sie ermöglichen vor allem auch eine Vielfalt von Wohnungstypen (1,5- bis 7,5-Zimmer-Wohnungen) für alle Generationen und Lebensformen. Im Hochparterre vernetzt sich die häusliche Sphäre mit der städtischen: Die innere Straße öffnet sich hier in die quer liegenden Eingangshallen und lädt über Treppen und Rampen in das Haus ein. Neben der entwurfsbestimmenden Ausdruckskraft der bestehenden Strukturen motiviert die ökologische Nachhaltigkeit dazu, sorgsam mit dem Bestand umzugehen. So können durch die Weiterverwendung der alten Konstruktion 42 Prozent an grauer Energie eingespart werden. Mittels einer Photovoltaikanlage und einer Grundwasser-Wärmepumpe wurden beim Gesamtenergieverbrauch zwei Drittel Autarkie erreicht.

The imposing mushroom-shaped columns of the former wine warehouse in Basel's Lysbüchel district reveal the building's history in an impressive way. They are the most striking elements of the existing structure and form the most important starting point for the design. In order to maintain their impact despite the detailed design of the new residential use, they are revealed and showcased in various ways: In the apartments perpendicular to the building's orientation, their unwieldy monumentality is an experience in itself—in the sequence, they can be felt in the two "rues intérieures" (inner streets) that run lengthwise through the building. They also form a starting point for the internal organisation of the building: The actual urban planning is dictated by the existing building, but along the rues intérieures you get the sense of a city within the building. They not only provide access to the staircase, the communal rooms, and the laundry rooms, but also allow for a variety of apartment types (1.5- to 7.5-room apartments) for all generations and life-styles. On the raised ground floor, the domestic sphere connects with the urban one—the rue intérieure opens into the transverse entrance halls and invites you into the house via stairs and ramps. In addition to the expressive power of the existing structure, which has shaped the design, ecological sustainability also motivates us to treat the existing building with care. Reusing the old structure saves 42% of grey energy. The photovoltaic system and the groundwater heat pump achieve two-thirds self-sufficiency in terms of total energy consumption.

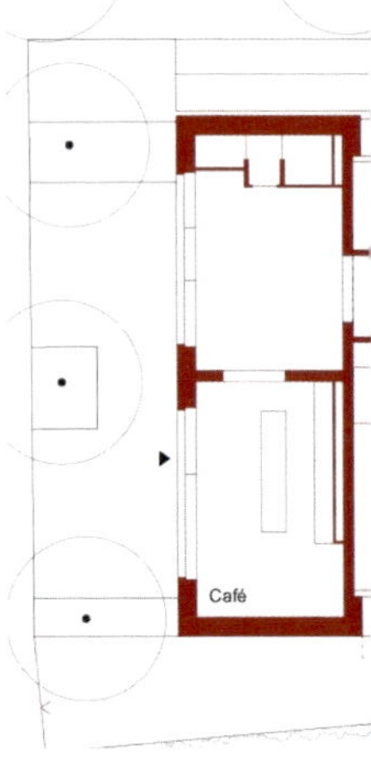

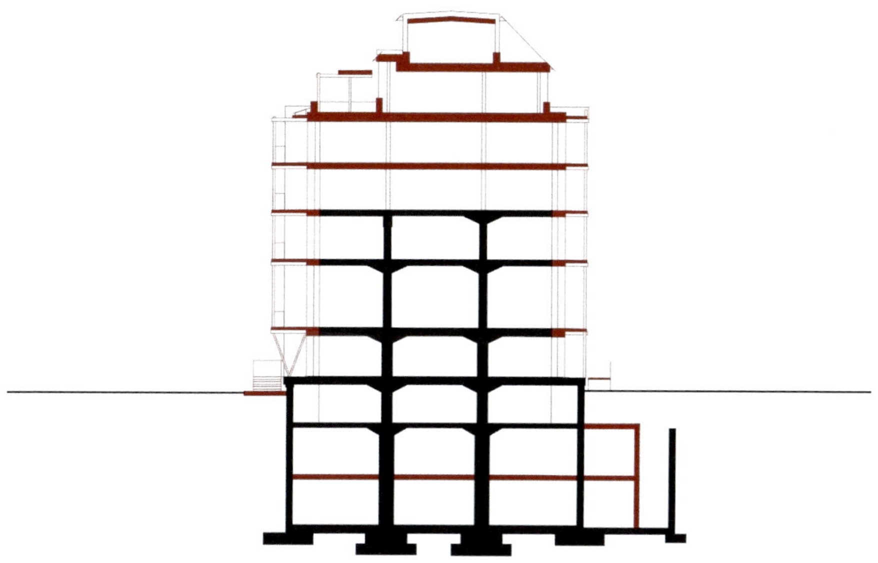

Schnitt | Sectional view

DAM Was finden Sie besonders gelungen an Ihrem Projekt?
Esch Sintzel Insbesondere finden wir den Einsatz der unverleimten Stützen aus Tannenholz als Pendant zu den bestehenden Pilzstützen und als Hinweis auf die temporäre Statik während des Rückbaus sehr gelungen. Im Allgemeinen war das Projekt in vielerlei Hinsicht eine Herausforderung für alle Beteiligten – wir finden, dass wir sie gemeinsam gut gemeistert haben.

DAM What do you find particularly well-executed about your project?
Esch Sintzel The use of the unglued fir columns as a counterpart to the existing mushroom columns and as an indication of the temporary statics during dismantling was particularly successful. For everyone involved, the project posed challenges in many respects—we think that we have overcome these challenges well.

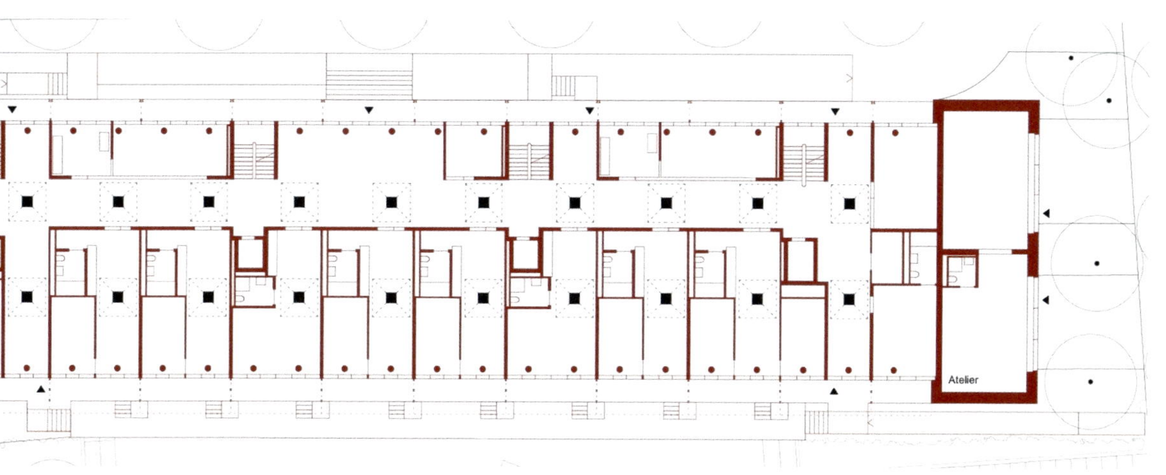

Grundriss Erdgeschoss | Floor plan—ground floor

Plusenergiehaus | Plus-energy house

Poschiavo, Schweiz
Poschiavo, Switzerland

Bauaufgabe | Task
Nachhaltiger Ersatzneubau eines Wohnhauses mit Nutzungsflexibilität | Sustainable new construction of a flexible-use residential building

Entwurf Hochbau | Architects
Nadia Vontobel Architekten, Zürich | Zurich

Auftrag | Client
Privat | Private

Fertigstellung | Completion
2021

Finanzierung | Financing
Privat | Private

Energie/Emissionen
Photovoltaikdach und -fassade; Wärmerückgewinnung; Wärmepumpe für Heizung; Gebäudehülle produziert rund sechsmal so viel Energie wie benötigt

Energy/Emissions
Photovoltaic roof and façade, heat recovery, heat pump for heating, building envelope produces around six times as much energy as is needed

Das Winter-Plusenergiehaus Sol'CH ist der Ersatzneubau für ein Wohnhaus am nördlichen Dorfrand von Poschiavo, der konsequent auf Energieeffizienz und Energiegewinnung ausgelegt ist. Die gesamte Gebäudehülle des Demonstrationsprojekts im Bereich BIPV (Building integrated photovoltaic) besteht aus Photovoltaikmodulen. Dank der Nutzung aller Fassaden- und Dachflächen werden auch in den Wintermonaten große Produktionsüberschüsse erzielt. Die volumetrische Idee des Neubaus mit seiner länglichen Ausrichtung spiegelt sich in der Organisation des Grundrisses wider. Während sich

sämtliche Wohnräume zum südlichen Garten hin orientieren, nimmt eine schmale Raumschicht im Norden Erschließung und Nasszellen auf. Die beiden Zonen werden durch eine lineare Möbelschicht unterteilt, welche je nach Bedarf Nutzungen von der einen oder der anderen Seite aufnimmt. Der Neubau mit zwei Eingängen kann ebenso als Einfamilienhaus wie auch als zwei separate Wohneinheiten genutzt werden. Die durch geringe Eingriffe mögliche Trennung erfolgt vertikal, sodass der direkte Zugang zu dem großen Garten für beide Wohneinheiten gewährleistet bleibt.

Die Produktionsmenge der BIPV-Anlage entspricht gemäß Modellrechnungen 47.770 kWh pro Jahr und beträgt das Sechsfache des Eigenbedarfs des gesamten Gebäudes. Die optimal ausgerichtete Südfassade erhöht den Ertrag im Winter und in der Übergangszeit, sodass auch in der kalten Jahreszeit erhebliche Energieüberschüsse erzielt werden. Der Energiebedarf für Geräte/Beleuchtung, Heizung und Warmwasser ist dank optimaler Dämmung, Komfortlüftung mit Wärmerückgewinnung, Wärmepumpe für Heizung und Warmwasser, Geräten der Energieklasse A und LED-Beleuchtung sehr gering. Die lokale Speicherung erfolgt über einen 3.000-Liter-Speicher für Heizung und Warmwasser. Der darüber hinaus ins Stromnetz eingespeiste Überschuss überkompensiert zudem die gesamte zur Herstellung der Baumaterialien und im Bauprozess eingesetzte Energie.

Fassade und Dach wurden als „hinterlüftete Fassade resp. Dach“ mit robusten Glas-Glas-Silizium-PV-Modulen realisiert. Während auf dem Dach hocheffiziente Module mit einer Antireflexbeschichtung zum Einsatz kamen, bestehen die Fassadenmodule aus satinierten, nicht spiegelnden und eingefärbten Gläsern. Aus wirtschaftlichen und energetischen Gründen war es wichtig, mit einer großen Repetition von Modulen zu arbeiten. Den Ausgangspunkt der Planung stellten die Standardmodule des Daches dar.

The Sol'CH house, a Winter Plus Energy project, was built to replace a residential building on the northern edge of the village of Poschiavo, and is specifically designed for energy efficiency and energy generation. A demonstration project in the field of BIPV (Building-Integrated Photovoltaics), the building's entire envelope consists of photovoltaic modules. By utilising every façade as well as the roof, large production surpluses are possible even in the winter months. The volumetric idea of the new building, with its elongated orientation, is reflected in the floor plan. While all living spaces face the southern garden, a narrow layer of rooms on the north side accommodates access and wet rooms. The two zones are divided by a linear layer of furniture, which accommodates uses from one or the other side as required. The new building with two entrances can be used as a single-family house or as two separate residential units. The separation, which is possible with only minor interventions, is vertical, so that both residential units still have direct access to the large garden.

According to model calculations, the BIPV system produces 47,770 kWh per year, which is six times the owner's needs. The optimally aligned south-facing façade increases production in winter and during the transitional periods, meaning that significant energy surpluses are also achieved during the cold season. The energy requirements for appliances, lighting, heating, and hot water are very low thanks to optimal insulation, comfort ventilation with heat recovery, a heat pump for heating and hot water, appliances in energy class A, and LED lighting. A 3,000-litre storage tank for heating and hot water is used for local storage. The surplus that is fed into the electricity grid more than compensates for the energy needed to manufacture the building materials and for the construction process.

The façades and roof were realised as a "back-ventilated façade and roof" with robust glass-glass-silicon photovoltaic modules. While highly efficient modules with an anti-reflective coating were used on the roof, modules with satin-finished, non-reflective, and coloured glass were used for the façades. For economic and energy-related reasons, it was important to work with a large repetition of modules. The starting point for the planning was the standard modules of the roof.

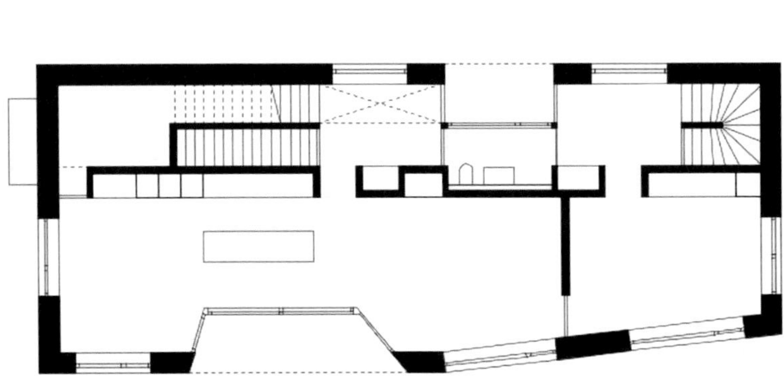

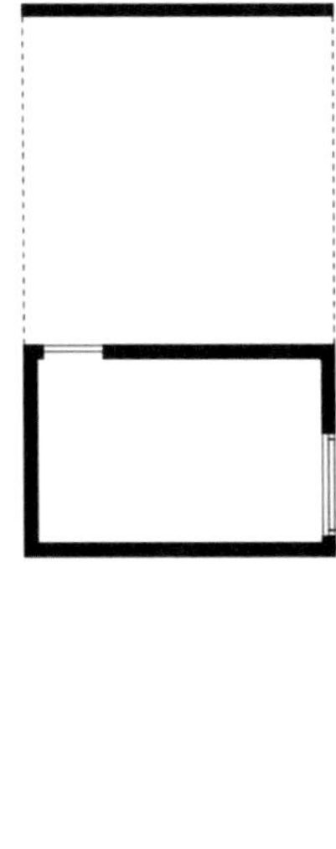

Grundriss Erdgeschoss | Floor plan—ground floor

DAM Was finden Sie besonders gelungen an Ihrem Projekt?
Nadia Vontobel Besonders gelungen finde ich das Zusammenspiel von Architektur und Technik. Vielen Elementen liegen sowohl technische als auch architektonische Überlegungen zugrunde, welche sich gegenseitig beeinflusst haben und in einem ausgewogenen Verhältnis zueinander stehen.

DAM Which aspects of your project do you consider particularly successful?
Nadia Vontobel I find the interplay between architecture and technology particularly successful. Many elements are based on both technical and architectural considerations, which have influenced each other and stand in a balanced relationship.

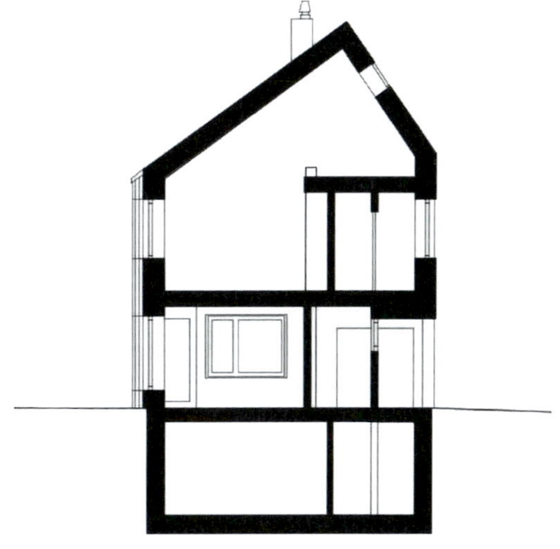

Schnitt | Sectional view

Brian Cody

Die Form folgt der Energie: Zusammenhänge von Energie, Form, Architektur und Stadtplanung

Form follows energy: Relationships between energy, form, architecture, and urban design

Die womöglich alles entscheidende Frage, die sich die Menschheit zum jetzigen Zeitpunkt stellen muss, ist, wie dem erwarteten globalen Bevölkerungswachstum Rechnung getragen werden kann und gleichzeitig die anthropogenen CO_2-Emissionen bis 2050 auf Null reduziert werden können. Die Strategie für die Lösung dieses Kernproblems muss so radikal wie ganzheitlich und ausgewogen sein. Ein nur moderater und gradueller Wandel ist nicht genug. Das ganze System muss in seiner Gesamtheit in die Betrachtung einfließen und es gilt ein Gleichgewicht zwischen den verschiedenen Elementen zu finden.

Perhaps the most important question facing humanity today is how to accommodate global population growth while simultaneously reducing anthropogenic carbon emissions to zero by 2050. The approach to this central problem must be radical, holistic, and balanced. Moderate and gradual change is not enough. The whole system must be considered in its entirety, and the correct balance between the various elements must be found.

Um nachvollziehen zu können, warum ein radikaler Ansatz notwendig ist, sollten wir uns vor Augen führen, dass alles, was bisher geschehen ist, nicht weniger radikal war. Besonders deutlich wird dies, wenn wir die Art von Veränderungen betrachten, die die Industrielle Revolution im 19. Jahrhundert hervorgebracht hat, oder die Agrarrevolution zuvor, der exponentielle Fortschritt in der Technologie des 20. Jahrhunderts oder im gegenwärtigen Digital- und Informationszeitalter. Für die Lösung der Problematik ist das gesamte Wissensfundament der westlichen Wissenschaft und Technologie erforderlich, aber es gibt mindestens genauso viel von der östlichen Philosophie zu lernen, mit ihrer Einsicht, dass alles miteinander zusammenhängt und die Aspekte von Gleichgewicht und Vergänglichkeit ebenso mitbedacht werden müssen. Wir sollten begreifen, dass alles auf einer grundlegenden Ebene miteinander verbunden ist und wir zwischen Mensch und Natur, aber auch zwischen Gegenwart und Zukunft wieder eine harmonische Ausgewogenheit herstellen müssen. Es gilt, mit der Natur und ihren Kräften zu agieren anstatt gegen sie.

Das massive Bevölkerungswachstum ist unvermeidlich. Die Weltbevölkerung wächst um 220.000 Menschen pro Tag und diese Entwicklung wird sich für den Rest des Jahrhunderts so fortsetzen. Ein Wachstum der Weltwirtschaft ist daher notwendig, um für die rund eine Milliarde Menschen auf der Erde, die nicht über ausreichend Nahrung, Wasser und Unterkünfte verfügen, einen angemessenen Lebensstandard sicherzustellen. Die Frage kann daher nicht lauten, ob wir bauen, sondern vielmehr was und wie wir bauen. Wir müssen für die rund eine Milliarde Menschen Unterkünfte schaffen, die zum jetzigen Zeitpunkt kein Dach über dem Kopf haben, sowie für die

To understand why a radical approach is necessary, we should remember that every global change up to this moment has been radical. If we reflect on the changes caused by the industrial revolution in the nineteenth century, the agricultural revolution before that, the exponential advancements in technology during the twentieth century, or those of the current digital and information age, this is readily understood. Solutions to current problems will require all we know from Western science and technology, but we can also learn enormously from Eastern philosophy and the principles of interconnectedness, balance, and impermanence. We need to realise that everything is connected at a fundamental level and reintroduce harmony, not only between mankind and nature, but also between present and future. We need to work with the forces of nature instead of against them.

The global population is growing at a rate of over 220,000 people per day, and it will continue to increase over the next half century or longer. An expanding global economy is necessary to provide a reasonable standard of living for the approximately one billion people on the planet today who lack adequate food, water, and shelter. The question is not if we should build, but rather what and how we build. We urgently need to provide shelter for people across the world who lack a home today along with the two billion people expected to join us on the planet over the next twenty-five years. Most of this population growth is expected in the tropical climate zone, especially in sub-Saharan Africa. Of course, this could change depending on global events and crises, such as massive migration driven by climate change.

2 Milliarden Menschen, die in den nächsten 25 Jahren noch dazukommen. Der größte Teil dieses Bevölkerungswachstums ist in der tropischen Klimazone zu erwarten, insbesondere in Subsahara-Afrika. Überdies könnte es zu unvorhergesehenen Entwicklungen kommen, wie beispielsweise zu einer durch den Klimawandel induzierten massiven Migration.

Um unerwünschte klimatische Veränderungen zu vermeiden, ist es wesentlich, das Ziel der CO_2-Neutralität zu erreichen. Nicht weniger entscheidend ist der Weg zu diesem Ziel. Das Klima wird durch die akkumulierten Emissionen in der Atmosphäre beeinträchtigt. Je länger der Kohlendioxidanteil erhöht ist, desto schwerwiegender sind die Folgen und die Veränderungen für das Klima. Daher muss der Fokus insbesondere auch auf Emissionen gerichtet werden, die durch den Bausektor inklusive der grauen Energie von Gebäuden verursacht werden. In diesem Zusammenhang ist zudem der Zeitpunkt der Emissionen maßgeblich, das heißt, dass der Ausstoß von Kohlendioxid heute größere Auswirkungen hat als derjenige in 25 Jahren. Das ist auf den Einfluss der kumulativen Emissionen zurückzuführen sowie auf die Erwartung, dass unser Energieversorgungssystem innerhalb dieses Zeitraums weitgehend dekarbonisiert wird. Zudem gehen wir davon aus, dass dieses Vierteljahrhundert eine Art Zeitpuffer darstellt, innerhalb dessen potenzielle Lösungen gefunden werden, die uns heute noch nicht zur Verfügung stehen.

Obwohl der gebundene Kohlenstoff im Vordergrund stehen muss, sollten wir die Bedeutung der operativen Emissionen dabei nicht außer Acht lassen. Wenn wir nicht aufpassen, könnte sich jene Form von Kurzsichtigkeit

To avoid undesired changes in our climate, achieving zero carbon emissions by 2050 is important. Equally important is the path to this goal. The climate is impacted by the accumulated emissions in the atmosphere. The longer carbon levels remain elevated, the higher the impact, and the greater the changes in our climate. Therefore, more emphasis must be placed on upfront emissions caused by building activities (the embodied energy of construction). Carbon emitted today has a greater impact than carbon emitted in twenty-five years due to cumulative emissions and the expectation that our energy supply system will be largely decarbonised within this time frame. Moreover, those twenty-five years represent a buffer period within which we can find solutions not available to us today.

Although our focus on embodied carbon must increase, we should not forget the importance of operational carbon. If we are not careful, a form of short-sightedness, typical of the way society has approached this challenge so far, can creep in. Operational energy will in many cases have the largest potential for carbon savings. For example, in a large airport project in the Middle East that our office is involved in, operational carbon is expected—due to typology and climate—to account for 80% of carbon emissions for the its entire life cycle, unless designed to operate on largely carbon-free energy sources.

It is a fallacy to think that at some time soon energy supply will be CO_2-free, and therefore operational energy in the future is unimportant and minimising energy demand unnecessary. As energy use increases, so does the demand on the infrastructure supplying renewable energy. Building this

einschleichen, wie sie für die Art und Weise typisch ist, in der wir als Gesellschaft bisher mit dieser Problematik umgegangen sind. In vielen Fällen werden die operativen Emissionen das größte Potenzial für CO_2-Einsparungen beinhalten. Bei einem großen Flughafenprojekt, an dem unser Büro im Nahen Osten beteiligt ist, wird beispielsweise davon ausgegangen, dass die operativen Emissionen – aufgrund der Typologie und des Klimas – einen Anteil von 80 Prozent der Kohlenstoffemissionen im gesamten Lebenszyklus haben werden, es sei denn, der Betrieb wird über eine weitgehend kohlenstofffreie Energiequelle versorgt.

Es ist ein Trugschluss zu glauben, dass die Energieversorgung bald CO_2-frei sein wird und damit der operationale Energieaufwand und dessen Minimierung zukünftig nicht mehr von Bedeutung sind. Je höher der Energiebedarf ist, desto höher sind die Anforderungen an eine Infrastruktur für erneuerbare Energien. Für deren Aufbau werden große Mengen an Materialien benötigt, darunter Mineralien, Metalle, seltene Erden und Land. Unsere Forschung hat ergeben, dass man die ultimative Ressource Land als Tauschwert zugrunde legen sollte, um Optionen miteinander vergleichbar zu machen – nicht Geld, Energie oder Kohlenstoff. Aktuelle Projekte, mit denen wir die Schaffung CO_2-neutraler Städte für die Zukunft anstreben, haben diese Erkenntnisse bestätigt.

Um zu verstehen, wie Land als ultimative Ressource betrachtet werden kann, stellen wir uns ein Szenario vor, bei dem eine neue, CO_2-neutrale Stadt in einer Wüste im Nahen Osten errichtet werden soll. Mit einer ausreichenden Verfügbarkeit von Land und den notwendigen Materialien lässt sich mit

infrastructure requires vast amounts of materials, including minerals, metals, rare earths, and land. Our research shows that land, as the ultimate resource, should be used as the currency to compare options, not money, energy, or carbon. Projects we are currently working on, which are aiming to be carbon-neutral cities of the future, have confirmed the results of this research.

To understand how land is to be seen as the ultimate resource, imagine building a new carbon-neutral city in a desert in the Middle East. With sufficient land and the necessary materials, you can construct the infrastructure for supplying renewable energy, allowing you to supply the city with the necessary energy for power, desalination plants for water, and vertical farming for food. The nexus of energy, water, and food must be central to our thinking, as these elements are inextricably interconnected.

According to the theory of relativity, matter can be converted into energy. Everything is energy. In accordance with the first law of thermodynamics, energy is constant and cannot be consumed. The total amount of energy in a closed system, such as the universe, is conserved. Energy is finite. The second law of thermodynamics, however, poses greater challenges. Every process on this planet leads to an irreversible increase in the total entropy of the system, with important consequences for us and the planet. Energy performance or efficiency is the relationship between input and output, benefit and cost, utility and expenditure. Human thermal comfort—as a basic requirement at the base of Maslow's hierarchy of human needs—must be at the forefront of considerations. At the end of the day, a city is about human experience. In the context of a building or a city, energy performance is the relationship

erneuerbaren Energien eine Versorgungsinfrastruktur schaffen, mit der die Stromversorgung sowie die Bereitstellung von Wasser mittels Entsalzungseinrichtungen und auch Nahrungsmitteln auf der Grundlage einer vertikalen Landwirtschaft sichergestellt werden können. Die Verflechtung der Aspekte Nahrung, Energie und Wasser muss dabei im Mittelpunkt der Überlegungen stehen, da sie untrennbar miteinander verbunden sind.

Nach dem Relativitätsgesetz kann Materie in Energie umgewandelt werden. Alles ist Energie. Laut des ersten Hauptsatzes der Thermodynamik ist Energie konstant und kann nicht verbraucht werden. Das heißt dass in einem geschlossenen System wie dem Universum die Gesamtenergiemenge konstant bleibt. Dennoch ist Energie endlich. Der zweite Hauptsatz bringt damit größere Herausforderungen mit sich, da jeder einzelne tatsächliche Prozess auf der Erde zu einer irreversiblen Veränderung der gesamten Entropie des Systems führt, mit erheblichen Folgen für uns und den Planeten. Energieleistung bzw. Effizienz bezeichnet das Verhältnis zwischen Input und Output, Nutzen und Kosten, Nutzen und Aufwand. Der Wärme, die gemäß der Maslowschen Bedürfnispyramide als Grundbedürfnis betrachtet wird, muss im Kontext dieser Überlegungen Priorität eingeräumt werden. Bei einer Stadt geht es letztlich immer um menschliche Erfahrungen. Im Kontext eines Gebäudes oder einer Stadt bezeichnet die Energieleistung das Verhältnis zwischen der erreichten Qualität und der Energie (Ressourcen), die zu ihrer Erhaltung erforderlich ist.

Bei der Lösungsfindung kann es hilfreich sein, die Art und Weise anzupassen, in der wir ein Problem angehen. Im Rahmen der Forschungstätigkeit

between the quality achieved and the energy (resources) required to maintain this quality.

An important step in finding solutions to a problem can be found in adapting the way we look at the problem. Through research performed at my institute, we have started to construct a new lens by which we can view our carbon footprint. Instead of breaking energy use and carbon emissions down into categories such as industry, transport, and buildings, we have begun to categorise according to human activities. Cars, planes, and buildings do not use energy—people do. We must understand which of our activities leads to which emissions. Sometimes, a new way of looking at a problem can lead to radical new solutions.

Human behaviour is at the root of the problem. We need radical solutions which will allow us to change our behaviour. We need radical visions for our society. We need to rethink the city and rethink society. We need to densify spatially and temporally. How can we use virtual infrastructure to replace and reconfigure our physical infrastructure? Can we share instead of owning? This includes everything: buildings, transport systems, equipment, clothing. Can software replace hardware? Flexibility and adaptability to future change are key elements of future-orientated solutions. We need to connect the elements of our society together in a way that nurtures symbiotic relationships between nature, mankind, and technology.

Due to the complexity and interconnectedness described above, dogmas and simple recipes are doomed to failure and may lead to a waste of valuable time. Timber construction, passive houses, vertical farming,

an meinem Institut haben wir damit begonnen, eine neue Betrachtungs-methodologie zur Bewertung des CO_2-Fußabdrucks zu entwickeln. Anstatt Energieverbrauch und Kohlenstoffemissionen in Kategorien wie Industrie, Transport und Gebäude zu unterteilen, sind wir dazu übergegangen, eine Kategorisierung nach menschlichen Aktivitäten vorzunehmen. Es sind die Menschen, die die Energie verbrauchen, und nicht etwa Autos, Flugzeuge und Gebäude. Wir müssen erfassen, welche unserer Aktivitäten zu welchen Emissionen führen. Eine andere Form der Betrachtung eines Problems kann mitunter zu radikal neuen Lösungen führen.

Menschliches Verhalten stellt die Wurzel des Problems dar. Wir brauchen radikale Lösungen, die es uns ermöglichen, unser Verhalten zu ändern. Wir brauchen radikale Visionen für unsere Gesellschaft. Wir müssen eine Neubetrachtung von Stadt und Gesellschaft vornehmen. Dazu müssen wir eine Verdichtung im räumlichen und zeitlichen Sinne einleiten. Wie können wir mithilfe der virtuellen Infrastruktur unsere physische Infrastruktur ersetzen und neu konfigurieren? Können wir Dinge teilen, anstatt sie zu besitzen? Das würde alles umfassen: Gebäude, Transportsysteme, Gerätschaften, Kleidung. Kann Software Hardware ersetzen? Flexibilität und Anpassungsfähigkeit an künftige Veränderungen sind Schlüsselelemente einer zukunftsorientierten Lösungsfindung. Wir müssen die verschiedenen gesellschaftlichen Bereiche so zusammenführen, dass sie für eine symbiotische Beziehung zwischen Natur, Mensch und Technologie förderlich sind.

Aufgrund der oben beschriebenen Komplexität und Verflechtung sind dogmatische Haltungen, aber auch einfache Rezepte zum Scheitern verurteilt

parametric design, BIM: All of these are at best a potential contribution. None of them is the answer. We should stick with physics and forget buzzwords and fashions. We need to think more critically. There are many items which are for the most part accepted as true by the professional and academic communities, which would benefit from critical reflection. To give a few examples of some such open questions:

Is burning waste ecological?
Is waste-heat use ecological?
Does district heating and cooling make sense?
Are energy concepts for neighbourhoods so much better? Why?
Do mixed-use developments save energy? Why?
Which is more sustainable, high tech or low tech? Why?

This list could easily be extended to fill a book. There is a lot to do.

und kosten uns womöglich wertvolle Zeit. Bauen mit Holz, Passivhäuser, vertikale Landwirtschaft, parametrisches Design, BIM – all das ist bestenfalls ein potenzieller Beitrag. Nichts davon an sich ist eine Antwort. Wir sollten bei der Physik bleiben und Schlagworte sowie Trends außen vor lassen. Wir müssen kritischer denken. Es gibt viele Dinge, die von Fachleuten und Wissenschaftlern weitestgehend als wahr akzeptiert werden, die aber von einer kritischen Betrachtung profitieren würden. Einige Beispiele für derartige offene Fragen sind:

> Ist die Verbrennung von Abfall ökologisch?
> Ist die Nutzung von Abwärme ökologisch?
> Sind Fernwärme und Fernkühlung wirklich sinnvoll?
> Sind Energiekonzepte für einzelne Viertel so viel besser und warum?
> Lässt sich mit gemischt genutzten Gebäuden tatsächlich Energie sparen und warum?
> Was ist nachhaltiger: Hightech oder Lowtech, und warum?

Die Fortführung dieser Auflistung könnte ein ganzes Buch füllen. Es gibt viel zu tun.

Rathaus | Town hall

Freiburg im Breisgau, Deutschland
Freiburg im Breisgau, Germany

Energie / Emissionen
Photovoltaikfassade und -dach erzeugt mehr Strom als benötigt; Solarthermieanlage liefert Warmwasser; Grundwassernutzung für passive Kühlung; Grundwasser-Wärmepumpe für Heizbedarf

Energy / Emissions
Photovoltaic façade and roof, generates more electricity than is needed, solar thermal system supplies hot water, groundwater use for passive cooling, groundwater heat pump for heating requirements

Bauaufgabe | Task
Rathausneubau mit Verwaltungszentrum und Kindertagesstätte | New town hall with administrative offices and daycare centre

Entwurf Hochbau | Architects
Christoph Ingenhoven Architects, Düsseldorf; ingenhoven associates, Düsseldorf

Entwurf Energiekonzept | Energy design
Drees & Sommer, Frankfurt am Main

Auftrag | Client
Stadt Freiburg im Breisgau, Freiburg i. Br.

Fertigstellung | Completion
2017

Finanzierung | Financing
Öffentliche Mittel | Public funds

Das neue Rathaus vereint 840 Mitarbeitende der Stadtverwaltung an einem zentralen Standort. Es ist das erste öffentliche DGNB Netto-Plusenergie-Haus weltweit. Die Fassade aus vertikalen Modulen mit Photovoltaikzellen, die zugleich Sonnenschutz bieten, wird ergänzt durch eine großzügige Photovoltaikanlage auf dem Dach. Das Gebäude erzeugt darüber mehr Energie aus regenerativen Quellen als es für Heizen, Kühlen, Lüften und Beleuchten benötigt. Überschüssiger Strom wird in das Stadtnetz eingespeist.

Nach Passivhausstandard unterschreitet der Primärenergiebedarf des neuen Rathauses denjenigen vergleichbarer Bürogebäude um 60 Prozent. Durch die Reduktion der CO_2-Emissionen weist es zudem eine positive Klimabilanz auf.

Die Bauweise setzt auf einfache, wirtschaftliche Lösungen sowie auf Baumaterialien von hoher Dauerhaftigkeit wie Glas, unbeschichtetes Holz und Aluminium. Das Gebäude erfüllt somit die essenziellen Anforderungen der Kreislaufwirtschaft. Die Lärchenholzfassade aus lokalem Waldbestand prägt das Gesamterscheinungsbild.

This new city hall brings together 840 city employees in one central location. It is the first public DGNB (German Sustainable Building Council) net-positive-energy building in the world. The façade of vertical modules with photovoltaic cells, which also provide solar shading, is complemented by a large-scale photovoltaic system on the roof. The building generates more energy from renewable sources than is needed for heating, cooling, ventilation, and lighting. Surplus electricity is fed into the city grid.

In accordance with the passive house standard, the primary energy requirement of the town hall is 60% lower than that of comparable office buildings. By reducing CO_2 emissions, it also has a positive carbon footprint.

The construction method relies on simple, economical solutions and highly durable building materials such as glass, uncoated wood, and aluminium, thus meeting the essential requirements of the circular economy. The larch wood façades from local forests characterise the overall appearance.

DAM Was finden Sie besonders gelungen an Ihrem Projekt?
Ingenhoven Das Rathaus als weltweit erstes öffentliches Netto-Plusenergie-Gebäude setzt neue Nachhaltigkeitsmaßstäbe und dient als Vorbild für zukünftige Projekte. Es verbindet innovative Technologie mit der Ästhetik natürlicher Materialien.

DAM Was würden Sie beim nächsten Mal anders machen?
Ingenhoven Beim zweiten Bauabschnitt verzichten wir auf die PV-Elemente an der Fassade zugunsten effizienterer Lösungen, ohne den Energiestandard zu senken. Den ersten Bauabschnitt würden wir jedoch unverändert wiederholen, um die Bau- und Diskussionskultur zu fördern.

DAM What do you find particularly remarkable about your project?
Ingenhoven As the world's first public net-positive-energy building, the town hall sets new sustainability standards and serves as a model for future projects. It combines innovative technology with the aesthetics of natural materials.

DAM What would you do differently next time?
Ingenhoven In the second construction phase, we are dispensing with the photovoltaic elements on the façade in favour of more efficient solutions, yet without lowering the energy standard. However, we would repeat the first construction phase unchanged in order to promote a culture of building and discussion.

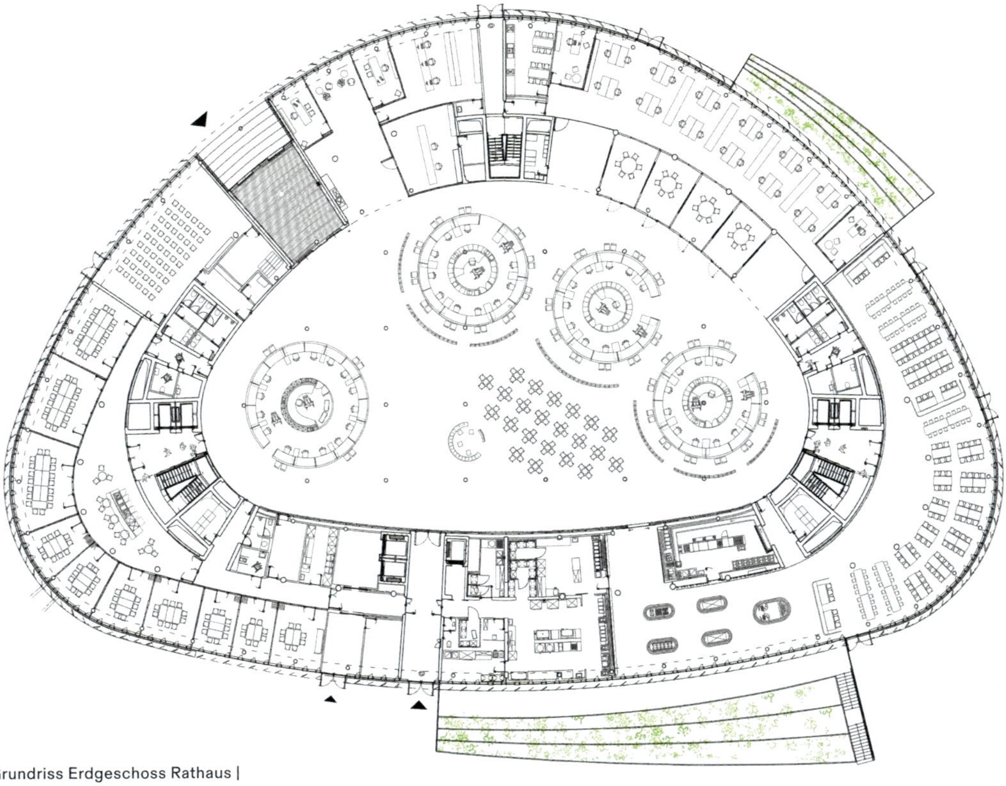

Grundriss Erdgeschoss Rathaus |
City hall: floor plan—ground floor

Rathaus (links) und Kindertagesstätte (rechts) | City hall (left) and childcare centre (right)

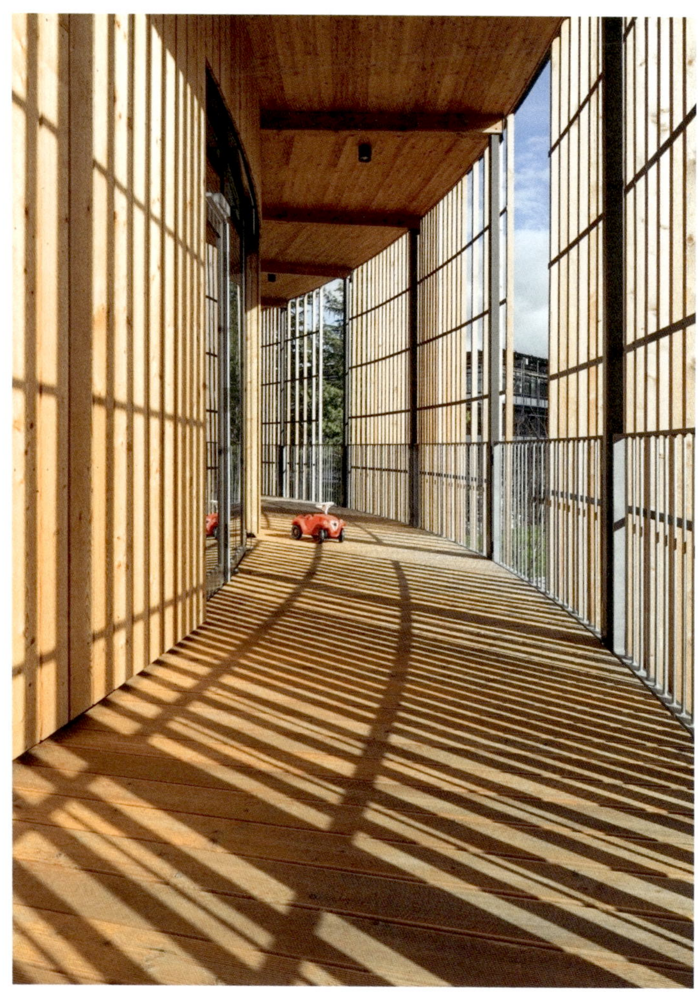

Laubengang Kindertagesstätte | Childcare centre: covered open walkway

Kindertagesstätte | Childcare centre

Innenraum Rathaus | City hall: interior

Besucherzentrum | Visitor centre

Legau, Deutschland
Legau, Germany

Bauaufgabe | Task
Neubau eines Besucherzentrums mit Biomarkt, Kaffeerösterei, Ausstellung, Bäckerei und Bistro, Kochwerkstatt und Weinkeller | New construction of a visitor centre with organic market, coffee roastery, exhibition space, bakery and bistro, cooking workshop, and wine cellar

Entwurf Hochbau | Architects
haascookzemmrich STUDIO2050, Stuttgart

Entwurf Energiekonzept | Energy design
Transsolar, Stuttgart

Auftrag | Client
Rapunzel Naturkost, Legau

Fertigstellung | Completion
2022

Finanzierung | Financing
Privat | Private

Energie / Emissionen
Nutzung von Abwärme, nachwachsenden oder wiederverwertbaren Baustoffen

Energy / Emissions
Utilisation of excess heat, renewable or recyclable building materials

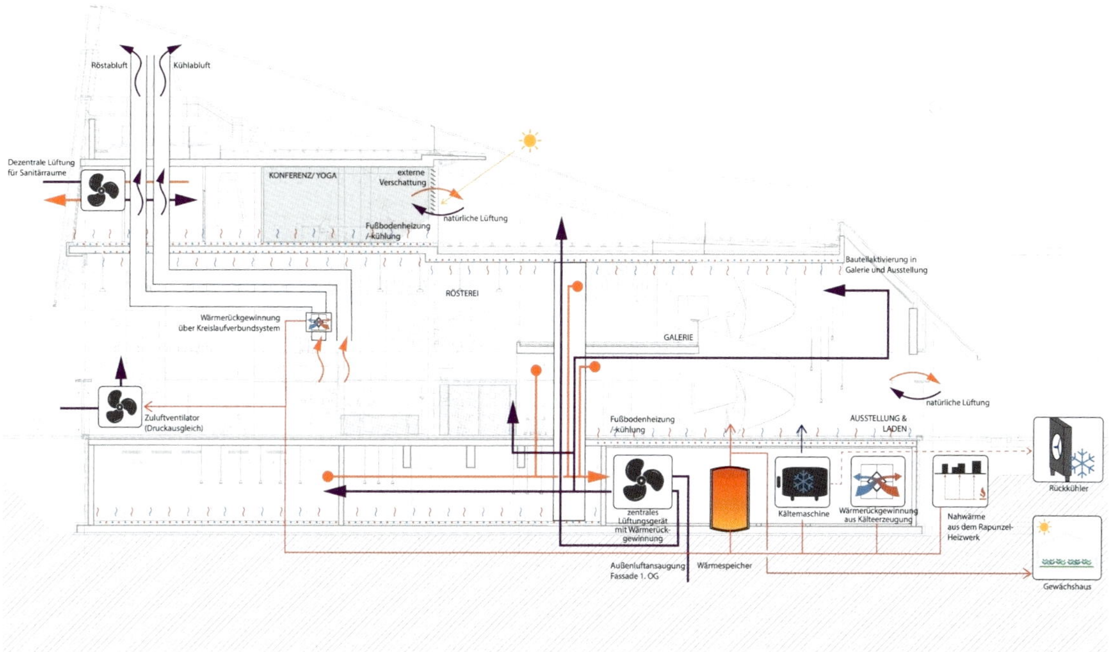

Energiekonzept | Energy concept

Natürliche und nachwachsende Baustoffe wie Holz und Ton wurden eingesetzt und die Haustechnik auf ein notwendiges Minimum reduziert. Für die Dämmung und den Unterboden wurde anstelle von Styropor recycelter Schaumglasschotter verwendet.

Bei diesem Projekt wurde genutzt, was in der Natur vor Ort als Mikroklima zur Verfügung stand, um ein robustes und somit dauerhaftes Haus zu errichten. Die Lage und Anordnung der Räume und die Fensteröffnungen wurden nach mikroklimatischen Gesichtspunkten festgelegt. Ein weiter Dachüberstand sorgt für die natürliche Verschattung der tageslichtoptimierten Räume. Auch die Belüftung erfolgt natürlich. Lediglich die Bereiche der Rösterei müssen mechanisch belüftet werden, da hier die Wärmelasten ein Normalmaß überschreiten. Das Gebäude wurde an das vorhandene gute Nahwärmenetz und die solare Stromgewinnung von Rapunzel angeschlossen. Eine Ökobilanz wurde erstellt, und bei der Wahl der Materialien waren die eingebundene Energie, die Wiederverwertbarkeit und der Transport entscheidende Faktoren. Nachwachsenden oder wiederverwertbaren Baustoffen wurde, wann immer möglich, der Vorzug gegeben. Während des Röstereibetriebs entsteht Abwärme durch die Röstanlage und die thermische Nachbehandlung mit Gasbrennern, die normalerweise über das Abgassystem abgeführt wird. Bei der geplanten jährlichen Röstmenge von 300 Tonnen Kaffee ergibt sich eine theoretisch nutzbare Abwärmemenge von mehr als 140 MWh. Dem steht ein Wärmebedarf des neuen Besuchergebäudes von nur 110 MWh/a gegenüber. Für die Beheizung ist daher eine Rückgewinnung der Abwärme aus dem Röstabgas vorgesehen. Mit welchem Anteil die Abwärme der Rösterei den Gesamtwärmebedarf des Gebäudes deckt, hängt vom Betrieb der Röstanlage ab.

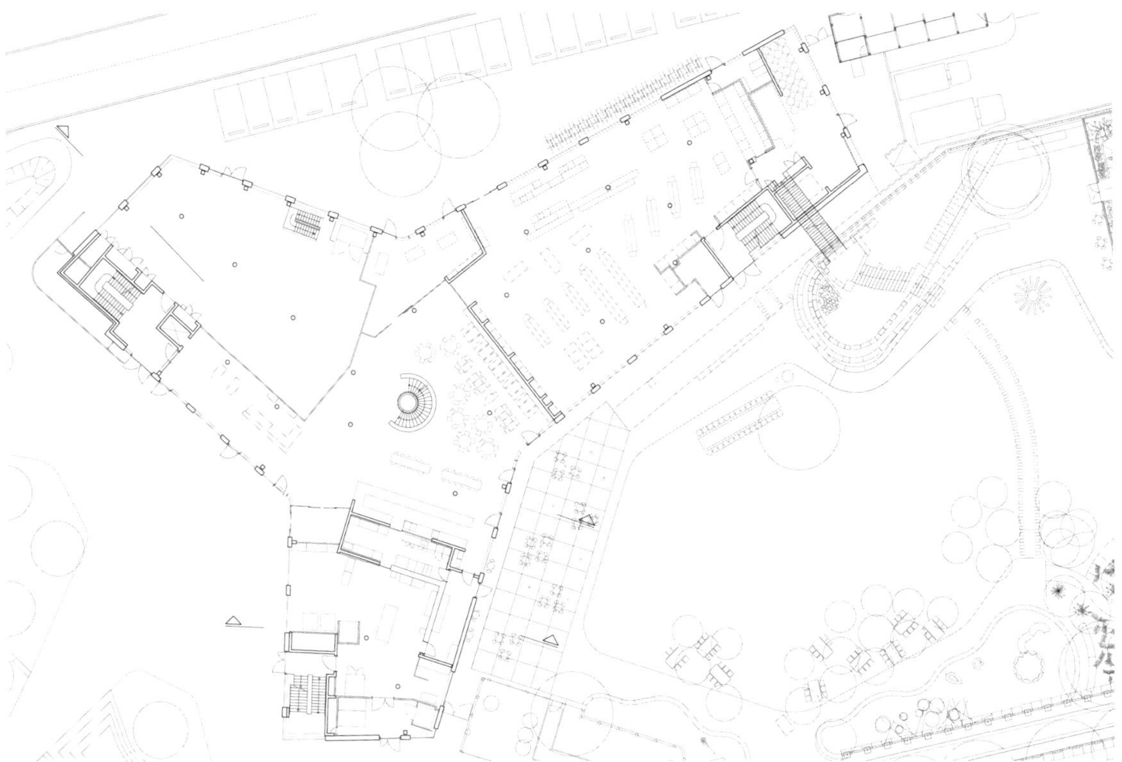

Grundriss Erdgeschoss | Floor plan—ground floor

The building was constructed using natural and renewable materials such as wood and clay, and its services were reduced to a necessary minimum. Instead of polystyrene, recycled foam glass gravel was used for the insulation and the subfloor. The microclimate provided by the local natural environment was used to construct a robust and durable house. The location and arrangement of the rooms and windows were determined according to microclimatic aspects. The wide roof overhang provides natural shading for the rooms, optimising the use of daylight. The ventilation is natural. Mechanical ventilation is only needed in the coffee roasting area, as the heat load there is higher. The building was connected to the already good-quality local heating network and to Rapunzel's solar power generation. All the materials used were selected based on the amount of energy required to produce them, their recyclability, and the transport involved. Whenever possible, renewable or recyclable building materials were given preference. Coffee roasting and thermal after-treatment with gas burners generate waste heat that is normally discharged via the exhaust gas system. Assuming a planned annual roasting volume of 300 tonnes of coffee, a theoretically usable amount of waste heat of more than 140 MWh is generated. The heating requirement of the new visitor centre is only 110 MWh per year. It was therefore planned to utilise the waste heat from the roasting exhaust gas for heating. The proportion of the roasting plant's total heat requirement covered by the waste heat depends on the operation of the roasting plant.

DAM Was war Ihnen bei der Erarbeitung des Projektes wichtig?
haascookzemmrich Wir haben von Anfang an auf die Einbindung lokaler Firmen und Handwerker gesetzt, um einerseits von deren Innovationskraft zu profitieren und um andererseits die lokale Akzeptanz und die Identifikation der Beteiligten mit dem Projekt zu stärken. Dies ermöglichte uns außerdem, kurze Wege während der Bauzeit für Mensch, Material und Transport im Sinne einer CO_2-Footprint-Reduzierung zu erzielen.

DAM What was important to you when developing the project?
haascookzemmrich Right from the start, we focused on involving local companies and craftsmen in order to benefit from their innovative strength on the one hand and to strengthen local acceptance and the identification of those involved with the project on the other. This also enabled us to achieve short distances during the construction period for people, materials, and transport in terms of reducing the CO_2 footprint.

Gustav Düsing
Katharina Volgger

Technosphären: Anforderungen an die nachwachsende Architektengeneration

Technospheres: Challenges for the next generation of architects

forecast_24

Das Studio forecast_24 am Lehrstuhl für Experimentelles Gestalten und Grundlagen des Entwerfens, Institut Architektur und Städtebau (IAS) der Universität der Künste Berlin unter der Leitung von Prof. Gustav Düsing und Dozentin Katharina Volgger soll einen Blick in die Zukunft werfen und sich auf die Suche nach experimentellen Ansätzen zu verschiedenen Themen unserer Zeit begeben. forecast_24 beschäftigt sich über den Zeitraum von zwei Semestern mit dem Thema Energie und Wetter.[1]

1 Entwurfsstudio Wintersemester 2024/25. Tutor: Felix Schuschan. Studierende: Merlin Thomas Augele, Louis Emil Baurmann, Cristiana Bombelaj, Benedikt Burkhardt, Carl Dissmann, Marcus Friede, Emma Holder, Agnieszka Kawalec, Linus Emil Klein, Helen Grace Niebuhr, Agustin Paschetta, Nathan Reichenthal, Paula Riebel, Anna Lisa Senius, Firas Tokdemir, Justus Voigt, Kilian Johannes Weber, Lan Hua Wenig.

forecast_24

The design studio forecast_24, headed by Prof. Gustav Düsing and lecturer Katharina Volgger, is attached to the Chair for Experimental Forms and Principles of Design at the Department of Architecture, Berlin University of the Arts.[1] Its task is to glance into the future in search of experimental approaches to some of today's crucial issues. For two semesters, forecast_24 will concern itself with the topic of energy and weather.

1 Design studio, winter semester 2024/25. Tutor: Felix Schuschan. Students: Merlin Thomas Augele, Louis Emil Baurmann, Cristiana Bombelaj, Benedikt Burkhardt, Carl Dissmann, Marcus Friede, Emma Holder, Agnieszka Kawalec, Linus Emil Klein, Helen Grace Niebuhr, Agustin Paschetta, Nathan Reichenthal, Paula Riebel, Anna Lisa Senius, Firas Tokdemir, Justus Voigt, Kilian Johannes Weber, Lan Hua Wenig.

Technosphäre

Der 2018 im *UNESCO Courier* erschienene Artikel „The unbearable burden of technosphere" von Jan Zalasiewicz betrachtet die Erde als ein Konglomerat von Schichten und beschreibt dabei die Technosphäre.[2] Ähnlich der Atmosphäre, Hydrosphäre oder Biosphäre können Systeme wie fossile Brennstoffe und andere Energieressourcen als geologische Phänomene betrachtet werden – ein Konzept, das von dem amerikanischen Geologen und Ingenieur Peter Haff, Professor Emeritus an der Duke University, so benannt wurde. Im Gegensatz zur Biosphäre umfasst die Technosphäre die von Menschen erzeugte technologische Masse. Sie stellt nicht nur eine immer weiter wachsende Sammlung technischer Mittel und Hilfsmittel dar, sondern beeinflusst auch unser biologisches und kulturelles Leben. Für das Entwurfsstudio wurde der Begriff „Technosphären" im Plural gewählt – als Ausdruck für verschiedene Möglichkeiten im Umgang mit ausgedienten Energieinfrastrukturen, die den Rahmen von forecast_24 bilden.

TECHNOSPHÄREN: Der sogenannte technologische Fortschritt der Vergangenheit wird mit der Energiewende zur unvermeidlichen Frage der Gegenwart

Der neue Wille und die Erkenntnisse im Umgang mit Technologien und dem Energieverbrauch manifestieren sich in der Energiewende – es ist der Übergang von fossilen zu erneuerbaren Energieträgern. Das soll nicht nur große dringliche Veränderungen im Klima, in der Wirtschaft und in der Industrie ausdrücken, sondern bringt auch einen Wandel in der gebauten Umwelt –

2 Vgl. Jan Zalasiewicz, The unbearable burden of the technosphere, in: *The UNESCO Courier*, April–Juni 2018.

Technosphere

"The unbearable burden of the technosphere" by Jan Zalasiewicz, published in the *UNESCO Courier*, sheds light on the Earth as a conglomerate of spheres and, in the process, describes the technosphere.[2] The concept was developed by US geologist and engineer Peter Haff, professor emeritus at Duke University, who suggests that, like the atmosphere, hydrosphere, or biosphere, systems such as fossil fuels and other energy resources can be construed as geological phenomena. The technosphere, unlike the biosphere, includes the technological mass produced by humans. It not only represents an ever-growing aggregation of technical means and tools but also influences our biological and cultural life. For forecast_24, the concept has been pluralised as "technospheres" in order to express the different opportunities for handling discontinued energy infrastructures.

Technospheres: With the energy transition, the so-called technological progress of the past becomes an inescapable issue of the present

The energy transition demonstrates a new drive for change in, and insights into, handling technologies and their energy consumption; it marks the transition from fossil fuels to renewable energy sources. It is not only meant to confront major, urgent changes in the climate, economy, and industry, but also to bring about a change in our built environment—not least in architecture and social infrastructure. In their current state of flux, the technospheres are making a creative space of possibilities.

2 Cf. Jan Zalasiewicz, "The unbearable burden of the technosphere", *UNESCO Courier* (April–June 2018).

nicht zuletzt in der Architektur und der sozialen Infrastruktur – mit sich. Die TECHNOSPHÄREN befinden sich im Wandel und stellen einen gestalterischen Möglichkeitsraum zur Verfügung.

Seit dem Atomausstieg und dem Kohleausstiegsgesetz, das die Beendigung der Kohleverstromung bis 2038 regeln soll, stellt sich die drängende Frage, wie die ausgedienten Energieinfrastrukturen künftig genutzt werden können. Ihr Weiterleben lässt sich seit Jahrzehnten an postindustriellen Landschaften wie dem Ruhrgebiet erahnen. Doch müssen die baulichen Über-

Abb. 1 | Fig. 1 **forecast_ Studio-Exkursion NRW: Besuch eines Kraftwerk-Verteilers** | forecast_ Studio excursion in North Rhine-Westphalia: visiting a power plant distribution station

reste der Energieerzeugung aus herkömmlichen Energieträgern zwangsläufig zu musealisierten (Techno-)Fossilien werden? In ihrer Materialität und Form sind sie fossile Objekte, stehen aber für einen neuen Umgang zur Verfügung.

Es ergibt sich die Frage, welches räumliche und kulturelle Erbe die Bauwerke des fossilen Zeitalters hinterlassen. Was geschieht mit diesen Monumenten der fossilen Energieerzeugung und den Menschen, die ihnen gedient haben, wenn wir in das Zeitalter der erneuerbaren Energien eintreten? Welche materiellen und immateriellen Hinterlassenschaften bleiben, sollten bewahrt werden oder vielleicht ganz verschwinden? Wie gehen wir mit kontaminierten Landstrichen, verstrahlten Reaktoren und endlosen Kilometern von Rohren, Kabeln und Schläuchen um? Welchen gestalterischen Wert haben chromglänzende Raffinerien, elegant geschwungene Kühltürme oder die steil aufsteigenden Dampfsäulen am Horizont?

Das forecast_24-Entwurfsstudio TECHNOSPHÄREN der Bachelor- und Masterstudierenden der UdK Berlin begibt sich auf eine Reise durch die Bundesrepublik, um stillgelegte Atomkraftwerke zu untersuchen, Abraumhalden zu besteigen und Raffinerien zu durchwandern. Der Zugang zu Steinkohlekraftwerken macht es möglich, die architektonischen, technischen und sozialen Dimensionen dieser mächtigen Infrastrukturen hautnah zu erleben. Gespräche mit ehemaligen und aktiven Mitarbeitenden geben Einblicke in die alltäglichen Abläufe und erzählen von den Rhythmen und Herausforderungen dieser industriellen Giganten, während zugleich die konstruktiven Prinzipien und die räumliche Organisation dieser Orte ergründet werden.

Since Germany's phase-out of atomic energy and the Coal Phase-Out Act, which is meant to regulate the exit from coal-fired power stations by 2038, the pressing question is how the decommissioned energy infrastructures should be used in future. For decades, it has been possible to intuit the consequences of redundant infrastructures by casting a glance at the post-industrial landscapes in the Ruhr region. But must the built leftovers of energy generation from conventional sources invariably morph into museumified (techno-)fossils? They are fossil objects in terms of materiality and shape and yet are available for a new approach.

The question must therefore be what spatial and cultural legacy the edifices of the fossil age will leave behind. What is to be done with these monuments of fossil energy generation and the people who served (in) them once we enter the age of renewable energy? What material and immaterial heritage will remain, is worthy of preservation, or should perhaps disappear completely? How do we deal with contaminated stretches of land, irradiated reactors, and endless kilometres of pipes, cables, and hoses? What design value do refineries gleaming in chrome, elegantly curved cooling towers, or smokestacks have on the horizon?

The forecast_24 design studio "Technospheres" for bachelor's and master's students at the Berlin University of the Arts embarks on a journey throughout Germany in order to delve into decommissioned atomic power stations, climb slag heaps, and wander around refineries. Access to coal-fired power stations offers an opportunity to experience the architectural, technical, and social dimensions of these massive pieces of infrastructure firsthand.

Durch diesen direkten Einblick entstehen ein umfassendes Bild und eine sinnliche Präsenz dieser Orte, die eine beeindruckende Vielfalt an Elementen, Texturen, Verbindungen und Formen beherbergen.

forecast_24 sieht darin Potenzial. Können wir aus diesen hochtechnisierten, innovativen und robusten Elementen fernab jeder Recyclingromantik Gestalt entwickeln? TECHNOSPHÄREN zielt darauf ab, das gestalterische und soziale Potenzial technisch redundanter Bauwerke und Bauelemente der Energieinfrastruktur in experimentellen, programmatischen und theoretischen

Abb. 2 | Fig. 2 **Modell Strommasten im Maßstab 1:50** | Model: pylon, scale 1:50

Erkundungen zu ergründen. Die Elemente der Technosphäre werden nicht nur als Relikte der Vergangenheit betrachtet, sondern als aktive Bestandteile einer ständig im Prozess befindlichen Kultur, Baukultur und Kulturlandschaft. Die Studierenden des Entwurfsstudios entwickeln eigene Positionen und artikulieren sie in diversen Medien, etwa Modellbau, filmischen Arbeiten und Texten. Weder spezifische Orte noch Programme werden vorgegeben, da dies als integraler Bestandteil der intellektuellen Auseinandersetzung und der kreativen Leistung gilt. Der Ansatz der „Musealisierung" wird dabei bewusst und kritisch hinterfragt. forecast_24 sucht nach sinnstiftenden und identitätsbildenden Ansätzen, die sowohl eine materielle Wiederverwendung als auch eine Transformation der Räume und Kulturlandschaften in den Fokus

Abb. 3 | Fig. 3 Modell einer Dampfturbine im Maßstab 1:10 | Model: steam turbine, scale 1:10

Discussions with past and present staff members on site offer insights into the daily routines and tell a story of the rhythms and challenges of these industrial giants. At the same time, there is time for exploration of the structural principles and spatial organisation of these places. This act of direct observation gives rise to a comprehensive overview and a feel for the sensory presence of these places, each of which is home to an impressive variety of elements, textures, connections, and shapes.

The forecast_24 studio sees potential here. Can we develop a design from these highly technological, innovative, and robust elements, while avoiding any romantic recycling? The "Technospheres" project focuses on fathoming the design and social potential of technically redundant edifices and construction elements relating to energy infrastructure from an experimental, programmatic, and theoretical point of view. The elements of the technosphere are considered not just as relics of the past, but as active components of a culture, built culture, and cultural landscape that is in a process of constant change. The students in the design studio devise their own positions and articulate them in various media, relying, for example, on model building, filmic works, and texts. No specific places or programmes are defined in advance,

nehmen, sowie nach hybriden Orten, die von funktionalen Zwängen ebenso wie von sozialen und emotionalen Narrativen geprägt sind.

Die ausgediente Energieinfrastruktur als „Materiallager der Zukunft“ zu betrachten, öffnet Perspektiven für ein zirkuläres Denken und Handeln, das nicht nur die physischen Komponenten, sondern auch die kulturelle Bedeutung der Infrastrukturen bewertet. Gleichzeitig zelebriert es neue Entwurfsprozesse und Darstellungsmethoden innerhalb der Architekturlehre.

Diese Reflexionen verdeutlichen, wie stark technologische Räume auch als kulturelle Artefakte wirken und nicht zuletzt zum Strukturwandel auch innerhalb der Architektur beitragen können.

as both are considered an integral part of the intellectual approach and creative activity and input. In this context, the “museumification” method is consciously subjected to critical review. Instead, forecast_24 searches for meaningful and identity-fostering approaches that hinge on both reusing materials and transforming spaces and cultural landscapes, as well as on hybrid spaces that are determined by functional constraints and by social and emotional narratives.

Viewing the decommissioned energy infrastructure as a “material store for the future” affords us new perspectives on circular thinking and action that evaluate not just the physical components but also the cultural significance of these infrastructures. At the same time, it celebrates new design processes and methods of representation within architectural teaching.

These reflections highlight the powerful impact that technological spaces can also have as cultural artifacts and, not least, contribute to structural change within architecture, too.

Sozialer Wohnungsbau | Social housing

Barcelona, Spanien
Barcelona, Spain

Bauaufgabe | Task
Neubau eines Sozialwohnungsbaus mit 47 Wohnungen in Erdgeschoss und fünf Obergeschossen | New construction of social housing with 47 apartments across the ground floor and five upper floors

Entwurf Hochbau | Architects
DATAAE, Barcelona; Narch, Barcelona; Maira Arquitectes, Barcelona

Auftrag | Client
Institut Municipal de l'Habitatge i Rehabilitació de Barcelona

Fertigstellung | Completion
2022

Finanzierung | Financing
Öffentliche Mittel | Public funds

Energie/Emissionen
Kein Bedarf an Heiz- oder Kühlsystemen; Nutzung des Treibhauseffekts im Winter, überdachter und gut belüfteter Schattenplatz im Sommer

Energy/Emissions
No need for heating or cooling systems, greenhouse in winter and hyperventilated shading shelter in summer

Das Gebäude wurde mit einem durchgehenden Innenhof geplant, der einen zentralen Raum in Form eines bioklimatischen Atriums schafft. Er dient als Treffpunkt für die Bewohner und gleichzeitig als Mechanismus für eine hohe Energieeffizienz. Das Projekt vertieft die Beziehung zwischen Wohngebäude und öffentlichem Bereich, indem es Zwischenräume nutzt, um den Übergang von der Straße zum Haus zu schaffen. Der zentrale Raum kann geöffnet, geschlossen und vor der Sonne geschützt werden: Er fungiert im Winter als Gewächshaus und im Sommer als stark belüfteter, schattenspendender Zufluchtsort. Im Ergebnis entstand ein thermisch optimaler Bereich, der die Form des Gebäudes an die Umweltanforderungen anpasst, die Durchlässigkeit der Innenfassade

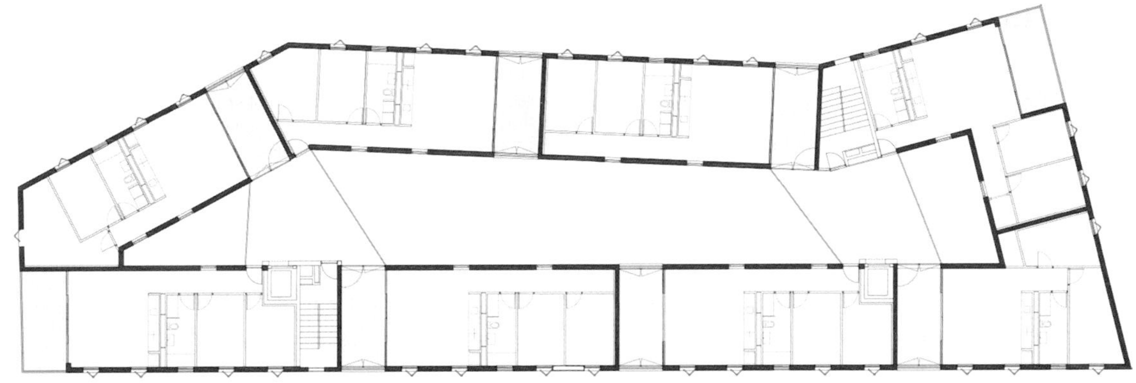

Grundriss Regelgeschoss | Floor plan—standard floor

verbessert und den Energieaustausch der Wohnungen ermöglicht, wodurch Verluste durch Belüftung und sanitäre Versorgung reduziert werden. Auf der typologischen Ebene verfügen alle Wohnungen über einen Zwischenraum in Form einer Terrasse oder Galerie zur passiven Nutzung: ein im Sommer offener, belüfteter Außenbereich, der durch Querlüftung zur Kühlung der Wohnungen beiträgt; im Winter ein geschlossener Raum, ein Kollektor, der durch den Treibhauseffekt für die Wohnräume Wärme gewinnt und so das Heizen überflüssig macht. Jede Terrasse wird zu einem privaten Raum, der als Puffer zwischen Innen- und Außenbereich dient. Entstanden ist eine einzigartige Typologie von Durchgangs-Terrassenwohnungen, bei denen sich alle Räume zur Fassade hin ausrichten, mit natürlicher Beleuchtung und Aussicht.

The building was conceived as a shallow and continuous perimeter of patio floors that creates a central space in the form of a collective and bioclimatic atrium, serving as a meeting space for inhabitants and a means for improving energy efficiency. The project deepens the relationship between the house and the public space, using intermediate spaces to make the transition between the street and the structure. The central space can be opened or closed and protected from the sun, functioning as a greenhouse in winter and as a hyper-ventilated shading shelter in summer. The result is a thermally favourable space, adapting the building's form factor to environmental needs, improving the transmittance of the interior façade, contributing to energy exchange with the dwellings, and reducing losses due to ventilation and sanitation. At the typological level, all the dwellings incorporate an intermediate terrace-gallery type space that functions as an area of passive use: an open, exterior, and ventilated space in summer, which collaborates in the cooling of the dwellings by taking advantage of cross ventilation. In winter, it is a closed space, a collector, which provides thermal gains, due to the greenhouse effect, to the living space, avoiding the need for heating. Each terrace becomes a private filter space between the interior and the exterior. We propose a unique typology of pass-through patio-flats where all the units are located along the façade, with natural lighting and views.

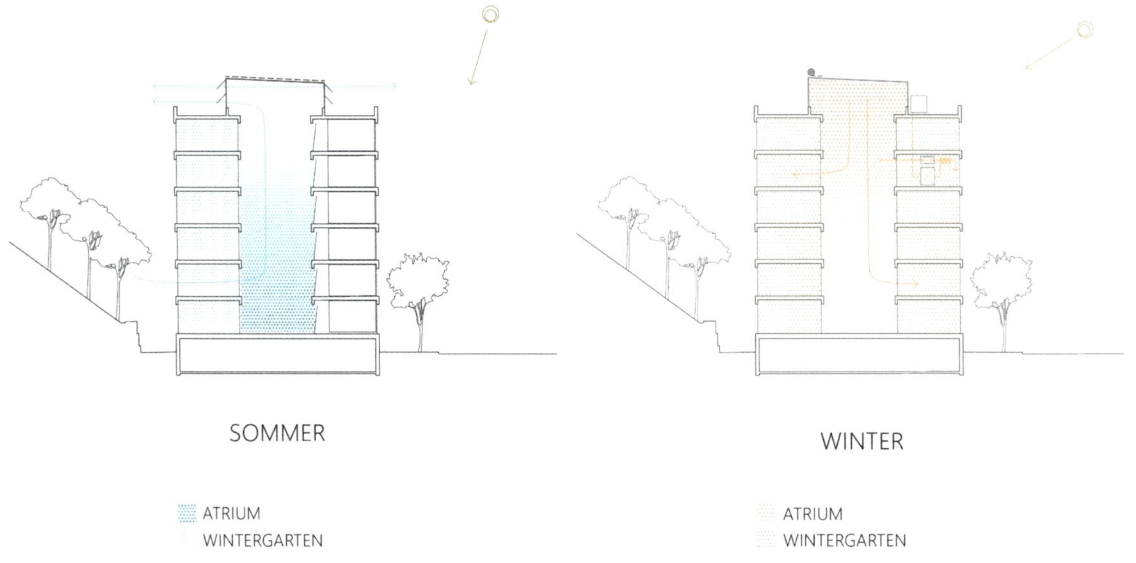

Klima-Schema | Climate—outline

DAM Was finden Sie an Ihrem Projekt besonders bemerkenswert?
DATAAE Der bemerkenswerteste Aspekt des Projektes ist die Nutzung der Zwischenräume wie des Atriums, des Treppenabsatzes und der Höfe am Eingang zu den Wohnungen als Strategien zur Energie- und sozialen Nutzung. Diese Räume begünstigen die Energieeffizienz, indem sie den Energiebedarf senken, und ermöglichen gleichzeitig die Erkundung unterschiedlicher Erfahrungen und die Nutzbarkeit des Raumes in Bezug auf verschiedene Komfortparameter.

DAM Welche Aspekte waren Ihnen bei der Entwicklung des Projektes wichtig?
DATAAE Der wichtigste Aspekt, der im Rahmen des Projektes bearbeitet und entwickelt werden sollte, war die Gewährleistung der dynamischen und anpassungsfähigen Eigenschaften der Bausysteme in den Übergangsräumen. Die Fassaden sollten sich im Sommer vollständig öffnen lassen, um eine Querlüftung zu ermöglichen, und im Winter geschlossen werden können, um den Treibhauseffekt zu nutzen, wobei stets ein Mindestmaß an Lüftung gewährleistet sein sollte.

DAM Was würden Sie beim nächsten Mal anders machen?
DATAAE Wir würden sicherlich eine andere Konstruktionslösung für die Fassade wählen. Dabei würden wir die Tatsache nutzen, dass die vertikale Struktur auf Betonwänden basiert, die senkrecht zur Richtung der Wohnungen verlaufen, und die Bodenplatte innen sichtbar bleibt. Für dieses Projekt wäre eine leichte, nicht-tragende Holzfassade mit hoher Dämmung und einem günstigeren CO_2-Wert erforderlich.

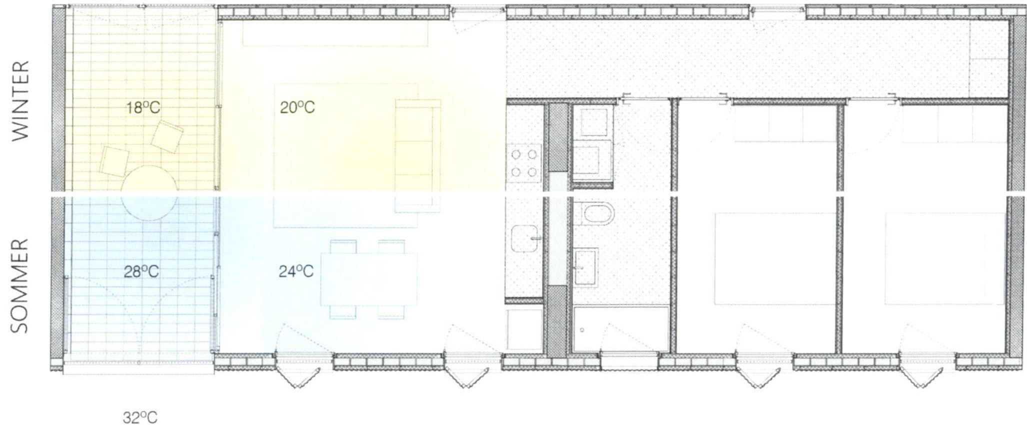

Klimazonen | Climate zones

DAM What do you find particularly remarkable about your project?
DATAAE The most remarkable aspect of the project is the use of the intermediate spaces such as the atrium, the staircase landing, and the courtyards at the entrance to the dwellings, both for their energy and social appropriation purposes. These spaces favour energy efficiency by reducing energy demand, while at the same time allowing the exploration of different experiences and usability of the space in relation to different parameters of comfort.

DAM Which aspects were important to you when developing the project?
DATAAE The main aspect to be worked on and developed in the project was to defend the dynamic and adaptive capacity of the construction systems of

the intermediate spaces. Enclosures capable of opening 100% in summer to ensure cross ventilation, and closing in winter to utilise the greenhouse effect, always maintaining a minimum level of ventilation.

DAM What would you do differently next time?

DATAAE We would certainly find a different construction solution for the façade, taking advantage of the fact that the vertical structure is based on concrete screens perpendicular to the direction of the dwellings and the floor slab is visible on the inside. This project would require a light, non-structural wooden façade with a high level of insulation and a more favourable CO_2 content.

Kultur- und Informationszentrum
Cultural and information centre

Ursprung, Deutschland
Ursprung, Germany

Bauaufgabe | Task
Neubau eines Kultur- und Informationszentrums als Versammlungsstätte | New construction of a cultural and information centre as a place for public assembly

Entwurf Hochbau | Architects
furoris X art, Chemnitz

Auftrag | Client
roger & ines, Ursprung

Fertigstellung | Completion
2021

Finanzierung | Financing
Privat und öffentliche Mittel | Private and public funds

Vertrauen und Zusammenarbeit sind nicht delegierbar. Aus dieser Erkenntnis heraus entstand ein neues Gebäude mit dem Namen „Zukunftshaus terra.hub“ als Ergänzung eines bestehenden Bauernhofs in Ursprung, das sich zu einem Nukleus für ein neues Zusammenleben in einer Dorfgesellschaft mit ihren kulturellen, sozialen und ökologischen Ansprüchen entwickelte. Wer durch diesen Ort bei Chemnitz schlendert, erwartet nicht, dass auf dem 300-jährigen Hofgelände ein Erweiterungsbau entstand, der nicht nur in seiner Reduzierung auf das Wesentliche besticht, sondern auch in Ergänzung des Gemeindelebens zu einem erneuerten Dorfkonzept beträgt. Nähert man sich dem Objekt, wird eine Gebäudegeometrie erkennbar, die sowohl eine Analogie zu den bestehenden

Energie / Emissionen
Stromversorgung durch Wasserstoffanlage mittels Photovoltaik; Beheizung durch Vergärung landwirtschaftlicher Reststoffe in einem Biomeiler

Energy / Emissions
Power is provided by a hydrogen plant using a photovoltaic system, heating is ensured by the fermentation of agricultural residues in a biopile plant

Gebäuden bildet als auch eine eigenständige Identität besitzt. Die Fassade, die den angrenzenden Platz raumfüllend einnimmt, zeigt sich durch das vertikal stehende Holzlamellenkleid eher zurückhaltend und verschlossen.

Die Suche nach einer traditionellen Beheizung des Gebäudes erwies sich als vergeblich. Durch die maßgeschneiderte PV-Anlage, die gleichzeitig einen gelungenen Dachabschluss bildet, wird die eigens entwickelte Wasserstoffanlage mittels selbstgewonnener Photovoltaikenergie betrieben. Damit die vollständige Autarkie des Gebäudes und des angrenzenden Dreiseitenhofs auch an sonnenarmen Tagen gesichert ist, wurde in unmittelbarer Nähe ein Biomeiler errichtet, der durch die entstehende Vergärung von landwirtschaftlichen Reststoffen eine behagliche und konstante Beheizung gewährleistet. Das Zukunftshaus terra.hub bildet nicht nur einen neuen Ankerpunkt in der dörflichen Struktur, sie setzt ebenso in der Umsetzung der Gebäudeanforderungen wie auch in der weiteren Bewirtschaftung der Immobilie eine wegweisende Systematik, die nicht im Verborgenen bleibt, sondern von der Bauherrin und der Ortsgemeinschaft weitergetragen und kommuniziert wird. Für die Bewohner der Gemeinde Ursprung hat die Zukunft schon begonnen.

Trust and cooperation cannot be delegated. Based on this realisation, a new building called Zukunftshaus terra.hub was built as an addition to an existing farm, which is developing into a nucleus for a new way of living together in a village, with its cultural, social, and ecological demands. If you take a stroll through the tranquil town of Ursprung, not far from the city of Chemnitz, Germany, you might find it hard to believe that an extension has been built on the 300-year-old farm grounds, which stands out for being reduced to the essentials, while also contributing to the community life of a new village concept—a new means of realising identity. As you approach the building, a new geometry emerges that forms an analogy to the existing buildings, but with an independent identity. The recognisable façade, which fills the adjacent square, appears rather reserved and closed due to the vertical wooden lamella cladding.

There is no traditional heating in the building. The specially developed hydrogen system is generated by the customised photovoltaic system, which also forms a successful roof finish. To ensure that the building and the adjacent outdoor area are fully self-sufficient even on days with little sunshine, a biopile plant has been built in the immediate vicinity, ensuring comfortable and constant heating through the resulting fermentation of agricultural residues. Zukunftshaus terra.hub not only forms a new anchor point in the village, but also sets a pioneering example for the implementation of building requirements and in the further management of the property, which is communicated and passed on by the client and the local community. For the residents of the community of Ursprung, the future has already begun.

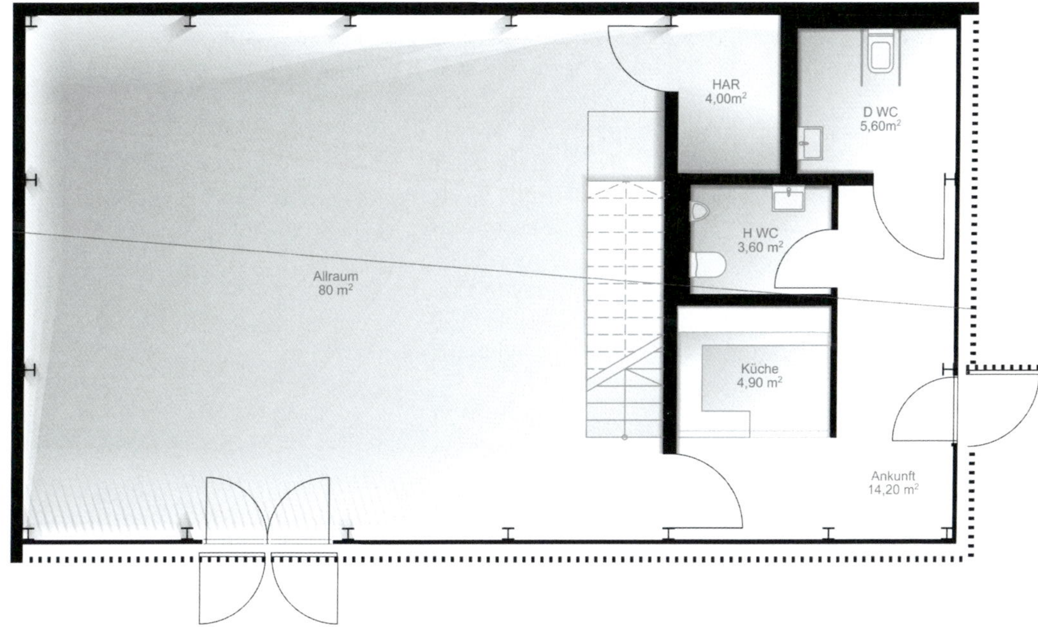

Grundriss Erdgeschoss | Floor plan—ground floor

DAM Was war Ihnen bei der Erarbeitung des Projektes wichtig?
furoris X art Durch Anordnung einer verdrehten Firstlinie entstanden unterschiedliche Neigungen und Schrägen im Fassadenbereich. Diese mit der Solartechnik und der vorstehenden Lamellenkonstruktion in eine bündige Ebene zu setzen, war geometrisch eine Herausforderung und handwerklich eine Meisterleistung.

DAM What was important to you when developing the project?
furoris X art The arrangement of a twisted ridge line creates different inclinations and slopes in the façade area. Aligning these with the solar technology and the protruding lamella construction in a flush plane was a geometric challenge and a feat of craftsmanship.

Bauen für die Stadt von morgen

Interview mit | with Cord Soehlke

Baubürgermeister und Erster Bürgermeister der Universitätsstadt Tübingen

City executive responsible for construction and First Deputy Mayor of Tübingen

Build for the city of tomorrow

DAM Energie ist ein allgegenwärtiges Thema, besonders im Gebäudebereich. Hat sich das Bewusstsein für Energiesparen und klimafreundliches Bauen in den letzten Jahren verändert?
Cord Soehlke Ja, das Bewusstsein ist deutlich gestiegen. In Städten wie Tübingen war das Thema schon immer präsent, aber besonders durch die Fridays-for-Future-Bewegung und die Energiekrise hat sich die Diskussion intensiviert. Die Herausforderungen sind vielfältiger geworden und wir erkennen zunehmend die Verknüpfung zwischen verschiedenen Bereichen wie Wärme, Verkehr und Stromproduktion. Gebäude sind heute nur ein Teil der umfassenderen kommunalen Klimaschutzstrategie.

DAM Energy is an omnipresent issue, especially when it comes to buildings. Has awareness of energy-saving and climate-friendly construction grown in recent years?
Cord Soehlke Yes, there is a far stronger awareness of the issue. In cities like Tübingen, the topic has always been on people's minds, but discussions have intensified, especially as a result of the Fridays-for-Future movement and the energy crisis. We now face a broader range of challenges, and it has become clear that various fields, such as heat, transportation, and electricity generation, are all interconnected. Today, buildings are only one part of the overall climate strategy that a local authority or municipality needs to pursue.

„Wir haben uns zu sehr auf Grenzwerte fokussiert, anstatt den breiteren Kontext von Emissionen und Ressourcenverbrauch zu betrachten“

DAM Was bedeutet für Sie persönlich Energiewende?

CS Für mich steht die Reduzierung von Emissionen im Vordergrund. Es geht darum, so schnell wie möglich aus der fossilen Energie auszusteigen und unseren CO_2-Footprint zu minimieren – sowohl individuell als auch kollektiv.

DAM Haben wir uns in den letzten Jahren zu stark auf die Energieeffizienz konzentriert und dabei die Emissionen vernachlässigt?

CS Ich denke, ja. In der Vergangenheit haben wir oft auf hochtechnisierte Lösungen gesetzt, etwa Passivhäuser, die viele Ressourcen verbrauchen. Wir haben uns zu sehr auf Grenzwerte fokussiert, anstatt den breiteren Kontext von Emissionen und Ressourcenverbrauch zu betrachten. Ein erweiterter Ansatz, der auch Themen wie graue Energie und Quartiersentwicklung einbezieht, wäre nachhaltiger gewesen.

DAM Wie sehen Sie die Balance zwischen Neubau und Bestand?

CS Es geht nicht um ein „Entweder-oder“, sondern um ein „Sowohl-als-auch“. Der Neubau ist oft energetisch effizienter, aber Bestandsgebäude enthalten bereits viel graue Energie, die wir nicht einfach ignorieren sollten. In Tübingen setzen wir auf Quartiersansätze, um beides

DAM To your mind, personally, what does the energy transition mean?

CS For me, the emphasis must be on reducing emissions. We need to exit fossil-fuel-generated energy as quickly as possible and minimise our carbon footprint—both as individuals and collectively.

DAM Have we concentrated too strongly on energy efficiency in recent years and neglected emissions in the process?

CS I think we have, yes. In the past, we have often opted for high-tech solutions, such as buildings constructed to the “passive house” standard, and that requires a lot of resources. We focused too strongly on the threshold values instead of considering the broader context of emissions and resource consumption. A broader approach that also included grey energy and neighbourhood development would have been more sustainable.

DAM In your opinion, what sort of a balance should be struck between new builds and the existing building stock?

CS It’s not about an “either/or” but about a “not only/but also”. New builds are often more efficient in energy terms, but existing buildings already contain a lot of grey energy that we should not simply ignore. In Tübingen, we have opted for neighbourhood-based approaches in order to forge an intelligent link between both fields, meaning modernising existing buildings where it makes sense and choosing new builds where necessary.

DAM How have the citizens responded to that?

CS There have been many emotional and controversial discussions, as preserving buildings is often bound up with personal memories.

intelligent zu verknüpfen: Bestandsgebäude sinnvoll zu sanieren und dort neu zu bauen, wo es notwendig ist.

DAM Wie reagiert die Bevölkerung darauf?

CS Es gibt natürlich gerade bei der Innenentwicklung viele emotionale und kontroverse Diskussionen. Andererseits gibt es auch eine große Akzeptanz, Wohnraum zu schaffen, besonders in wachsenden Städten wie Tübingen. Der Quartiersansatz hat sich hier als besonders wichtig erwiesen, da viele Herausforderungen – Energie, Mobilität oder soziale Fragen – auf dieser Ebene besser gelöst werden können. Es ist effizienter, über größere Flächen und Systeme nachzudenken, etwa bei der Fernwärme oder Mobilität, als nur einzelne Gebäude zu betrachten.

DAM Wie schätzen Sie die Zukunft des Quartieransatzes ein?

CS Ich bin überzeugt, dass städtisches Wohnen in Quartieren die nachhaltigste Form des Wohnens ist. Quartiere bieten soziale und funktionale Durchmischung, sparen Fläche und reduzieren den Verkehr. Projekte wie das Französische Viertel in Tübingen zeigen, dass diese Form des Bauens dichter, flächensparender und gleichzeitig energetisch sinnvoller ist.

DAM Welche Rolle spielt die soziale Dimension in Quartieren?

CS Quartiere sind mehr als nur Gebäude – sie sind soziale Lebensräume. Die Durchmischung von verschiedenen Wohnungstypen und Nutzungen, soziale Infrastruktur und Begegnungsräume spielen eine zentrale Rolle, besonders bei angespannten Wohnungsmärkten. Durch eine ganzheitliche Quartiersentwicklung können wir nachhaltige

At the same time, there is pressure to create new housing, particularly in growing cities such as Tübingen. The neighbourhood-based approach has proved to be really important, as many challenges such as energy, mobility, or social issues can be better solved at that level. It is more efficient to think about larger areas and systems, for example when it comes to remote heat or mobility, than it is to focus on an individual building.

DAM What role does the social dimension play in neighbourhoods?

CS Neighbourhoods are more than just buildings; they are social spaces where people live. So it is essential to achieve a vibrant mixture of different apartment types and usages, social infrastructure, and spaces of encounters, and this is particularly true when housing markets are tight. A holistic approach to developing neighbourhoods can spawn sustainable solutions that then function in the long term.

DAM How do you rate the future prospects of this neighbourhood-based approach?

CS I'm convinced that urban living in distinct neighbourhoods is the most sustainable form of living. It ensures a social and functional mixture, and reduces the overall volume of land required and traffic. Neighbourhoods like Französisches Viertel in Tübingen demonstrate that this form of building is denser and uses less land, and also makes more sense in energy terms.

“We focused too strongly on the threshold values instead of considering the broader context of emissions and resource consumption”

„Quartiere sind mehr als nur Gebäude – sie sind soziale Lebensräume“

Lösungen schaffen, die auf lange Sicht funktionieren.

DAM Gibt es ein Projekt in Tübingen, das besonders hervorzuheben ist?

CS Es sind weniger einzelne Projekte, sondern eher die Gesamtheit unserer Quartiersentwicklungen wie das Französische Viertel oder die Alte Weberei. Diese basieren auf einem ganzheitlichen Ansatz, der soziale, bauliche und energetische Überlegungen integriert. Auch unser Klimaschutzprogramm, das Klimaneutralität bis 2030 anstrebt, ist ein Modell, von dem andere Städte lernen können.

DAM Was bedeutet klimaschonendes Bauen für Sie in einem Wort?

CS Robustheit.

DAM Was motiviert Sie bei Ihrer Arbeit?

CS Mich motiviert die Frage, wie wir als Gesellschaft in Städten leben und Strukturen schaffen, die den gesellschaftlichen Zusammenhalt fördern. Generationengerechtigkeit spielt dabei eine große Rolle, besonders im Umgang mit dem Klimawandel.

DAM Was wünschen Sie sich von der nächsten Generation der Architekten und Ingenieure?

CS Ich wünsche mir, dass sie sich auf Machbarkeit konzentrieren. Otto Rehhagel sagte mal: „Die Wahrheit liegt auf dem Platz.“ Das heißt, es geht darum, realisierbare und umsetzbare Lösungen zu entwickeln.

DAM In a nutshell, what does climate-friendly construction mean to you?

CS Robustness. We must try and plan so that structures will still function in thirty or forty years' time, without unnecessary technical solutions.

DAM Is there a project in Tübingen you would especially like to emphasise?

CS Well, it's less about individual projects and more about the totality of our neighbourhood development efforts, such as Französisches Viertel or Alte Weberei. They are both based on a holistic methodology that integrated social, structural, and energy issues. Our climate protection programme, which aspires to achieve climate neutrality by 2030, is likewise a model from which other cities could learn.

DAM What motivates you at work?

CS I'm motivated by the question of how we as a society live in cities and create structures that foster social cohesion. Intergenerational justice plays a major role here, particularly in how we tackle climate change.

DAM What would you like to see from the next generation of architects and engineers as regards climate-conscious construction?

CS I would hope that they focus on feasibility. Football trainer Otto Rehhagel once said: "The truth is on the pitch." Meaning, the emphasis is on developing solutions that can be realised

"Neighbourhoods are more than just buildings; they are social spaces where people live"

Die zweite wichtige Sache ist Haltung. Es ist wichtig, sich selbst zu fragen: „Was will ich eigentlich?“ Haltung und Umsetzungsleidenschaft sind entscheidend.

DAM Hinterfragen Sie manchmal, ob Ihre Maßnahmen wirklich zum Klimaschutz beitragen?

CS Täglich. Zum Beispiel haben wir das historische Rathaus saniert und eine hochkomplexe Heizungssteuerung eingebaut, die auf dem Papier perfekt ist, aber in der Praxis manchmal versagt. Oder wir bauen Fahrradbrücken, die verkehrspolitisch sinnvoll sind. Aber wenn man den Materialaufwand berechnet, ist es nicht immer sicher, ob sie auch kurzfristig dem Klima nutzen. Auch bei großen Bauprojekten wie der Fahrradtiefgarage unter dem Europaplatz müssen wir uns stets die Frage stellen, ob sich der Aufwand lohnt. Diese Zweifel begleiten mich bei fast jedem Projekt.

in practice. The second important thing is our outlook. It's key to ask yourself: "What do I really want?" Outlook and a passion for implementation are decisive, I believe.

DAM Do you ever ask yourself whether your measures do actually help protect the climate?

CS Day in and day out. For example, I modernised our historical city hall and had a highly complex heating management system installed; it is perfect on paper but sometimes fails in practice. And I have had bridges for cycle paths built, which make sense in terms of climate policies but, in light of the material inputs, it gets pretty hard to justify them. And it bears asking, even with major construction projects such as the underground car park at Europaplatz, whether the effort and outlays are worth it. I have similar doubts with regard to almost every project.

Sozialer Wohnungsbau | Social housing

Ibiza, Spanien
Ibiza, Spain

Bauaufgabe | Task
Sozialer Wohnungsbau aus 43 Wohnungen mit ein bis drei Schlafzimmern |
Social housing construction with 43 apartments having one to three bedrooms

Entwurf Hochbau | Architects
Peris+Toral Arquitectes, Barcelona

Entwurf Energiekonzept | Energy design
Societat Orgànica, Barcelona

Auftrag | Client
IBAVI – Institut Balear de l'Habitatge, Palma de Mallorca

Fertigstellung | Completion
2022

Finanzierung | Financing
Öffentliche Mittel |
Public funding

Energie/Emissionen
Verzicht auf Heiz- und Kühlsysteme durch Atrium und Sonnenkamin; hohe thermische Trägheit der Konstruktion aus kohlenstoffarmen, gepressten Erdblöcken

Energy/Emissions
No need for heating or cooling systems thanks to the atrium and the solar chimney, high thermal inertia of the construction made of low-carbon pressed-earth blocks

Der Vorschlag für Sozialwohnungen in einem heterogenen Umfeld zielt darauf ab, sich an das Klima anzupassen und Energiearmut ohne aktive Heiz- und Kühlsysteme zu bekämpfen. Drei Einheiten sind um einen Innenhof herum angeordnet, was eine Querlüftung in allen Wohnungen ermöglicht. Das Konstruktionssystem besteht in tragenden Wänden aus gepressten Erdblöcken (CEB) mit einer Dicke von 20 Zentimetern und einer Dichte von ca. 2.000 kg/m³, die eine hohe thermische Trägheit und genügend Masse bieten, um mit einer einzigen Schicht den Schallschutz zu verbessern, und zugleich einen geringen Kohlenstoffausstoß aufweisen. Darüber hinaus besitzen die Tone ein hygrothermisches Verhalten, das zur Regulierung der Umgebungsfeuchtigkeit beiträgt. Um den Energiebedarf sowohl im Winter als auch im Sommer zu senken, ist der Innenhof mit einer Überdachung versehen, die im Winter als Atrium und im Sommer als Sonnenkamin dient.
In der Winterperiode nimmt das Gebäude eine kompakte Form an, wobei die Wärme durch die Galerien und Atrien aufgefangen wird, und ist mit einer Korkdämmung geschützt, um Wärmebrücken und Infiltration zu verhindern. Die thermische Trägheit trägt dazu bei, die Wärme über Nacht zu halten.
In der Sommerzeit wird das Atrium geöffnet und der Sonnenschutz genutzt, wodurch die Wärme abgeleitet und die Luftgeschwindigkeit erhöht werden kann, um den thermischen Komfort zu verbessern.

The proposal was to build social housing in a heterogeneous context while adapting to the climate and addressing energy poverty without employing active heating and cooling systems. Three units are organised around a courtyard, allowing cross ventilation in all the dwellings. The construction system employs load-bearing walls of compressed earth blocks (CEB) 20 centimetres thick and with a density of approximately 2,000 kg/m^3, providing high thermal inertia, enough mass to absorb acoustics between neighbours with a single layer, and a low carbon footprint. In addition, the clay has a hygrothermal behaviour that helps to regulate ambient humidity. To reduce energy demands in both winter and summer, a covering is provided for the courtyard, which then acts as an atrium in winter and solar chimney in summer. During the winter, the building adopts a compact form, capturing heat through the galleries and atriums, and is protected with a cork ETICS system to prevent thermal bridges and infiltration. Thermal inertia helps to retain heat at night, while in summer the atrium opens up and sunscreens are deployed, allowing heat dissipation and increasing air velocity to improve thermal comfort.

Grundriss 3. Obergeschoss | Floor plan—third floor

DAM Was finden Sie besonders gelungen an Ihrem Projekt?
Peris+Toral Es gewährleistet Behaglichkeit ohne die Notwendigkeit aktiver Systeme mit einer Strategie der Nachfragereduzierung, die zur Bekämpfung der Energiearmut beiträgt.

DAM Was war Ihnen bei der Erarbeitung des Projektes wichtig?
Peris+Toral Minimierung des Materialverbrauchs und eine Reduzierung von 60 Prozent im Vergleich zu einem konventionellen Gebäude.

DAM What do you consider a highlight of your project?
Peris+Toral It ensures comfort without the need for active systems, with a strategy of demand reduction that helps to combat energy poverty.

DAM What was important to you when developing the project?
Peris+Toral Minimising the consumption of materials and achieving a 60% reduction compared to a conventional building.

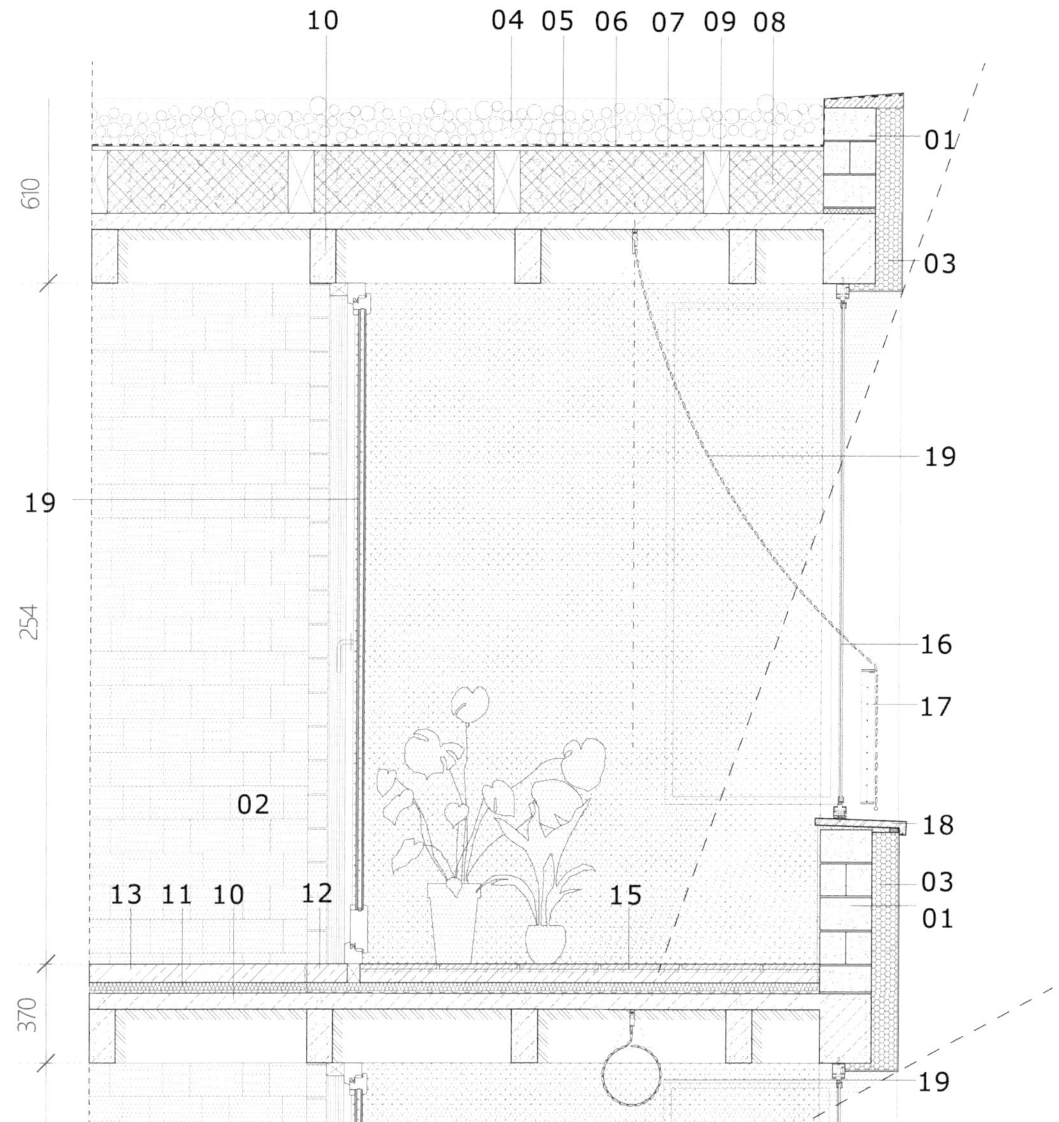

01. Gepresste Lehmziegel (CEB)
02. Gepresste Lehmziegelwand (CEB)
03. Korkplatte mit Kalkputzoberfläche
04. Kiesschicht, Recycleter Kies
05. Geotextil (150gr/m²)
06. Abdichtung EPDM d=1.5mm
07. OSB-Platte D=20mm
08. Seegras-Dämmung
09. Kiefernholzsparren
10. Betonplatte auf 20x10cm Trägern
11. Trittschalldämmung Steinwolle d=30mm
12. Zugangsschwelle (CEB)
13. Polierte Betondecke d=8cm
14. Faltschiebetüren Lärche
15. Bodenbelag aus weißem Marmor 60x30x2cm
16. Sonnenschutzglasvorhang mit vertikaler Profilen, seitlich faltbar
17. verzinkter und lackierter Handlauf aus Kunststoffgewebe
18. Fensterbank aus säuregewaschenem Kunststein
19. Rolläden aus Kiefernholz

Fassadenschnitt | Sectional view of the façade

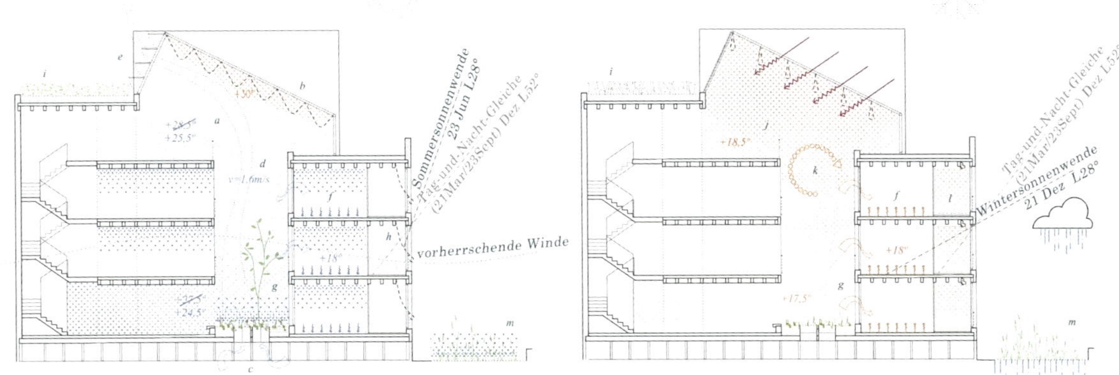

Klima-Schema | Climate—outline

Gemeinschaftliches Wohnen
Community housing

München, Deutschland
Munich, Germany

Bauaufgabe | Task
Neubau eines Wohngebäudes mit 35 Wohneinheiten unterschiedlicher Größe, Gemeinschaftsräumen und einem Gemeinschaftsgarten | New residential building with 35 units of different sizes with community rooms and a community garden

Entwurf Hochbau | Architects
ArchitekturWerkstatt Vallentin, München | Munich

Entwurf Energiekonzept | Energy design
IBP Ingenieure, München | Munich

Auftrag | Client
StadtNatur WEG, München | Munich

Fertigstellung | Completion
2020

Finanzierung | Financing
Baugemeinschaft und ihre Mitglieder | Building community and its members

Energie / Emissionen
Zertifiziertes Passivhaus Plus in Holzhybridbauweise; erzeugt durch Photovoltaik mehr Strom als die Bewohner verbrauchen

Energy / Emissions
Certified Passive House Plus in hybrid timber construction, generating more electricity through photovoltaic system than the residents consume

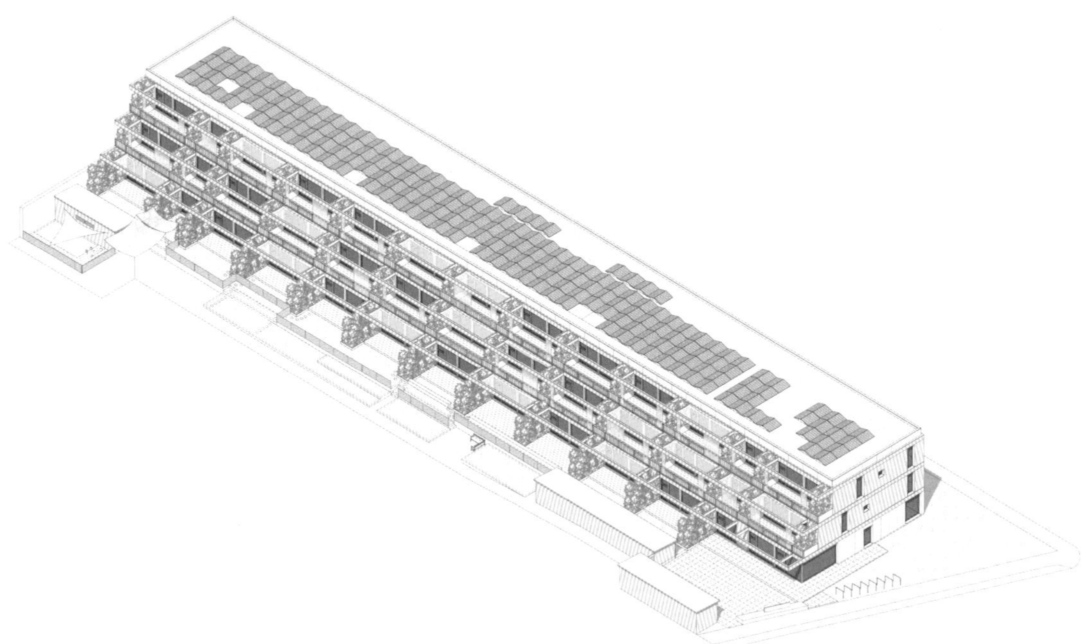

Isometrie | Isometric diagram

Im Münchner Stadtteil Alt-Riem wurde ein Grundstück an die Baugemeinschaft StadtNatur vergeben, initiiert von der ArchitekturWerkstatt Vallentin. Gemeinsam mit den zukünftigen Bewohnern wurde ein klimagerechtes und kostengünstiges Wohnkonzept entwickelt. Das Gebäude verfügt über eine Terrassierung, was unterschiedliche Wohnungsgrößen ermöglichte. Die Wohnungen sind über einen Laubengang als Kommunikationsfläche miteinander verbunden. Flex- und Schalträume erlauben spätere Anpassungen des Wohnungsmixes. Ein Gemeinschaftsraum öffnet sich zu einem Platz im Quartier. Das Mobilitätskonzept umfasst Ladestationen für Elektrofahrzeuge, zusätzliche Fahrradstellplätze und eine Fahrradwerkstatt. Naturnahe Gestaltung, ein Teich und Fassadenbegrünung tragen zur Kühlung im Sommer bei. Ein Gemeinschaftsgarten mit Gemüsebeeten, Sauna, Spielplatz und Hühnerstall belebt den Außenbereich.

In the Alt-Riem district of Munich, a piece of land was given to the StadtNatur building association, initiated by ArchitekturWerkstatt Vallentin. A climate-friendly and cost-effective living concept was developed together with the future residents. The building is terraced, allowing different apartment sizes. The apartments are connected to each other via a pergola, and flexible rooms allow the apartment layouts to be adjusted in the future as needed. A community room opens onto a neighbourhood square. The mobility concept includes charging stations for electric vehicles, additional bicycle parking, and a bicycle repair shop. A natural design, a pond, and green façades help to keep the building cool in summer. A community garden with vegetable plots, a sauna, a playground, and a chicken coop add life to the outdoor area.

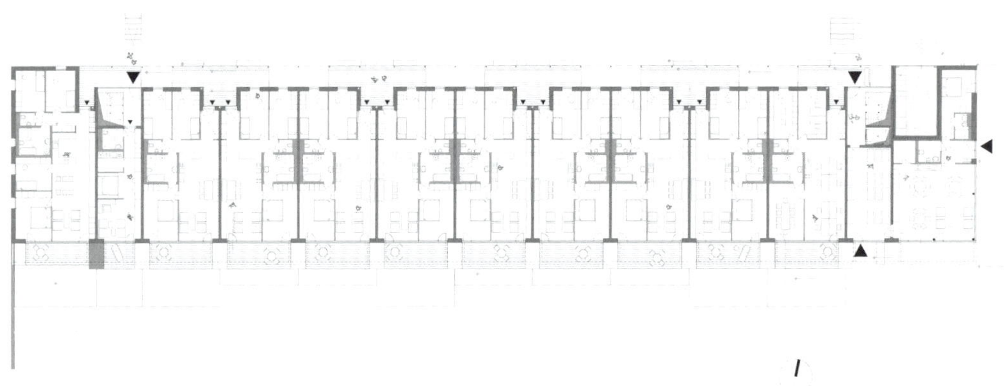

Grundriss Erdgeschoss | Floor plan—ground floor

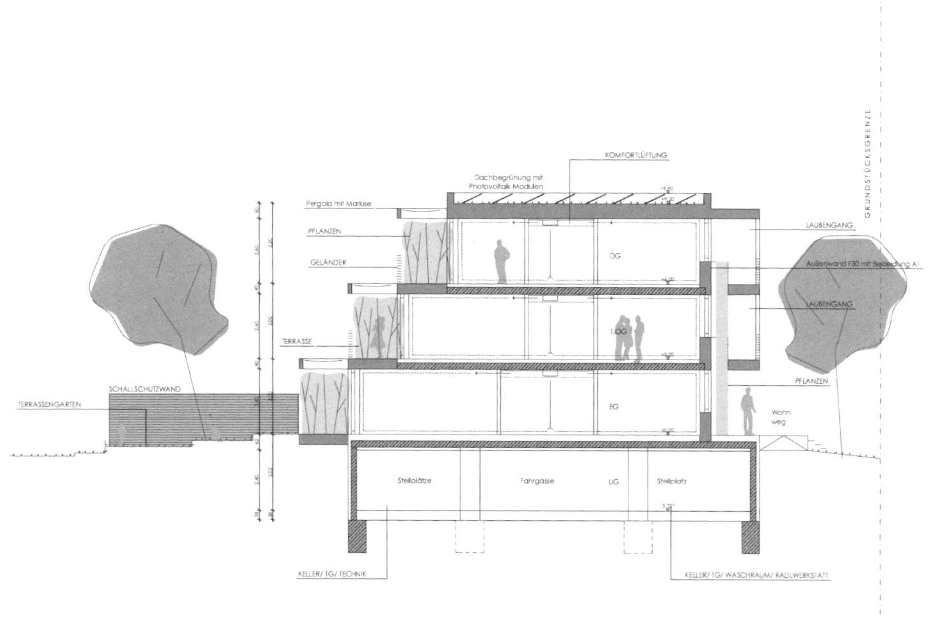

Schnitt | Sectional view

DAM **Was finden Sie besonders gelungen an Ihrem Projekt?**
ArchitekturWerkstatt Vallentin Das energetische Konzept in Kombination mit der Holzhybridbauweise bei gleichzeitig kostengünstigem Bauen sowie die Verknüpfung von Architektur und Außenbereich durch die Terrassierung des Gebäudes und der Freianlagen mit Urban Gardening, außerdem die Fassadenbegrünung.

DAM **Was war Ihnen bei der Erarbeitung des Projektes wichtig?**
ArchitekturWerkstatt Vallentin Das Schaffen einer lebendigen Baugemeinschaft, die auch über den Planungs- und Bauprozess hinaus eine starke Gemeinschaft bildet. Beim Bau eine ästhetische Einfachheit in der Konstruktion und den Details, die zu kostengünstigen und beispielhaften Lösungen führte.

DAM **What do you consider to be the highlights of your project?**
ArchitekturWerkstatt Vallentin The energy concept in combination with the timber hybrid construction and the cost-effective construction. The connection between architecture and open spaces through the terracing of the building and the open spaces with urban gardening, as well as the greenery on the façade.

DAM **What was important to you when developing the project?**
ArchitekturWerkstatt Vallentin The creation of a vibrant building community that continues to form a strong community beyond the planning and construction process. An aesthetic simplicity in the construction and details that lead to cost-effective and exemplary solutions.

Maxim von Gagern

Vom Wind bewegt: Landschaftsgestaltung im Zeitalter der Energiewende

Moved by the wind: Designing the landscape in the energy transition age

Die Energiewende beschäftigt die Bundesrepublik bereits seit fast einem Vierteljahrhundert und doch steht ein Großteil des Wandels erst bevor. Angestoßen wurde die Transformation hin zu erneuerbaren Energien mit dem Beschluss des Erneuerbare-Energien-Gesetzes (EEG) im Jahr 2000, die Reaktorkatastrophe von Fukushima elf Jahre darauf beschleunigte zusätzlich den damit einhergehenden Ausstieg aus der Atomkraft. Heute ist dieses Ziel in der Bundesrepublik erreicht, doch der Weg zur Klimaneutralität ist noch weit. Um das EEG zu erfüllen, muss der Anteil an erneuerbaren Energien am Bruttostromverbrauch weiter spürbar steigen, von derzeit 52,5 Prozent[1] auf 80 Prozent bis 2030. Dafür soll sich die Ausbaugeschwindigkeit bei den Erneuerbaren verdreifachen.[2] Der Windenergie an Land kommt dabei aus Sicht der Bundesregierung eine wichtige Rolle zu, da es sich dabei aktuell und langfristig um eine der günstigsten Energietechnologien in Deutschland handelt, die sich mit Photovoltaik optimal ergänzen lässt.[3] Zweifellos einen starken Impuls

1 Vgl. Bundesministerium für Wirtschaft und Klimaschutz (BMWK): Entwicklung der erneuerbaren Energien in Deutschland im Jahr 2023. Grafiken und Diagramme unter Verwendung aktueller Daten der Arbeitsgruppe Erneuerbare Energien-Statistik (AGEE-Stat; 2023); https://www.bmwk.de/Redaktion/DE/Downloads/Energie/entwicklung-dererneuerbaren-energien-in-deutschland-2023.pdf?__blob=publicationFile&v=10 [Abruf: 15.11.2024].

2 Vgl. Bundesregierung: Fragen und Antworten zur Energiewende. Anteil der Erneuerbaren Energien steigt (2024); https://www.bundesregierung.de/breg-de/aktuelles/faq-energiewende-2067498 [Abruf: 15.11.2024].

3 Vgl. Bundesministerium für Wirtschaft und Klimaschutz (BMWK): Windenergie-an-Land-Strategie – Wir stellen die Weichen für 160 Gigawatt Wind an Land bis 2035 (2023); https://www.bmwk.de/Redaktion/DE/Publikationen/Energie/windenergie-an-land-strategie.pdf?__blob=publicationFile&v=11 [Abruf: 15.11.2024].

Germany has been concerned with energy transition for almost a quarter of a century now, and yet a large part of the transformation still lies ahead. The transition to renewable energies was triggered in 2000 by the resolution of the Renewable Energies Act (EEG), and the reactor disaster in Fukushima pushed the pace of the related phase-out of nuclear power eleven years later. Today, Germany has finished phasing out nuclear power, but the path to climate neutrality is still a long one. In order to achieve the target set in the EEG, renewable energy must account for a considerably higher proportion of gross energy consumption, rising from its current 52.5%[1] to 80% by 2030. To that end, the speed at which renewable energy is expanded needs to be increased by a factor of three.[2] The German federal government assigns a key role here to wind turbines, as they are at present and in the long term one of the most inexpensive energy technologies in Germany and can optimally be combined with photovoltaic sources.[3] The Onshore Wind Energy Law (WindBG), which came into

1 Cf. Bundesministerium für Wirtschaft und Klimaschutz (BMWK: Entwicklung der erneuerbaren Energien in Deutschland im Jahr 2023. Grafiken und Diagramme unter Verwendung aktueller Daten der Arbeitsgruppe Erneuerbare Energien-Statistik (AGEE-Stat; 2023); https://www.bmwk.de/Redaktion/DE/Downloads/Energie/entwicklung-dererneuerbaren-energien-in-deutschland-2023.pdf?__blob=publicationFile&v=10 (accessed 15 November 2024).

2 Cf. Bundesregierung: Fragen und Antworten zur Energiewende. Anteil der Erneuerbaren Energien steigt (2024); https://www.bundesregierung.de/breg-de/aktuelles/faq-energiewende-2067498 (accessed 15 November 2024).

3 Cf. Bundesministerium für Wirtschaft und Klimaschutz (BMWK): Windenergie-an-Land-Strategie – Wir stellen die Weichen für 160 Gigawatt Wind an Land bis 2035 (2023); https://www.bmwk.de/Redaktion/DE/Publikationen/Energie/windenergie-an-land-strategie.pdf?__blob=publicationFile&v=11 (accessed 11 August 2023).

stellt in diesem Zusammenhang das im Februar 2023 in Kraft getretene Windenergieflächenbedarfsgesetz (WindBG, auch „Wind-an-Land-Gesetz") dar. Es gibt den Ländern verbindliche Flächenziele für den Ausbau der Windenergie bis 2032 vor, die je nach Bundesland zwischen 1,8 und 2,2 Prozent der Landesfläche variieren. Vor diesem Hintergrund werden in den kommenden Jahren deutlich mehr Flächen allein für die Nutzung von Windenergie an Land ausgewiesen werden müssen. Da Anlagen zur Erzeugung erneuerbarer Energien einen großen visuellen Einfluss auf ihr Umfeld haben, ist die Energiewende ebenso ein wesentlicher Faktor des Landschaftswandels – gestern wie heute.[4]

Das heißt, dass sich die Frage nach der Gestaltung im Zusammenhang mit klimafreundlicher Energie nicht nur für die Architektur stellt und nicht allein in bebauten Räumen. Sie bedeutet zugleich eine Herausforderung für den Freiraum: Auch hier gilt es, dem gestalterischen Anspruch bei der Umsetzung der Energiewende gerecht zu werden. Windkraft- und Solaranlagen, aber auch der Anbau von Biomasse haben über sogenannte Wirkfaktoren Auswirkungen auf das Landschaftsbild, die in hohem Maß abhängig von der spezifischen Empfindlichkeit des landschaftlichen Umfeldes sind.(Abb. 1) Die Wirkfaktoren beziehen sich dabei auf die bloße Anwesenheit (anlagebedingte Faktoren) und den Betrieb (betriebsbedingte Faktoren). Aber auch der räumlich-gestalterische Umgang, also die Anzahl und Anordnung der Anlagen stellt eine Gruppe von Faktoren dar, die die Wirkung beeinflussen. Während erstere, zu denen die Formgebung, die Dimension, die Bewegung der Rotoren oder der Schattenwurf zählen, durch ihre technogene Anmutung

4 Vgl. Schmidt et al., Landschaftsbild und Energiewende. Ergebnisse des gleichnamigen Forschungsvorhabens FKZ 3515823400 im Auftrag des Bundesamtes für Naturschutz, Bd. 1: Grundlagen, Bonn/Bad Godesberg 2017, S. 7.

force in February 2023, has doubtless stimulated this. It specifies binding state-level land allocation targets for the expansion of wind power through 2032; these targets vary across the larger states, ranging from 1.8% to 2.2% of the total land area. In this context, considerably more land will need to be allocated solely for use by onshore wind farms in the coming years. Since plants that generate renewable energy have a high visual impact on the surrounding countryside, the energy transition has been and still is a key factor driving the change in the countryside.[4]

In other words, the question of design in connection with climate-friendly energy arises not just in relation to architecture and not only in built-up areas. It also constitutes a challenge for open spaces, and design standards need to be met in the realisation of the energy transition, too. Whether they generate wind power, solar power, or exploit biomass, these plants have an impact on the countryside via so-called effect factors, depending to a large degree on the specific sensitivity of the local countryside.(fig. 1) The effect factors relate here to the mere presence (plant-related factors) and to operations (operational factors). That said, the spatial-design approach, meaning the number and layout of the plants, encompasses a group of factors that influence the impact. Plant- and operations-related effect factors (which include shape, size, movement of rotors, and shading) all cause a change in the specifics of the seemingly natural or historical, nurtured countryside in particular, owing to their technological feel. The effect factors of the spatial-design approach, by contrast, offer an opportunity for designing in a countryside-compatible idiom. For example, in the case of wind turbines, a deliberate

4 Cf. Schmidt et al., Landschaftsbild und Energiewende. Ergebnisse des gleichnamigen Forschungsvorhabens FKZ 3515823400 im Auftrag des Bundesamtes für Naturschutz, vol. 1: Grundlagen (Bonn/Bad Godesberg, 2017), p. 7.

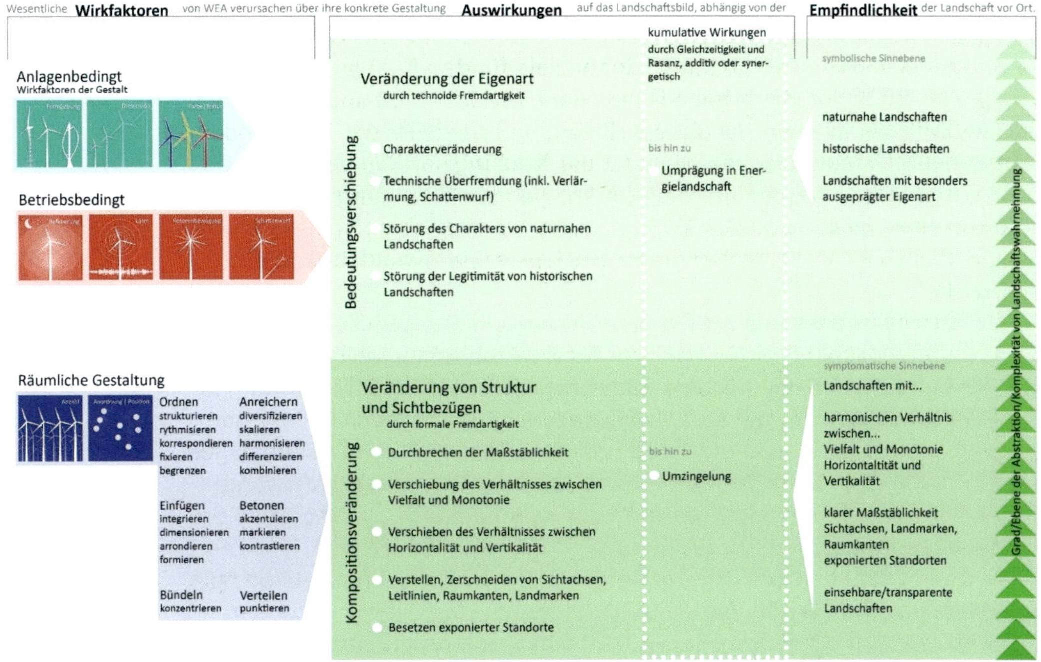

Abb. 1 Wesentliche landschaftsästhetische Wirkfaktoren von Windenergieanlagen |
Fig. 1 Key factors determining the aesthetic impact of landscaping for wind farms

choice of layout can ensure that the turbines are designed to emphasise aspects of the countryside, such as existing lines of vision, transitions, or eye-catching points. This means that, while it is not possible to use a design approach to prevent changes to the specifics of sensitive countryside by the erection of wind turbines, in less sensitive settings the design can have a favourable influence. To this end, however, two conditions must be met: On the one hand, the change must entail a conscious and recognizable design thrust that responds to the specific qualities of the countryside, such as lines of vision, landmarks, or borderlines. On the other hand, only such countryside comes into question that does not have an especially pronounced, seemingly natural or historically nature-specific feel to it. Even if these design options do not lead to renewable-energy power plants being hidden in the country-side, precisely their visual dominance and the related impact on the face of the countryside would speak in favour of their being deployed in line with a conscious design idea derived from the particular countryside.

This design focus contrasts in practice with the fact that the distribution of power plants from renewable energy sources in open spaces is subject to a series of legal and technical restrictions, such that the final shape of the corresponding sites leaves little scope for design. Nevertheless, there are design ideas as to how the plants can be shaped in order to do justice to the particular landscape. By way of example, here I would like to describe a cross-university student competition for the “Oederan Energy Landscaping” held in 2016 in the context of the “Face of the Countryside & the Energy Transition” research project. Students at the University of Kassel and the Dresden

eine Veränderung der Eigenart insbesondere von natürlich erscheinenden oder historisch gewachsenen Landschaften herbeiführen, bieten die räumlich-gestalterischen Wirkfaktoren eine Chance für landschaftsverträglicheres Design. So eröffnet beispielsweise bei Windrädern eine bewusste Anordnung Möglichkeiten, mit denen sie sich gestalterisch als Betonung einsetzen lassen, etwa durch den Bezug auf bereits vorhandene Linien, Übergänge oder markante Punkte. Das heißt, während eine Veränderung der Eigenart durch Windenergieanlagen in entsprechend sensiblen Landschaften auch durch einen gestalterischen Ansatz nicht zu verhindern ist, kann die Gestaltung in einem weniger empfindlichen Umfeld eine positive Wirkung haben. Dafür müssen allerdings zwei Voraussetzungen erfüllt sein: Einerseits muss diese Veränderung mit einem bewussten und erkennbaren Gestaltungswillen einhergehen, der auf landschaftliche Eigenheiten wie Sichtachsen, Landmarken, Raumkanten reagiert. Außerdem kommen nur solche Landschaften in Frage, die keine besonders ausgeprägte natürlich anmutende oder historisch gewachsene Eigenart aufweisen. Auch wenn diese gestalterischen Möglichkeiten nicht dazu führen, dass sich Anlagen zur Erzeugung erneuerbarer Energien verstecken lassen, spricht gerade ihre visuelle Dominanz und der damit verbundene Einfluss auf das Landschaftsbild dafür, sie im Sinne einer bewussten, aus der jeweiligen Umgebung abgeleiteten Gestaltungsidee einzusetzen.

Diesem Anspruch steht in der Praxis entgegen, dass die Verteilung der Anlagen im Freiraum einer Reihe von rechtlichen und fachlichen Einschränkungen unterliegt, sodass letztendlich bei der Ausgestaltung der

University of Technology addressed the task in a design study that looked at incorporating a renewable-energy plant into the countryside for a predefined volume of energy to supply the community of Oederan in Saxony, and doing so in such a way that not only was the requisite volume of energy considered, but ecological, legal, and in particular aesthetic criteria were also taken into account. The object was to explore whether energy transition projects could be staged in terms of landscape architecture.[5] The jury deemed the proposals then submitted to be extraordinarily diverse and creative, in particular as regards combining innovation and tradition, and unique aspects of the nurtured countryside were highlighted. The latter was a method successfully applied in many of the proposals. The use of synergies and tying in participatory methods also proved conducive to good outcomes. For example, the proposal entitled *Landschaft ma(h)len* by Maren Zipperlen marvellously references the long-standing nurtured countryside by locking into names and sites of former mills and resorting to planting energy crops on historical farming fields in order to breathe new life into the typical picture of ancient farming villages.(fig. 2) The proposal by Mary Meier, meanwhile, paid special attention to multiple uses for the renewable-energy plants. In particular, linking the potential for activities and the presence of renewable-energy plants is inspiring, and on the basis of a well-thought-out analysis it was tailored to specific target groups.(fig. 3) Carolin Gallacher's proposal, by contrast, was persuasive thanks to her focus on grasping the windfarm as a park in the literal sense, while incorporating the experience of the wind. The study relied on a very inspiring graphic that highlights in a quite unprecedented manner the design

5 Cf. ibid., pp. 205ff.

entsprechenden Gebiete wenig gestalterischer Spielraum besteht. Dennoch gibt es Entwurfsideen, wie eine landschaftsgerechte Gestaltung aussehen kann. Hier soll beispielhaft auf die Beiträge zum hochschulübergreifenden studentischen Wettbewerb „Energielandschaft Oederan" eingegangen werden, der 2016 im Rahmen des Forschungsvorhabens „Landschaftsbild & Energiewende" durchgeführt wurde. Studierende der Universität Kassel und der Technischen Universität Dresden stellten sich dabei der Aufgabe, für die sächsische Gemeinde Oederan hinsichtlich eines vorab definierten Energiebedarfs in einer entwurflichen Arbeit erneuerbare Energien so in die Landschaft einzubinden, dass neben dem zu erreichenden Energieerzeugungsziel auch ökologische, rechtliche und insbesondere ästhetische Aspekte berücksichtigt werden. Es galt zu ergründen, ob Vorhaben der Energiewende landschaftsarchitektonisch inszeniert werden können.[5] Die eingereichten Arbeiten wurden von der Jury als außerordentlich vielfältig und ideenreich eingeschätzt. Insbesondere die Verknüpfung von Innovation und Tradition durch die Inszenierung von kulturlandschaftlicher Eigenart war ein Ansatz, der in vielen der Arbeiten erfolgreich angewendet wurde. Auch die Nutzung von Synergieeffekten und die Verknüpfung mit partizipativen Ansätzen erwiesen sich als zielführend. So besitzt etwa die Arbeit *Landschaft ma(h)len* von Maren Zipperlen einen herausragenden kulturlandschaftlichen Bezug, indem sie Namen und Standorte ehemaliger Mühlen aufgreift und beim Anbau von Energiepflanzen auf historische Ackerschlagstrukturen zurückgreift, um das typische Bild der Waldhufendörfer neu zu beleben.(Abb. 2) Ein besonderes Augenmerk auf die Mehrfachnutzung von Anlagen für erneuerbare Energien

5 Vgl. ebd., S. 205ff.

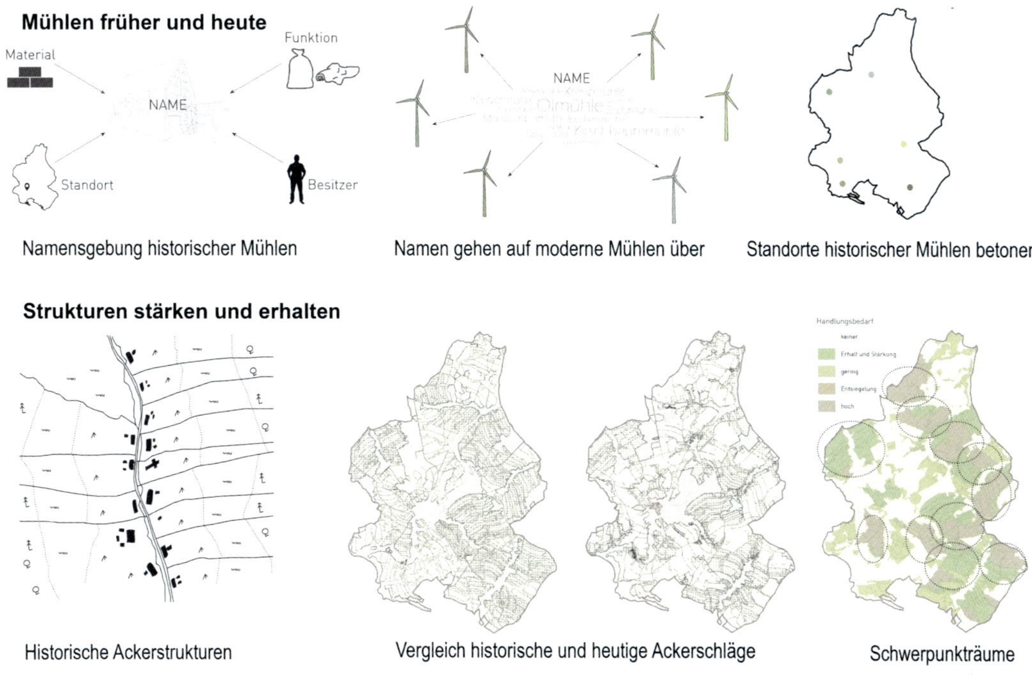

Abb. 2 Ausschnitt aus der Arbeit *Landschaft ma(h)len* von Maren Zipperlen (1. Preis im Wettbewerb) | Fig. 2 Extract from the project "Landschaft ma(h)len" by Maren Zipperlen (awarded first prize)

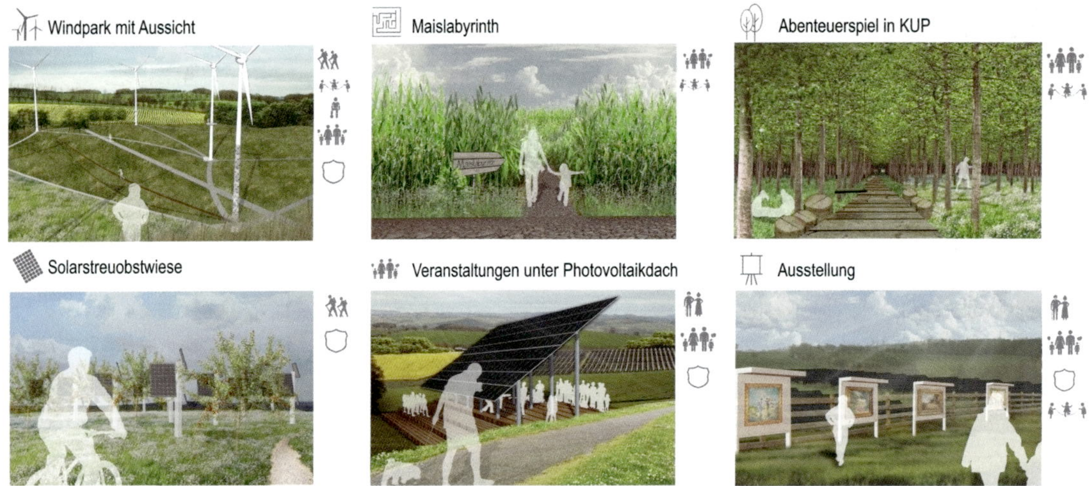

Abb. 3 Ausschnitt aus der Arbeit *Energie Erleben* von Mary Meier (2. Preis im Wettbewerb) |
Fig. 3 Extract from the project "Energie Erleben" by Mary Meier (awarded second prize)

Abb. 4 Visualisierung aus der Arbeit *Windpark* von Carolin Gallacher (3. Preis im Wettbewerb) |
Fig. 4 Visualisation from the project "Windpark" by Carolin Gallacher (awarded third prize)

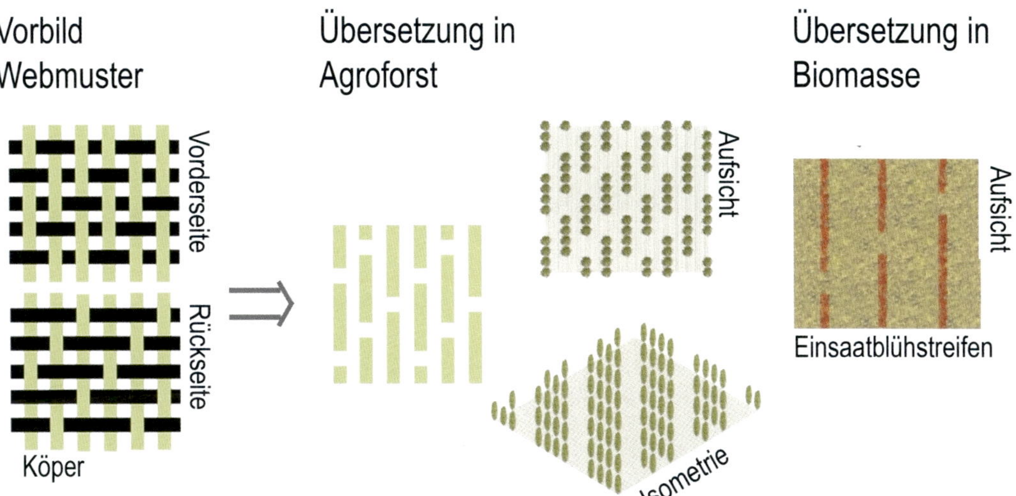

Abb. 5 | Fig. 5 Verknüpfung von Tradition mit Innovation durch die Übersetzung historischer Webmuster in Agroforst- und Biomasseanbauflächen, Entwurfsbeitrag von Ulrike Schmidt | Linking tradition and innovation by translating historical weave patterns into agroforestry and biomass areas—in the proposal by Ulrike Schmidt

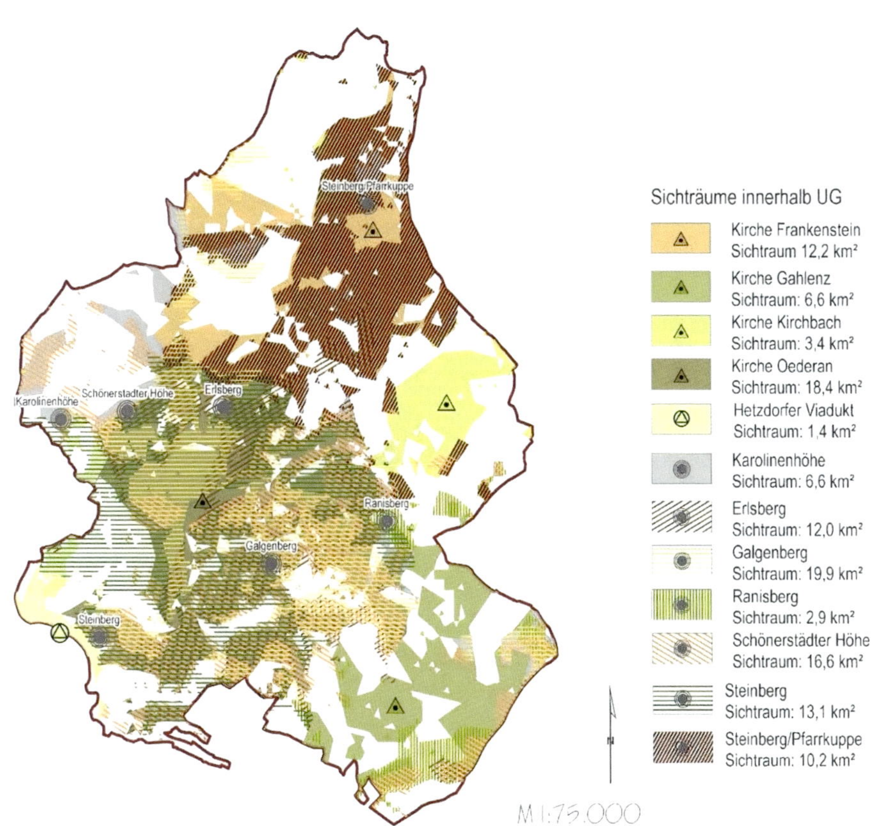

Abb. 6 | Fig. 6 Einsatz von GIS-basierten Sichtraumanalysen für natur- und kulturbedingte Landschaftselemente im Untersuchungsraum, Entwurfsbeitrag von Mary Meier | Use of GIS-based visual spatial analysis for nature and culture-determined landscaping elements in the area being studied in the proposal by Mary Meier

setzt die Arbeit von Mary Meier. Insbesondere die Verknüpfung des Potenzials für Aktivitäten und den Aufenthalt von Erneuerbaren ist inspirierend, wobei dies durch eine gut durchgearbeitete Analyse auch auf spezifische Zielgruppen zugeschnitten werden konnte.(Abb. 3) Die Arbeit von Carolin Gallacher überzeugt hingegen mit dem Anspruch, über das Erlebnis des Windes einen *Windpark* als Park im eigentlichen Sinne zu verstehen. Dabei bedient sich die Arbeit einer überaus inspirierenden Grafik, die das entwerferische Potenzial im Umgang mit diversen Anlagen wie keine andere herausstellt. Für die Jury stellte es einen fruchtbaren Impuls dar, Energielandschaften aus einem Blickwinkel zu betrachten, der dem Landschaftsbild in besonderer Weise gerecht wird.(Abb. 4)

Aus den Ergebnissen des Wettbewerbs lassen sich Impulse für die Gestaltung neuer Energielandschaften ableiten, die mit der aktuellen Beschleunigung des Ausbaus wieder von besonderer Relevanz sind:[6] Das **Aufgreifen von kulturlandschaftlicher Eigenart,** auf der materiellen wie auf der assoziativen Ebene, ist eine Möglichkeit, Tradition mit Innovation, gewachsene Besonderheiten des Umfeldes mit modernen Nutzungen zu verknüpfen. Der gestaltete Wandel könnte so eine Inszenierung von verblassenden landschaftlichen Zusammenhängen sein. Beispielsweise wurden in der Arbeit von Ulrike Schmidt die im Entwurfsgebiet tradierte Weberei und deren Webmuster als Inspiration für die Struktur von Pflanzungen genutzt.(Abb. 5) Auch birgt die **Mehrfachnutzung** ein großes Potenzial für die Gestaltung. Die genannten Arbeiten werfen insbesondere ein Licht auf die damit verbundene Möglichkeit, Energielandschaften erlebbar zu machen. Die Entwürfe setzten

6 Vgl. ebd., S. 208ff.

potential that lies in renewable-energy power plants. The jury felt this was a fruitful way of stimulating a consideration of energy systems in a manner that did special justice to the face of the countryside.(fig. 4)

We can derive various ideas for the design of new energy worlds from the results of the competition, findings that are of special relevance when it comes to speeding up the pace of installing such a plant:[6] **Resorting to the specifics of the nurtured countryside,** at both the material and the associative levels, is one way of linking tradition and innovation, long-standing specifics of the countryside, and modern usages. The designed transition can thus offer a way of staging slowly fading aspects of the countryside. For example, Ulrike Schmidt's proposal took the tradition of weaving and the woven patterns in the respective region as inspiration for the structure of plant crops.(fig. 5) The **multiple use** of land also affords great design potential. The student proposals mentioned all highlight in particular the related opportunity for enabling us to experience energy systems in the countryside. The projects focused intensively on the **visual impact of the design.** For example, GIS-driven analyses of the visual space were deployed in relation to both the impact of the new plant and the existing, defining landscape elements.(fig. 6) Although criticism could justifiably be levelled at all the proposed ideas, for example with respect to their ability to be realised or the approach to certain energy crops, the results nevertheless illustrate that it is also worthwhile searching for design answers to the question of how we approach renewable-energy plants in open spaces.

6 Cf. Ibid., pp. 208ff.

sich zudem intensiv mit der **Sichtwirkung ihrer Gestaltung** auseinander. So wurden GIS-gestützte Sichtraumanalysen eingesetzt, sowohl in Bezug auf die Wirkung der neuen Anlagen als auch von bestehenden, prägenden Landschaftselementen.(Abb. 6) Selbst wenn bei allen Entwurfsideen berechtigte Kritik bestand, etwa hinsichtlich der Umsetzbarkeit oder beim Umgang mit bestimmten Energiepflanzen, zeigen die Ergebnisse doch, dass es sich lohnt, auf die Frage nach dem Umgang mit erneuerbaren Energien im Freiraum auch gestalterische Antworten zu suchen.

Energieberg Georgswerder
Energy mountain Georgswerder

Hamburg, Deutschland
Hamburg, Germany

Bauaufgabe | Task
Öffentliche Erschließung und Einrichtung einer Aussichtspromenade auf einer gesicherten Deponie, die mit Nutzung der Abgase, Windkraft- und Photovoltaikanlagen durch die BSU zu einem „Energieberg“ entwickelt wurde | Public development and establishment of a viewing promenade on a secured landfill site, which was developed into an "energy mountain" by the Ministry for Urban Development and the Environment using exhaust gases, wind power, and photovoltaic systems

Entwurf Landschaft | Landscape design
häfner jiménez betcke jarosch landschaftsarchitektur, Berlin

Auftrag | Client
Behörde für Stadtentwicklung und Umwelt Hamburg

Fertigstellung | Completion
2013

Finanzierung | Financing
Öffentliche Mittel | Public funding

Lageplan | Site plan

Der Berg in Georgswerder ist eine stillgelegte, gesicherte Mülldeponie, auf der bis 1979 Bauschutt, Haus- und Industrieabfälle abgelegt wurden – Symbol für den ehemals sorglosen Umgang mit der Umwelt und entsprechend negativem Image. Als Teil der Internationalen Bauausstellung Hamburg ist er nun als „Energieberg" für das Publikum geöffnet. Erschlossen durch Wege, Treppen und vor allem den erhöhten Horizontweg mit seiner signifikanten Form eröffnen sich spektakuläre Blicke über Landschaft, Stadt und Hafen. Der Berg wandelte sich zu einem Ausflugsziel, das die Geschichte der Deponie und ihrer Transformation zum Energieberg veranschaulicht. Ergänzt wird das Projekt durch ein Ausstellungsgebäude und eine Ausstellung, die sich mittels verschiedener Medien vom Innenraum bis auf den Horizontweg erstreckt. Nachts macht die Außenfläche der Reling des Weges den Berg zur weithin sichtbaren Landmarke.

The hill in the Georgswerder district of Hamburg is an inoperative, secured landfill site where construction waste as well as domestic and industrial waste were deposited until 1979—a symbol of the careless treatment of the environment and a correspondingly poor image for the city. As part of the International Building Exhibition in Hamburg, it has now been opened to the public as an "energy mountain". With paths, steps, and especially the elevated Horizon Path, it offers spectacular views over the countryside, city, and harbour. The project has transformed the hill into a tourist attraction where the history of the landfill and its transformation are vividly demonstrated. A visitor centre and exhibition presents the project through various media, extending from the Horizon Path to the interior. At night, the railing's outer surface makes the hill a widely visible landmark.

DAM **Was finden Sie besonders gelungen an Ihrem Projekt?**
häfner jiménez betcke jarosch Der Horizontweg als Aufenthalts- und Bewegungsort funktioniert auch als horizontale Landmarke, eröffnet Ausblicke und fördert den Imagewechsel des Berges.

DAM **Was war Ihnen bei der Erarbeitung des Projektes wichtig?**
häfner jiménez betcke jarosch Geringe Eingriffe in die Substanz und Oberflächenvegetation des Berges, einer gesicherten Deponie.

DAM **Was würden Sie beim nächsten Mal anders machen?**
häfner jiménez betcke jarosch Die Beleuchtung des Horizontwegs ausschließlich aus vor Ort erzeugter Energie sicherstellen.

DAM **What do you find particularly successful about your project?**
häfner jiménez betcke jarosch The Horizon Path as a place to linger and exercise also functions as a horizontal landmark, opening up views and helping to change the image of the area.

DAM **What was important to you when developing the project?**
häfner jiménez betcke jarosch Minimal intervention in the substance and surface vegetation of the hill, a secured landfill site.

DAM **What would you do differently next time?**
häfner jiménez betcke jarosch Ensure that the lighting for the Horizon Trail is powered exclusively by energy generated on site.

Platz an der Basilika Saint-Sernin
Public space by the Saint-Sernin Basilica

Toulouse, Frankreich
Toulouse, France

Bauaufgabe | Task
Umgestaltung der Freiflächen des zwei Hektar großen Geländes um die Basilika Saint-Sernin | Redesign of the two-hectare public space by the Saint-Sernin Basilica

Entwurf Landschaft | Design landscape
BAU – B. Arquitectura | Urbanisme, Barcelona + MDP Michel Desvigne Paysagiste, Paris

Auftrag | Client
Toulouse Métropole

Fertigstellung | Completion
2020

Finanzierung | Financing
Öffentliche Mittel | Public funding

Die imposante Basilika Saint-Sernin ist ein Meisterwerk der romanischen Baukunst und gehört zum UNESCO-Weltkulturerbe. Jahrelang wurde ihre Pracht durch einen weitläufigen asphaltierten Parkplatz überdeckt, der eine unansehnliche städtische Wärmeinsel im historischen Stadtzentrum bildete. Die Neugestaltung dieses einzigartigen öffentlichen Raumes stellt die Bedeutung der Basilika heraus, indem sie den Zugang für Fußgänger priorisiert, natürliche Elemente wieder einführt und die Alltagserfahrung der Menschen verbessert. Der Boden besteht aus grauen Porphyrpflastersteinen, Kalkstein aus Comblanchien und Schotter; die Materialien wurden so ausgewählt, dass sie die Aufheizung durch Sonneneinstrahlung minimieren. Die Natursteine spiegeln das Erbe des Ortes

wider und sorgen mit ihren unterschiedlichen Mustern und Texturen für eine besondere Atmosphäre auf dem Platz. Darüber hinaus bilden der erweiterte und überarbeitete Apsidengarten und der neu gestaltete mittelalterliche Kreuzgang offene Grünflächen. Der höher gelegene Kiesboden, auf dem einst das Palais Abbatial stand, bietet einen schattigen Bereich, der zu gelegentlichen Boule-Spielen und zur weiteren gemeinschaftlichen Nutzung einlädt. Insgesamt verbesserte sich die Durchlässigkeit des Bodens erheblich, sodass Wasser versickern kann und die Oberflächentemperaturen sinken. Es wurden 82 neue Bäume gepflanzt, ausgewählt nach ihrer Widerstandsfähigkeit gegenüber den örtlichen Bedingungen. Sie bilden den Grundriss des ehemaligen Abteigebäudes nach und spenden im Sommer Schatten und Abkühlung, während sie im Winter das Sonnenlicht durchlassen. Die Vegetation kühlt nicht nur den Bereich, sie reinigt gleichzeitig die Luft und verbessert ihre Qualität. Mit der Zeit wird das wachsende Grün den Platz weiter bereichern. Ein neugebauter Brunnen sorgt für Verdunstungskühlung und erzeugt angenehme Hintergrundgeräusche, was den akustischen Komfort erhöht.

The imposing Basilica of Saint-Sernin is a masterpiece of Romanesque architecture and is listed as a UNESCO World Heritage Site. For years, its grandeur was obscured by a sprawling asphalted parking lot, creating an unsightly urban heat island in the historic city centre. The redesign of this unique public space restores the basilica's significance by prioritising pedestrian access, reintroducing natural elements, and enhancing the day-to-day human experience.

The ground features grey porphyry pavers, Comblanchien limestone, and crushed gravel, materials chosen to minimise solar absorption. These natural stones echo the site's heritage, with varied patterns and textures that enhance the distinct atmosphere within the plaza. Additionally, open green spaces are formed by the expanded and redesigned apsidal garden and the reimagined medieval cloister. The "raised gravel ground", where the Palais Abbatial once stood, offers a shaded area that encourages casual games of pétanque, further inviting community use. Altogether these changes substantially improve the permeability of the soil, allowing water to percolate and lowering surface temperatures.

In total, eighty-two new trees have been planted, selected for their resilience to local conditions. These trees form the ground plan of the former abbey building and provide shade and cooling in summer while allowing sunlight to filter through in winter. The vegetation not only cools the area but also purifies the air, improving atmospheric quality. Over time, the maturing greenery will further enrich the space. A new fountain adds evaporative cooling and generates pleasant background sounds, enhancing acoustic comfort.

DAM **Was finden Sie an Ihrem Projekt besonders bemerkenswert?**

BAU Die Place Saint-Sernin ist zu einem vielseitigen öffentlichen Platz geworden, der die städtische Hitze mildert und eine einladende Umgebung für verschiedene Nutzungsmöglichkeiten bietet. Die Kombination aus der Einfachheit des Entwurfs, der Verwendung von für die Region charakteristischen Materialien und der Anerkennung des außergewöhnlichen kulturellen Erbes des Ortes machen dieses Projekt zu etwas Einzigartigem, das es geschafft hat, einen Raum, der einst von Autos eingenommen war, neu zu beleben und für die Bürger der Stadt zurückzugewinnen.

DAM Welche Aspekte waren Ihnen bei der Entwicklung des Projektes wichtig?
BAU Ein Gleichgewicht zu finden zwischen der Würdigung der historischen Bedeutung dieses monumentalen Ortes und der Schaffung eines neuen städtischen öffentlichen Raumes, der die Lebensqualität der Menschen erhöht (anpassungsfähig für verschiedene Nutzungen wie spielen, entspannen, treffen etc.) und gleichzeitig die atmosphärischen und klimatischen Bedingungen für das umliegende dichte historische Viertel verbessert.

DAM What do you find particularly remarkable about your project?
BAU Place Saint-Sernin has become a versatile public square that mitigates urban heat, providing a welcoming environment for varied uses. The simplicity of the proposal, the use of materials characteristic of the surroundings, and the recognition of the exceptional heritage value of the site make this a unique project that has succeeded in reactivating a space that was once taken over by vehicles, recovering it for use by the city's residents.

DAM Which aspects were important to you when developing the project?
BAU Striking a balance between honouring the historic significance of this monumental site and creating a new urban public space that enhances users' quality of life (adaptable for various uses—play, relaxation, gathering, and more) while also improving atmospheric and climatic conditions for the surrounding dense historic neighbourhood.

Stadtplanung aus der Landschaft heraus denken

Interview mit | with Andrea Gebhard

Stadtplanerin sowie Landschaftsarchitektin und Präsidentin der Bundesarchitektenkammer

Urban planner, landscape architect, and President of the German Federal Chamber of Architects

Thoughtful landscape-based urban planning

DAM Hat sich das Bewusstsein für Energiesparen gewandelt und führt das zu einem neuen Verständnis des Bauens?
Andrea Gebhard Ja, das Bewusstsein hat sich stark verändert. Die Klimakrise ist offensichtlich – denken Sie an die vermehrt auftretenden Starkregenereignisse. Es geht darum, unseren CO_2-Ausstoß zu reduzieren. Im Bauen sind wir einen großen Schritt weitergekommen, zum Beispiel durch die Einführung der Umbauordnung. Es gibt viele Möglichkeiten, Energie selbst zu erzeugen, wie im Ort Wildpoldsried, der weitaus mehr Energie produziert als er benötigt. Leider hat die Politik noch nicht überall erkannt, wie wichtig die Energiewende ist, vor allem beim Bauen.

DAM Has awareness around energy efficiency grown, and has this led to a new understanding of construction?
Andrea Gebhard Yes, overall awareness has changed significantly. The climate crisis is obvious for all to see—just think of the increase in torrential storms. The focus must be on reducing our CO_2 emissions. We've made real progress in the field of construction, for example with the introduction of the Conversion Decree. There are many different options for generating energy yourself, as the example of the township of Wildpoldsried shows. After all, it produces much more energy than it requires. Unfortunately, politicians have not yet realised how important the energy transition is everywhere, especially in the construction sector.

„Wir müssen weniger überbordende Technik einbauen und uns auf einfachere Lösungen konzentrieren“

DAM Wie definieren Sie persönlich den Umgang mit Energie?

AG Wichtig ist, sich zu überlegen, wie viel Energie wir bei verschiedenen Tätigkeiten verbrauchen und wie wir sie anders erwirtschaften können, sei es durch Solar-, Wind- oder Wasserkraft. Die zweite Möglichkeit ist es, Energie einzusparen. Wenn wir beides kombinieren, können wir große Veränderungen erreichen.

DAM Haben wir im Bauwesen zu viel Wert auf Energieeffizienz gelegt und die Emissionen vernachlässigt?

AG Rückblickend können wir sagen, dass der Fokus nicht ganz richtig war. Statt immer mehr Technik und Dämmung zu verwenden, sollten wir auf einfacheres Bauen setzen. Wie viel Technik brauchen wir wirklich? Eine Anekdote: In einem Holzgebäude in Berlin, in dem die Lüftung noch nicht funktionierte, öffneten wir einfach die Fenster – und es hat niemanden gestört. Wir müssen weniger überbordende Technik einbauen und uns auf einfachere Lösungen konzentrieren.

DAM Welche politischen Impulse wünschen Sie sich auf diesem Weg?

AG Ich wünsche mir eine enge Zusammenarbeit, insbesondere mit dem Wirtschaftsministerium, um den Umgang mit Energie und Baustoffen ehrlich und umfassend anzugehen. Wir müssen Materialströme genau betrachten, besonders beim Einsatz von Holz. Es ist wichtig, die Herkunft der Materialien zu hinterfragen.

DAM How do you personally define our approach to energy?

AG It is important to consider how much energy we consume in various activities and how we could generate that amount differently, be it from solar, wind, or hydropower. The second option is to save energy. If we combine the two, we can bring about major changes.

DAM Have we attached too much importance to energy efficiency in the construction sector and neglected emission levels?

AG Looking back, we could say that the focus was not exactly right. Instead of using ever-increasing quantities of technology and insulation, we should prioritise building simply. How much technology do we really need? I'd like to cite an anecdote in this context: In a wooden building in Berlin where the ventilation did not yet function, we simply opened the windows, and nobody minded. We need to concentrate less on installing excessive technology and instead opt for more simple solutions.

DAM What political action would you like to see for this?

AG I would like to see close cooperation in particular with the Ministry of Economic Affairs in order to tackle how we approach energy and construction materials honestly and comprehensively. We need to study the material flows accurately, especially the use of wood. It is essential to question where materials come from.

DAM How do you rate the conflict between low-emission construction and the need to create more housing, especially in cities such as Munich?

DAM Wie bewerten Sie den Konflikt zwischen emissionsarmem Bauen und der Notwendigkeit, neuen Wohnraum zu schaffen, besonders in Städten wie München?

AG Wir müssen neu überlegen, wie wir bauen. Wie groß müssen Wohnungen sein, und wie viele Gemeinschaftsflächen können wir entwickeln? Wir brauchen Kataster der Potenziale, um Flächen besser zu nutzen. Das bedeutet, auch gemeinschaftliche Wohnlösungen zu entwickeln. Einfamilienhäuser sind oft nicht zukunftsfähig, wenn ältere Menschen darin allein bleiben. Wir sollten gemeinschaftlich denken – große Waschküchen oder Gärten teilen, wie in früheren Zeiten. Das wäre auch eine Antwort auf soziale Probleme wie Einsamkeit.

DAM Als Stadtplanerin beschäftigen Sie sich mit der Klimaneutralität unserer Städte und Quartiere. Was sind dabei die dringendsten Aufgaben für die Landschaftsarchitektur?

AG Landschaftsarchitektur befasst sich mit allem, was außerhalb oder auf Gebäuden ist. Es ist entscheidend, Freiräume zu nutzen und die Stadtplanung stärker aus der Landschaft heraus zu denken. Wir haben ein Freiraumquartierkonzept für München entwickelt, das zeigt, wo diese Freiräume liegen und wie wir sie nutzen können. Themen wie Denkmalschutz und Grün müssen neu betrachtet werden, und die Zusammenarbeit zwischen der Architekturplanung, der Landschaftsarchitektur und der Stadtplanung ist dabei entscheidend.

DAM Wie können Fachplanende Einfluss auf Windparks und Solarfelder nehmen und die Akzeptanz für die Klimawende erhöhen?

AG We need to rethink how we construct things. How big must apartments be and how many communal areas can we develop? We need a cadastral record of what is available in order to better use existing space. That means we must also develop communal housing solutions. Detached homes will often not be viable going forward, if older people end up living there on their own. We should think in terms of community—sharing large laundry rooms or gardens, as was once the case. That would itself also be an answer to social problems such as loneliness.

DAM As an urban planner, you concern yourself with the climate neutrality of our cities and neighbourhoods. What are the really urgent tasks as regards landscape architecture?

AG Landscape architecture addresses everything that is outside or on buildings. It is crucial that we make use of outdoor spaces, and that urban planning is construed more strongly on the basis of the landscape. We developed a concept for outdoor spaces in neighbourhoods in Munich that shows where these outdoor spaces are and how they can be used. Topics such as heritage protection and greenery need to be revisited, and it is imperative that architects, landscape architects, and urban planners collaborate.

DAM How can specialist planners influence wind and solar farms and boost acceptance of the energy transition?

> “We need to concentrate less on installing excessive technology and instead opt for more simple solutions”

„Eine gute Landschaftsplanung, wie in Frankreich, kann die Akzeptanz von Windparks und Solaranlagen erhöhen“

AG Landschaftsplanung ist querschnittsorientiert und muss soziale und ökologische Aspekte gleichermaßen berücksichtigen. Landschaftspläne sind für alle Städte notwendig. Eine gute Planung, wie in Frankreich, kann die Akzeptanz von Windparks und Solaranlagen erhöhen. Es geht um einen holistischen Ansatz, bei dem wir alle Elemente – vom Moor bis zur Stadt – in unsere Planung einbeziehen.

DAM Verändert sich durch den Klimawandel der kulturelle Stellenwert von Architektur und Bauen?

AG Ja, Architektur und Stadtplanung gewinnen an Bedeutung. Leider ist uns bisher nicht gelungen, diesen Stellenwert in der Gesellschaft vollständig zu verankern. Wir arbeiten daran, Nachhaltigkeitsregister für Architektinnen und Architekten einzuführen, um deren Weiterbildung in diesem Bereich zu fördern. Der Beruf hat großes Potenzial, die Bauwende erfolgreich zu gestalten.

DAM Was bedeutet klimaschonendes Bauen für Sie in einem Wort?

AG Naturbasierte Lösungen.

DAM Haben Sie einen Tipp für Architekten und Bauende, die emissionsärmer und energieeffizienter bauen wollen?

AG Landscape planning is interdisciplinary in thrust and must equally consider social and ecological aspects. Landscape plans are necessary for all our cities. Good planning, such as in France, can enhance the acceptance of wind and solar farms. You require a holistic approach, where all the elements, from the marshlands to the city, are factored into the planning.

DAM Is climate change affecting the cultural significance of architecture and construction?

AG Yes, architecture and urban planning are becoming more important. Unfortunately, we have not yet ensured that society as a whole recognises this. We're working to introduce sustainability indexes for architects to promote advanced training in this field. The profession has great opportunities to successfully design the transition in the construction industry.

DAM To your mind, what does climate-friendly construction mean?

AG Nature-based solutions.

DAM Do you have a tip for architects and developers on how they can build in a way that causes fewer emissions and is more energy efficient?

AG Consult good architects and landscape architects in order to develop sustainable solutions together. Building Type E is an example of how we can cut

“Good planning, such as in France, can enhance the acceptance of wind and solar farms”

AG Sie sollen gute Fachleute für Architektur und Landschaftsarchitektur hinzuziehen, um gemeinsam nachhaltige Lösungen zu entwickeln. Der Gebäudetyp E ist ein Beispiel, wie wir sowohl Kosten als auch Energie sparen können. Es ist wichtig, dass wir Projekte nicht als Adler starten und als Spatz beenden.

DAM Was wünschen Sie sich von der nächsten Generation der Architekten und Ingenieure im Hinblick auf klimaschonendes Bauen?

AG Sie sollen das Potenzial erkennen und sehen, wie schön Städte und Gebäude werden können, wenn sie klimafreundliche Ansätze integrieren. Und dass sie so viel Freude an ihrer Arbeit haben wie ich.

costs and save energy. It is important that we do not start our projects as an eagle and finish as a sparrow.

DAM What would you like to see from the next generation of architects and engineers as regards climate-friendly construction?

AG They should recognise the potential and see how beautiful cities and buildings can be if they integrate climate-friendly methods. And that they can have as much fun with their work as I do.

Wildpoldsried, Deutschland

Wildpoldsried ist eine Gemeinde im Landkreis Oberallgäu mit rund 2.600 Einwohnern. Bekannt geworden ist sie als Energiedorf, das ca. 60 Prozent des Wärme- und mehr als 800 Prozent des Strombedarfs des Ortes regenerativ erzeugt.

So sind mittlerweile über 400 Bürgerinnen und Bürger (nur Einwohner von Wildpoldsried) an Windkraftanlagen beteiligt; 125 Privathäuser, alle öffentlichen Gebäude und 8 Betriebe werden mit regenerativer Wärme aus der Dorfheizung versorgt; 160 thermische und mehr als 300 private Solaranlagen wurden installiert. Die Erträge aus diesen Anlagen kommen fast ausschließlich Privatpersonen und örtlichen Vereinen der Gemeinde zugute.

Mit dem Energiemix aus Wind, Sonne, Biomasse und Wasser ist die Gemeinde jederzeit (auch an wind- und sonnenarmen Tagen) in der Lage, mehr als 100 Prozent des gesamten Energiebedarfs regenerativ abzudecken. Durch weitere Projekte zur Energieerzeugung ist es gelungen, nicht nur eine Wertschöpfung von mittlerweile rund 7 Millionen Euro pro Jahr für den Ort und seine Bürger zu erzielen, sondern auch zahlreiche Projekte zur Steigerung der Lebensqualität und Verbesserung der Infrastruktur umzusetzen.

Neben vielen erfolgreichen Umweltmaßnahmen zeichnet sich Wildpoldsried durch vorbildliche Projekte in den Bereichen Bürgerbeteiligung, Energieeinsparung, Verwendung regionaler Baustoffe und Energiebildung aus.

Wildpoldsried zeigt: Jedes kleine Dorf kann seine Entwicklung in die Zukunft selbst in die Hand nehmen. Was es dazu braucht, sind engagierte und motivierte Akteure, die mit Mut und Ausdauer einfach anfangen, sich Unterstützer suchen und sich nicht entmutigen lassen, ihre Visionen in die Tat umzusetzen.[1]

1 www.wildpoldsried.de

Wildpoldsried, Germany

Wildpoldsried is a township in Germany with about 2,600 inhabitants. Located in the district of Oberallgäu, it has become known as an "energy village" where about 60% of the heat and more than 800% of the electricity requirement is obtained from regenerative sources.

Today, over 400 citizens (all of them inhabitants of Wildpoldsried) have a stake in wind turbines; 125 private homes, all the public buildings, and eight commercial operations are supplied with regenerative heat from the village heating plant; and a total of 160 thermal and more than 300 private solar systems have been installed. The revenue from these facilities go almost exclusively to private individuals and clubs from the township.

With the energy mix of wind, solar, biomass, and hydropower, the community is able to cover more than 100% of its overall energy needs from regenerative sources at all times (even on days where there is little wind or solar). Thanks to additional energy generation projects, Wildpoldsried has managed not only to garner a total of some €7 million per year for the township and its citizens but also to realise countless projects to enhance the local quality of life and the infrastructure.

Alongside many successful eco-measures, Wildpoldsried stands out for exemplary projects in the fields of civic participation, energy saving, the use of regional construction materials, and energy generation.

Wildpoldsried shows that, in the future, every small village can take charge of its own development and destiny. What is needed are committed and motivated participants who have the courage and endurance to get started, look for supporters, and not get discouraged.[1]

1 www.wildpoldsried.de

Autoren und Autorinnen

Heinrich Bökamp ist Prüfingenieur für Baustatik und öffentlich bestellter und vereidigter Sachverständiger für konstruktiven Ingenieurbau. Seit 2009 ist er Präsident der Ingenieurkammer-Bau NRW und seit Oktober 2020 auch Präsident der Bundesingenieurkammer. Seit 2004 leitet er die Ingenieurgesellschaft Thomas & Bökamp in Münster.

Brian Cody ist Universitätsprofessor an der Technischen Universität Graz und leitet seit 2004 das Institut für Gebäude und Energie. Er ist Gründer und CEO des Beratungsunternehmens Energy Design Cody, das für die Entwicklung innovativer Energie- und Klimakonzepte für Bauprojekte weltweit verantwortlich ist.

Gustav Düsing ist Architekt in Berlin. Seine Arbeit wurde unter anderem mit dem EUMies Award ausgezeichnet. Seit 2024 ist er Professor für Experimentelles Entwerfen an der Universität der Künste Berlin.

Maxim von Gagern ist wissenschaftlicher Mitarbeiter an der TU Dresden, Lehrbeauftragter an der Hochschule Anhalt und er promovierte zu landschaftlicher Bildung.

Andrea Gebhard ist Stadtplanerin und Landschaftsarchitektin und langjährig berufspolitisch engagiert, u. a. im bdla und in der DASL. Seit 2012 ist sie Mitglied im Kuratorium für Nationale Stadtentwicklung. 2022 wurde sie als stellvertretende Vorsitzende in den Stiftungsrat der Bundesstiftung Baukultur gewählt. Seit 2022 ist sie Präsidentin der Bundesarchitektenkammer.

Oliver Geden ist Leiter des Forschungsclusters Klimapolitik der Stiftung Wissenschaft und Politik sowie Vize-Vorsitzender der IPCC-Arbeitsgruppe III.

Authors

Heinrich Bökamp is a test engineer for structural analysis as well as a publicly accredited and certified expert for structural engineering. Since 2009 he has been President of the Chamber of Construction of North Rhine-Westphalia and since October 2020 also President of the German Federal Chamber of Engineers. Since 2004, he has headed the Thomas & Bökamp engineering company in Münster.

Brian Cody is Professor at the Graz University of Technology and has been Director of the Institute of Buildings and Energy there since 2004. He is founder and CEO of the consultancy Energy Design Cody, which develops innovative energy and climate concepts for building projects the world over.

Gustav Düsing is a Berlin-based architect. He has won a European Union Prize for Contemporary Architecture, among other awards. Since 2024 he has been Professor of Experimental Design at the Berlin University of the Arts.

Maxim von Gagern is a research assistant at the Dresden University of Technology and a lecturer at Anhalt University of Applied Sciences. He received his PhD for a dissertation on landscape formation.

Andrea Gebhard is an urban planner and landscape architect. She has for many years been involved in policymaking in these professions at the German Federation of Landscape Architects and the German Academy for Urban and Land Planning, among other organisations. Since 2012 she has been a member of the Board of Trustees for National Urban Development. In 2022, she was elected Deputy Chair of the Foundation Council of the Federal Foundation for Built Culture. Since 2022 she has been President of the German Federal Chamber of Architects.

Andres Herzog ist Architekt, Publizist und Journalist. Er leitet die Kommunikation am Departement Architektur der ETH Zürich. 2021 hat er das Buch *Klima bauen. Ein Lexikon zu Architektur, Landschaftsarchitektur und Raumplanung unterwegs zu Netto-Null* herausgegeben.

Claudia Kemfert leitet seit 2004 die Abteilung Energie, Verkehr, Umwelt am Deutschen Institut für Wirtschaftsforschung und ist Professorin für Energiewirtschaft und Energiepolitik an der Leuphana Universität Lüneburg. Sie ist Co-Vorsitzende im Sachverständigenrat für Umweltfragen beim Bundesministerium für Umwelt, Naturschutz, Bau und Reaktorsicherheit sowie Mitglied im Präsidium der deutschen Gesellschaft des Club of Rome.

Regine Leibinger ist Mitbegründerin des Architekturbüros Barkow Leibinger, Gründerin der Experimental Foundation und lehrt derzeit an der Harvard University.

Werner Sobek ist Architekt und Bauingenieur. Er ist Gründer des Instituts für Leichtbau Entwerfen und Konstruieren (ILEK) der Universität Stuttgart und der Werner Sobek AG. Seine Arbeiten zeichnen sich durch ihre Gestaltung und ihre Konzepte zur Minimierung von Energie- und Materialverbrauch aus. Im Jahr 2022 wurde er von der Zeitschrift *Cicero* als einziger Architekt und Ingenieur in die Liste der 500 wichtigsten deutschsprachigen Intellektuellen aufgenommen.

Cord Soehlke leitete von 2001 bis 2010 das Stadtsanierungsamt der Universitätsstadt Tübingen, 2003 wurde er zudem Geschäftsführer der WIT, Geschäftsbereich Grundstücksentwicklung. Seit 2010 ist er Baubürgermeister der Universitätsstadt Tübingen. Im Februar 2018 wurde er für weitere acht Jahre im Amt bestätigt. Seit Oktober 2018 ist Soehlke auch Erster Bürgermeister der Universitätsstadt Tübingen.

Oliver Geden is Head of the Climate Policy and Politics Research Cluster at the German Institute for International and Security Affairs and Vice Chairperson of Working Group III in the Intergovernmental Panel on Climate Change (IPCC).

Andres Herzog is an architect, publicist, and journalist. He is Head of Communications at the Department of Architecture at ETH Zurich. In 2021, he edited the book *Klima bauen. Ein Lexikon zu Architektur, Landschaftsarchitektur und Raumplanung unterwegs zu Netto-Null* [Building climate: A lexicon of architecture, landscape architecture, and spatial planning on the path to net zero].

Claudia Kemfert has since 2004 been Head of the Department of Energy, Transportation, and Environment at the German Institute for Economic Research in Berlin and Professor of Energy Economics and Energy Policy at Leuphana University Lüneburg. She is Co-Chair of the Expert Council for Environmental Issues at the German Federal Ministry for the Environment, Nature Conservation, Building, and Nuclear Safety, as well as a member of the Executive Committee of the German Society of the Club of Rome.

Regine Leibinger is co-founder of the architecture practice Barkow Leibinger and founder of the Experimental Foundation. She currently teaches at Harvard University.

Werner Sobek is an architect and construction engineer. He is founder of the Institute for Lightweight Structures and Conceptual Design at Stuttgart University and of Werner Sobek AG. His works stand out for their design and concepts for minimising energy and materials consumption. In 2022, the magazine *Cicero* included him as the only architect and engineer in its list of the 500 most important intellectuals in Germany, Austria, and Switzerland.

Angèle Tersluisen promovierte an der TU Darmstadt und war Juniorprofessorin / apl. Professorin an der TU (heute RPTU) Kaiserslautern, Fachbereich Architektur, Fachgebiet Hauskybernetik, ab 2017 ee concept GmbH Darmstadt. Seit 2025 ist sie Professorin an der TU Berlin, Institut für Architektur, Fachgebiet Architektur, Gebäudetechnik und -systeme.

Katharina Volgger ist Architektin und Dozentin. Nach ihrer Zusammenarbeit mit verschiedenen Architekturbüros ist sie heute freiberuflich unter dem Namen katharinavolgger.studio in Berlin und Brixen/Bressanone (Italien) tätig. Seit Oktober 2024 ist sie zudem Gastdozentin im Fachgebiet Experimentelles Gestalten und Grundlagen des Entwerfens an der Universität der Künste Berlin.

Annette Becker
Kuratorin am Deutschen Architekturmuseum in Frankfurt am Main

Peter Cachola Schmal
Direktor des Deutschen Architekturmuseums in Frankfurt am Main

Kjell Reiter
Wissenschaftlicher Mitarbeiter am Deutschen Architekturmuseum in Frankfurt am Main

Cord Soehlke was Director of the Office of Urban Renewal at the University of Tübingen from 2001 to 2010. In 2003 he was also appointed Managing Director of the Real Estate Development Unit in Tübingen's business development corporation. Since 2010 he has been the city executive responsible for construction in Tübingen, and, in February 2018, he was reappointed to this position for a further eight years. Since October 2018, Soehlke has also been First Deputy Mayor of Tübingen.

Angèle Tersluisen was awarded a PhD at the Technical University of Darmstadt and was Junior and Extraordinary Professor at TU Kaiserslautern (now RPTU Kaiserslautern-Landau), Department of Architecture, House Cybernetics section. Since 2017 she has been with ee concept GmbH Darmstadt. In 2025, she was appointed professor at the Technical University Berlin, Institute of Architecture, Department of Architecture, Facilities Technology and Systems.

Katharina Volgger is an architect and lecturer. After working with various architecture practices, today she works freelance under the name of katharinavolgger.studio in Berlin and in Brixen (Bressanone), Italy. Since October 2024 she has been visiting lecturer in the Department of Experimental Forms and Principles of Design at the Berlin University of the Arts.

Annette Becker
Curator at the Deutsches Architekturmuseum, Frankfurt am Main

Peter Cachola Schmal
Director of the Deutsches Architekturmuseum in Frankfurt am Main

Kjell Reiter
Research assistant at the Deutsches Architekturmuseum, Frankfurt am Main

Weiterführende Literatur Bibliography

ARCH+ 184 Architektur im Klimawandel, Berlin 2007

ARCH+ 196/197 Post-Oil City, Berlin 2010

ARCH+ 257 Umbau – Maßstäbe der Transformation, Berlin 2024

Agora Energiewende (Hg. | Ed.): Die Energiewende in Deutschland: Stand der Dinge 2023. Rückblick auf die wesentlichen Entwicklungen sowie Ausblick auf 2024, Berlin 2024

Braham, William/Willis, Daniel: Architecture and Energy. Performance and Style, New York 2013

Broermann, Elisabeth et al.: Baupolitik im Wandel. Architektonische, soziale und klimapolitische Positionen, Berlin 2025

Brunnengräber, Achim/Leitschuh, Heike (Hg. | Eds.): Das Zeitalter der Städte. Die entscheidende Kraft im Anthropozän (Jahrbuch Ökologie), Stuttgart 2022

Bundesstiftung Baukultur: Baukultur Bericht. Neue Umbaukultur, Berlin 2022/23

Bundesstiftung Baukultur: Baukultur Bericht. Infrastrukturen, Berlin 2024/25

Bunting, Philip: Wie wir Energie erzeugen, Hamburg 2023

Chan, Carson/Wagstaffe, Matthew: Emerging Ecologies. Architecture and the Rise of Environmentalism, New York 2023

Cody, Brian: Form Follows Energy. Using natural forces to maximize performance, Basel/Berlin/Boston 2017

Deutsche Bau Zeitschrift (01–02): Energieoptimierte urbane Räume der Zukunft, Berlin 2023

Die Architekt 2/24. Weiterbauen Weiterdenken. Annäherungen an eine Theorie des Umbaus, Berlin 2024

Dixson-Declève, Sandrine/Gaffney, Owen/Ghosh, Jayati: Earth for all. Ein Survivalguide für unseren Planeten: Der neue Bericht an den Club of Rome, München | Munich 2022

Fraunhofer IRB-Verlag: Vom Bauen mit erneuerbaren Materialien. Die Natur als Rohstofflager, Stuttgart 2024

Green, Jared: Good Energy: Renewable Power and the Design of Everyday Life, Princeton 2021

Hauke, Bernhard (Hg. | Ed.): Nachhaltigkeit, Ressourceneffizienz und Klimaschutz. Konstruktive Lösungen für das Planen und Bauen – Aktueller Stand der Technik, Berlin 2021

Hebel, Dirk E./Heisel, Felix: Besser – Weniger – Anders Bauen: Energiewende und Digitale Transformation. Grundlage – Fallbeispiele – Strategien, Basel/Berlin/Boston 2023

Hegger, Manfred et al.: Energie Atlas. Nachhaltige Architektur, München | Munich 2007

Heiduk, Ernst et al.: Neues Bauen. Sparsame Räume für die Zukunft, Salzburg 2024

Heinlein, Frank: Recyclable by Werner Sobek, Stuttgart 2019

Herzog, Andres: Klima bauen. Ein Lexikon zu Architektur, Landschaftsarchitektur und Raumplanung unterwegs zu Netto-Null, Zürich 2021

Hofmeister, Sandra: Architektur und Klimawandel. 20 Interviews zur Zukunft des Bauens, München | Munich 2024

Holler, Christian et al.: Erneuerbare Energien zum Verstehen und Mitreden, München | Munich 2021

Hönger, Christian: Das Klima als Entwurfsfaktor, Luzern 2009

Jarmer, Tilmann: Innovation. Einfach Bauen. Material, Recyclingfähigkeit und Lebenszyklus, München | Munich 2024

Krautheim, Mareike et al.: City and Wind. Climate as an Architectural Instrument, Berlin 2014

Lucas, Dorian: Sustainable Buildings. Environmental Awareness in Architecture, Salenstein 2023

Mäckler, Christoph/Kaune, Michael/Motz, Markus (Hg. | Eds.): Stadtbild und Energie: Nachhaltige Stadtentwicklung durch energetische Optimierung, dauerhaftes Bauen und identitätsfähige Stadtbilder, Dortmund 2014

Malterre-Barthes, Anne-Charlotte: On Architecture and Greenwashing: The Political Economy of Space Bd. | Vol. 1, Berlin 2024

Meadows, Dennis L. et al.: Die Grenzen des Wachstums. Bericht des Club of Rome zur Lage der Menschheit, Stuttgart 1972

Ménard, Raphaël: Énergie Légères. Usages, architectures, paysages, Paris 2023

Mertens, Elke: Die resiliente Stadt. Landschaftsarchitektur für den Klimawandel, Basel 2021

Petzet, Muck: Reduce, Reuse, Recycle: Ressource Architektur: Deutscher Pavillon, 13. Internationale Architekturausstellung, Berlin 2012

Rahm, Philippe: Climatic architecture, New York/Barcelona 2023

Roth, Michael et al. (Hg. | Eds.): Renewable Energy and Landscape Quality, Berlin 2018

Sijmons, Dirk: Landscape and Energy: Designing Transition, Rotterdam 2014

Sobek, Werner: non nobis – über das Bauen in der Zukunft, Bd. | Vol. 1: Ausgehen muss man von dem, was ist, Stuttgart 2022

Sobek, Werner: non nobis – über das Bauen in der Zukunft, Bd. | Vol. 2: Über die Randbedingungen des Zukünftigen, Stuttgart 2023

Stockhammer, Daniel (Hg. | Ed.): Upcycling. Wieder- und Weiterverwendung als Gestaltungsprinzip in der Architektur, Zürich 2021

Unruh, Tina (Hg. | Ed.): Das Klima als Entwurfsfaktor. Architektur und Energie, Luzern 2013

Van Aubel, Marjan: Solar Futures. How to Design a Post-Fossil World with the Sun, Prinsenbeek 2022

Impressum

Colophon

Diese Publikation erscheint anlässlich der Ausstellung | This catalogue is published to accompany the exhibition

Architecture and Energy. Bauen in Zeiten des Klimawandels | Building in the age of climate change

14. Juni bis 5. Oktober 2025 | 14 June to 5 October 2025

Deutsches Architekturmuseum, Frankfurt am Main

Katalog | Catalogue

Herausgegeben von Werner Sobek, Annette Becker und Peter Cachola Schmal im Auftrag des Dezernats für Kultur und Wissenschaft, Kulturamt der Stadt Frankfurt am Main | Edited by Werner Sobek, Annette Becker, and Peter Cachola Schmal on behalf of the Department of Culture and Science, City of Frankfurt am Main Cultural Affairs Department

Buchkonzept | Book concept
Annette Becker, Kjell Reiter

Wissenschaftliche Mitarbeit | Research associate
Rebekka Dietz

Wissenschaftlicher Beirat | Scientific advisory board
Heinrich Bökamp, Bundesingenieurkammer, Berlin
Brian Cody, Technische Universität Graz, Institut für Gebäude und Energie
Gustav Düsing, Gustav Düsing GmbH, Berlin
Dietmar Eberle, Baumschlager Eberle Architekten, Lustenau, Österreich | Austria
Maxim von Gagern, TU Dresden und | and Hochschule Anhalt
Andrea Gebhard, Bundesarchitektenkammer, Berlin
Oliver Geden, Stiftung Wissenschaft und Politik, Forschungscluster Klimapolitik, Berlin
Andres Herzog, ETH Zürich | Zurich, Departement Architektur
Claudia Kemfert, Deutsches Institut für Wirtschaftsforschung e. V., Abteilung Energie, Verkehr, Umwelt und | and Leuphana Universität Lüneburg, Institut für Nachhaltigkeitssteuerung
Regine Leibinger, Barkow Leibinger Gesellschaft von Architekten mbH, Berlin
Florian Lesch, Erneuerbare Energien und Energietechnik
Mari Randsborg, Cobe A/S, Nordhavn, Dänemark | Denmark
Andreas Schulte, Henning Larsen GmbH, München | Munich
Cord Soehlke, Stadt Tübingen
Angèle Tersluisen, Technische Universität Berlin

Die technischen Angaben zu den einzelnen Projekten wurden von den jeweiligen Architekturbüros zur Verfügung gestellt. | The technical details of the individual projects were provided by the respective architectural offices.

Bibliothekarische Recherche | Library research
Christiane Eulig

Projektmanagement | Project management, Hirmer Verlag
Cordula Gielen

Lektorat Deutsch | German copyediting
Susanne Ibisch, Leipzig

Übersetzungen ins Englische | Translations from the German
Jeremy Gaines

Lektorat Englisch | English copyediting
James Copeland, Berlin

Gestaltung und Herstellung | Design and production
Lukas Winkler, Leipzig

Reproduktionen | Prepress
Ralf Lenk, ScanColor Leipzig

Papier | Paper
Munken Lynx Rough 300 g/m²
Magno Matt 135 g/m²

Schriften | Typefaces
Diatype (Dinamo), Untitled Serif (Klim Type)

Druck und Bindung | Printing and binding
F&W Druck- und Mediencenter GmbH, Kienberg

Printed in Germany

HIRMER VERLAG
Geschäftsführerin | Managing director:
Kerstin Ludolph
Bayerstraße 57–59
80335 München | Munich

hirmerverlag.de
hirmerpublishers.com
hirmerpublishers.co.uk

Bibliografische Information der Deutschen Nationalbibliothek: Die Deutsche Nationalbibliothek verzeichnet diese Publikation in der Deutschen Nationalbibliografie; detaillierte bibliografische Daten sind im Internet über https://www.dnb.de abrufbar. | Bibliographic information published by the Deutsche Nationalbibliothek: The Deutsche Nationalbibliothek lists this publication in the Deutsche Nationalbibliografie; detailed bibliographic data is available on the internet at https://www.dnb.de.

ISBN 978-3-7774-4516-8

Umschlagabbildung | Cover image
Rathaus | Town hall, Freiburg

Titelseite | Frontispiece
Bildungszentrum | Educational centre, Weil der Stadt

Seite | page 248
Gemischter Quartiersblock | Mixed neighbourhood block, Wuppertal

Ausstellung | Exhibition

Museumsleitung | Museum directorate
Peter Cachola Schmal, Andrea Jürges

Kuratoren | Curators
Werner Sobek, Annette Becker

Ausstellungskonzeption | Exhibition concept
Annette Becker, Kjell Reiter

Wissenschaftliche Mitarbeit | Research associate
Rebekka Dietz

Bibliothekarische Recherche | Library research
Christiane Eulig

Ausstellungsdesign und -grafik | Exhibition design and graphics
DESERVE Wiesbaden Mario Lorenz
und | and Laura Risse

Medien | Media
Jochen Krimm
Anatoli Skatchkov, Kinobrigada

Presse- und Öffentlichkeitsarbeit | Public relations
Brita Köhler, Anna Wegmann
Beratung Büro Sobek | Consulting office Sobek
Frank Heinlein

Übersetzungen ins Englische | Translations from the German
Jeremy Gaines

Sekretariat und Verwaltung | Office administration
Inka Plechaty, Katharina Neugebauer

Architekturvermittlung | Architectural education
Rebekka Kremershof, Confiyet Aydin, Nienke Wüst, Iman Adil Dilla, Alexander Bailey, Sara Biegler, Melinda Nasedy, Ruth Schlögl, Michèle Zeuner
FSJ: Juliia Gedvilo, Joris Van Santen

Führungen | Guided tours
Yorck Förster

Registrar | Registrar
Wolfgang Welker

Produktion der Ausstellungsarchitektur | Exhibition production
inditec GmbH, Bad Camberg
imb: Troschke GmbH & Co. KG, Mörfelden-Walldorf
Schreinerei Christian Dörner, Offenbach

Ausstellungsrealisation | Installation
Christian Walter, Marina Barry, Hans Brückner, Caroline Krause, Jörn Schön, Katharina Sckommodau, Ömer Simsek, Gerhard Winkler

Haustechnik | Museum technicians
Giancarlo Rossano, Daniel Sarvari

Bildnachweis | Image credits

Cover: Foto © HGEsch. **2:** Foto © Volker Schrank. **7:** Foto © Rademacher/de Vries. **9:** Foto, oben | above © Thilo Ross Urh., Quelle: DGJ Architektur GmbH; Foto, unten | below IBA Thüringen. **12:** Foto, oben | above © Rasmus Hjortshøj; Foto, Mitte | centre © Thomas Meyer/OSTKREUZ; Foto, unten | below © Fred Delangle. **27:** Grafik © Werner Sobek. **32:** Grafik, © Umweltbundesamt (UBA), Entscheidungsbaum GEG, Berlin, 2024. **35:** Grafik, oben | above © Statistisches Bundesamt (DeStatis), Energieverbrauch der privaten Haushalte für Wohnen, Berlin, 2024; Grafik, unten | below © Deutsche Energie Agentur (DENA), Gebäudereport 2024, Berlin, 2024, S. 64. **38:** Grafik © Deutsche Energie Agentur (DENA), Gebäudereport 2024, Berlin, 2024, S. 50. **44, 46, 47, 48/49:** Foto © Rasmus Hjortshøj. **45, 46:** Grafik © Lendager Studio. **50, 52, 53:** Foto © Volker Schrank. **51, 53:** Grafik © lohrmannarchitekten. **54, 55:** Foto © Dietmar Strauss. **56, 57:** Grafik © Freivogel Mayer Architekten. **69:** Foto, Grafik © Barkow Leibinger. **70, 72, 73:** Foto © Sebastian Schels. **73:** Grafik © Florian Nagler Architekten. **74:** Foto © Heipler Brunier. **76:** Foto © Jeva Griskjane. **77:** Grafik © ACME. **79, 80:** Foto © Sepideh Farvardin. **80, 81:** Grafik © 51N4E/Lacaton & Vassal. **88, 91, 92/93:** Foto © Jens Willebrand. **89, 90:** Grafik © raumwerk.architekten. **94, 95, 97:** Foto © Eibe Sönnecken. **96:** Grafik, © opus Architekten. **105, 106, 108/109:** Foto © Aldo Amoretti. **106, 107:** Grafik © Dietrich Untertrifaller. **110, 111, 114:** Foto © Nicolas Felder. **112, 113, 115:** Foto, Grafik © heilergeiger architekten. **115:** Foto unten | below © LATZ+PARTNER LandschaftsArchitektur Stadtplanung. **116, 118, 119:** Foto © Rasmus Hjortshøj. **117:** Grafik © Henning Larsen. **126/127:** Foto © Gitte Gylling Hammershøj Olesen. **136, 139, 140, 141:** Foto © The Pk. Odessa Co/Lanz, Schels. **138, 141:** Grafik, unten | below © Element A. **142, 143, 144, 145:** Foto © Dimitri und René Dürr. **145:** Grafik © Baumschlager Eberle. **154, 155, 156, 158/159:** Foto © Philip Heckhausen. **157:** Grafik © Esch Sintzel. **160, 161, 162, 163:** Foto, Grafik © Nadia Vontobel Architekten. **172, 173, 174, 175, 176, 177:** Foto © HGEsch. **175:** Grafik © Christoph Ingenhoven Architects/ingenhoven associates. **178:** Foto © Markus Guhl. **179:** Grafik © haascookzemmrich STUDIO2050/Transsolar. **180:** Grafik © haascookzemmrich STUDIO2050. **181:** Foto © Roland Halbe. **185:** Foto © Agustin Paschetta. **187:** Foto © forecast_ Student:Innen Cristiana Bombelaj und Helen Grace Niebuhr. **188:** Foto © forecast_ Student:Innen Lan Hua Weng und Kilian Johannes Weber. **190, 193, 194/195:** Foto © Adrià Goula. **191, 192, 193:** Grafik © dataAE/Narch/Maria Arquitectes. **196, 197, 198, 199:** Foto © Christian Reuther. **199:** Grafik © furoris X art. **206, 208, 211:** Foto © José Hevia. **209, 210, 211:** Grafik © Peris+Toral. **212, 214:** Foto © Sebastian Schels. **213, 214, 215:** Grafik © ArchitekturWerkstatt Valentin. **219:** Grafik © Schmidt et al., Landschaftsbild und Energiewende, Bonn-Bad Godesberg, 2017, S. 28. **221:** Grafik © TU Dresden, Maren Zipperlen, 2017. **222:** Grafik, oben | above © TU Dresden, Mary Meier, 2017; Grafik, unten | below © TU Dresden, Carolin Gallacher, 2017. **223:** Grafik, oben | above © TU Dresden, Ulrike Schmidt, 2017; Grafik, unten | below © TU Dresden, Mary Meier, 2017. **226, 228, 229:** Foto © Hanns Joosten. **227:** Grafik © haefner jiménez betcke jarosch landschaftsarchitektur. **230, 231, 232, 233:** Foto © BAU. **240/241:** Foto © Alexander Rochau. **248:** Foto © Jens Willebrand.